A Broken Path Restored
by True Love

Michelle Gustafson

TEACH Services, Inc.
P U B L I S H I N G
www.TEACHServices.com • (800) 367-1844

World rights reserved. This book or any portion thereof may not be copied or reproduced in any form or manner whatever, except as provided by law, without the written permission of the publisher, except by a reviewer who may quote brief passages in a review.

The author assumes full responsibility for the accuracy of all facts and quotations as cited in this book. The opinions expressed in this book are the author's personal views and interpretations, and do not necessarily reflect those of the publisher.

This book is provided with the understanding that the publisher is not engaged in giving spiritual, legal, medical, or other professional advice. If authoritative advice is needed, the reader should seek the counsel of a competent professional.

Copyright © 2025 Michelle Gustafson
Copyright © 2025 TEACH Services, Inc.
ISBN-13: 978-1-4796-1762-3 (Paperback)
ISBN-13: 978-1-4796-1763-0 (ePub)
Library of Congress Control Number: 2024918914

All scripture quotations are taken from the New King James Version®. Copyright © 1982 by Thomas Nelson. Used by permission. All rights reserved.

Note that some names have been changed to protect the privacy of characters in this true story.

Published by

Dedication

Above all, I thank God and Jesus Christ for carrying me through all my trials—past and future.

To my husband Bob, who never left my side during my darkest moments. Your unwavering love, constant prayers, and guidance back to faith sustained me when the pain seemed endless. You are truly a gift from God, and I will love you always.

To my mother Ruth, whose hours of phone conversations helped me piece together our shared past. Thank you for the prayers we offered as we revisited times of pain, loss, hardship, laughter, and joy. Our journey back in time brought healing, and without your memories, this book would not exist.

To my daughter Nautasha, for your courage in sharing both strengths and vulnerabilities during difficult times. Though words cannot fully capture your pain, I pray for God's continued healing of your heart with each passing day.

To my son Tristin (TJ), whose wit and humor brightened even my darkest days. Your ability to find positivity in life's challenges inspires me. Continue seeking Jesus, and He will guide your path.

To my grandmother Alice, whose unwavering support touched generations of our family. Your strength during troubled times and boundless love for Jesus remain an inspiration. I look forward to our reunion at our Savior's return.

Lastly, to my great aunt Genevieve (Gen/Meatball) Fetterhoff, who sparked my passion for writing. I cherish our conversations about God, our nature walks, your oatmeal raisin cookies, and snuggling in the big chair while gazing at the horse picture. I cannot wait to walk the streets of gold with you.

Table of Contents

Chapter 1:　　Guardian Angel................9
Chapter 2:　　Great Aunt Meatball................13
Chapter 3:　　Attention................16
Chapter 4:　　Vacation Bible School................21
Chapter 5:　　VBS Impact................25
Chapter 6:　　Moving................29
Chapter 7:　　The Old Gray House................33
Chapter 8:　　Don't Blackmail................35
Chapter 9:　　Out of Control. The Solution? 4H................38
Chapter 10:　　The Horse Shows................43
Chapter 11:　　A Gift................47
Chapter 12:　　Answered Prayer................51
Chapter 13:　　The Loss, and Turning to Rebellion................55
Chapter 14:　　The Bible Study................60
Chapter 15:　　Rivalries................63
Chapter 16:　　New School................67
Chapter 17:　　A Lesson Learned the Hard Way................71
Chapter 18:　　A Big Mistake................78
Chapter 19:　　Pregnant and Depressed................87
Chapter 20:　　The Birth................90

Chapter 21:	The Accident, and A Vision from God	95
Chapter 22:	Visit from Aunt Lu	102
Chapter 23:	Learning to Drive, and Breaking the Rules	105
Chapter 24:	Going to College, and Moving On	112
Chapter 25:	Baptism: God Is Working	119
Chapter 26:	Unevenly Yoked	125
Chapter 27:	Prison: The Truth Revealed	133
Chapter 28:	A New Job: The Casino	136
Chapter 29:	The Dealer	139
Chapter 30:	Lessons Still Not Learned: The Second Marriage	142
Chapter 31:	God is Still Calling Amidst the Trials, "Oh, Sinner, Come Home!"	149
Chapter 32:	Pregnant!	157
Chapter 33:	The Flight to Germany	163
Chapter 34:	Arrival of Household Goods, and Moving Again!	171
Chapter 35:	Baby in Distress, and an Unfaithful Husband	175
Chapter 36:	Birthday Request	182
Chapter 37:	The Birth of Tristin	185
Chapter 38:	Depression Sets In	192
Chapter 39:	Flood, Loss, New Job, and Church at Last	197
Chapter 40:	Another Vision	201
Chapter 41:	The Fire	205
Chapter 42:	Flight Back to the United States	208
Chapter 43:	The Power Struggle	212
Chapter 44:	Charley	217

Chapter 45:	Trenary: Home Again	220
Chapter 46:	Marriage Troubles	222
Chapter 47:	Fort Polk: Sam's House	229
Chapter 48:	New Apartment	235
Chapter 49:	New Jobs	239
Chapter 50:	I Can't Take Any More!	243
Chapter 51:	Moving Back to Michigan	247
Chapter 52:	Trailer in the Country	252
Chapter 53:	Hurricane Rita	259
Chapter 54:	Finding the Right House	263
Chapter 55:	Back to the War Zone, and Slowly Backsliding	266
Chapter 56:	Family Reunited, and Nautasha's Unhappiness	272
Chapter 57:	Back to the Farm	278
Chapter 58:	Phil's Surgery	283
Chapter 59:	Home Again	285
Chapter 60:	Selfishness and Heartache	288
Chapter 61:	Nautasha's Secret Revealed	296
Chapter 62:	Action Taken	302
Chapter 63:	Falling Apart and Angry	306
Chapter 64:	The Move to Escanaba	310
Chapter 65:	Emotional Turmoil	313
Chapter 66:	My Friend Bob, and The Proposal	318
Chapter 67:	A Wedding and a Hearing	323
Chapter 68:	You Want Me to Do *What?*	329
Chapter 69:	Evidence Recovered	334

Chapter 70: The Death of My Brother	338
Chapter 71: The Trial	342
Epilogue	347
Bibliography	355
About Never Alone Ministry	357

CHAPTER 1
Guardian Angel

I remember that when I was a little girl, I just loved to be outside. There was a peace about being in God's nature. I first realized it when I was about five years old, even if I did not truly understand that God gave us that beautiful peace.

I think that living in a two-bedroom trailer with up to six other people is what drove me outside: out where it was peaceful, and I could pretend to be whomever I wanted and go wherever I wanted; whether the middle of the cornfield, the hayfield, the apple orchard, or our tree fort just across the dirt road from our family's houses.

The cornfield became my woods, and I was a princess waiting to be rescued by a gallant prince on his horse. He would take me away to a big castle, where nothing could harm me ever again.

In the tree fort, I was a warrior protecting my home. Sticks were my sword and shield; I was invincible to anything and everyone.

But I think that my favorite places were the apple orchard and the hayfield. I would sit in the apple trees and listen to the birds sing. I wished that I could sound as pretty as they did when I sang.

> *I didn't understand how to pray when I was a little girl, so talking to my guardian angel was my way of communicating with God.*

I didn't understand how to pray when I was a little girl, so talking to my guardian angel was my way of communicating with God. In the trees, I would tell my angel how pretty the birds sounded and how I wanted to sing like them. I would ask why some birds didn't sound as pretty as the others. In the hayfield I would lay daydreaming and talking to my guardian. I don't remember everything I used to say, but I do remember feeling peace come over me.

I realize now that God was giving me that peace, but back then I only remember feeling safe, and when I wasn't in that place, longing to go there to get away from my family. I also remember always looking for my guardian angel, but never being able to find him.

My mother and grandmother had told me that I had a guardian angel, whom God had sent to watch over me. Grandma said that he watched over me wherever I went: whatever I did, he saw, and he would tell God if I was being good or bad. I asked my grandma one day, "How come I can't see my angel if he is with me all the time?"

She told me that only God could see all the angels. We could only feel their presence.

Of course, being a small child, I asked her what the word "presence" meant.

Grandma said that it was when you could feel that someone was with you, but when you looked, no one was there; so you feel their *presence*, and that is how you know your guardian angel is with you.

Now I was becoming confused, and I asked many more questions. My grandma answered them the best that she could. She loved God, but she still didn't have all the answers.

Let me back up and explain just a little bit about my family. We lived in what we called "The Yard." This property was about three acres of land on the outskirts of Trenary, Michigan, down a dirt road that was back in the woods.

We used to call this road "the old gravel road," because there were no signs back then on roads like that to tell you where you were driving. Today, however, there is a little green sign that reads *June Road*.

Down this gravel lane, on this plot of land, lived my grandma. Grandma Alice had fourteen children, some of whom died at birth and others which died early in life, leaving her with nine living children.

I'm not sure how she did it back in those days. Today I understand that raising just three children is a challenge. What I do know is that Grandma loved each one of her kids unconditionally. God's love is a big part of raising a family, and that is something she had: His love. Grandma Alice may have had flaws in other areas, but she was an example to me about how much we need to love one another.

The love in our family was so great that we all lived on that same plot (or close by) for years. Thus when I was a child it was Grandma, her kids, and her sister, Genevieve, known to us as Aunt Gen or Aunt Meatball (she got the nickname from Uncle Doyle, who was autistic and who could not remember how to say her name when he was young, thus he decided to call her Meatball; the name stuck, and that is what all the nieces and nephews called her).

In our yard there were four trailer houses: my grandma's, my mom's, Great Aunt Gen's, and Uncle Kent and Aunt Bell's. My uncles Dale and Doyle lived with Grandma Alice. Aunt Nancy lived with Great Aunt Gen. Uncle Dean (Uncle Dale's twin brother) lived with my mom, along with my two brothers, Scott and Robin, and me. Uncle Kent and Aunt Bell lived in the last trailer, along with their four children: Misty, Donna, Connie, and Junior.

Our family attended the Methodist Church in town occasionally. We did not go every Sunday, but when we did, it was nice to sit in the pew next to my mom. Even then I could feel the presence of God; I just didn't know that it was Him I was sensing. I only knew that I felt a sense of peace which I really liked and didn't want to let go of.

Still, I longed for answers to questions that no one in my family could really answer. After a while I just stopped thinking about it and tried to understand what

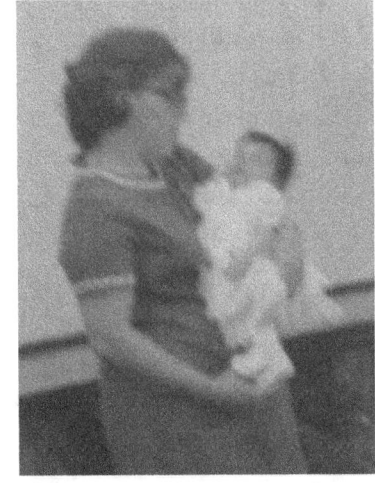

Mom with me as a newborn.

I did know: I had a guardian angel who was with me, and I could talk to him all of the time.

This is not a good thing to do when you are around other children. They used to ask me, "Who are you talking to?"

I would smile and say, "My guardian angel!"

The other kids thought I was nuts and started to tease me. After that, I decided to only talk to him when I was at home, or if I knew that no one could hear me.

Of course, just when you think you're alone, someone is always listening. My mom heard me all the time and just smiled at me. My brothers, on the other hand, teased me for talking to myself. It hurt, but I knew my brothers loved me. They could push me around and mistreat me, but if someone else tried, they would protect me.

It is funny how that works: family can hurt you, but no one else can. I truly wonder how that works out in one's mind. Jesus doesn't want us to be hurtful to anyone, and the ones whom we love the most ought to be the ones we are the nicest to … or so you would think. But it doesn't work out that way.

Later in life I would watch my children do the same things to each other that my brothers and I used to do, and I would ask them, "Would Jesus treat you that way?"

Of course they would tell me, "No, mom."

I would ask them, "How would Jesus treat you?"

"He would be kind or be nice," they would say.

It's funny how we know that Jesus wouldn't say or do unkind things, but we think it is okay for us to speak rudely or do unkind deeds or gestures, then we justify those actions. At the same time we condemn those whom we see hurting our family … in the same way that we do. It makes a person stop and think: *how am I representing my Savior, Jesus?*

I am reminded of Matthew 7:12: "Therefore, whatever you want men to do to you, do also to them." If we wouldn't want unkind things said about us or done to us, we shouldn't say or do anything that would be unkind to others. Rather, we should always have the love of Christ in our hearts.

CHAPTER 2

Great Aunt Meatball

Living in a two-bedroom trailer with four other people would seem to some people to be a bit much, but I loved it, even when Grandma Alice moved in while she was waiting for her new trailer to be delivered.

I hated not having my own room at times, but the family closeness was really nice. And when it rained, I would fall right to sleep to the tapping on the tin roof of the trailer. It was like God was singing all of us a lullaby. I think we all loved the rainy nights.

We had three people per bedroom while Grandma was there, and it did feel a bit crowded until she moved out into her new trailer. After that the bedroom was just mine and mom's. I remember thinking, "Good, I get her all to myself."

I look back and laugh at some of my thoughts back then. Most of the time I did not really think my ideas through. It is funny

> *It is funny how a child can believe everything will work out the way they plan it in their minds, and then become very disappointed when reality doesn't turn out that way.*

how a child can believe everything will work out the way they plan it in their minds, and then become very disappointed when reality doesn't turn out that way.

I planned all sorts of fun time with my mom: cuddling and talking at night, maybe reading some books together, and just plain having the alone time with her that I always wanted. But my mom had other things on her mind.

My mom liked to drink. When she got off of work, she would go to the bar and have a few drinks before coming home (the bars were only a few blocks from her workplace). On weekends, she went out to bars with my aunts and uncles and stayed out until they closed. We only went to church on Sunday if my mom wasn't suffering from a major hangover.

It was not all bad. Mom worked a lot at the Trenary Home Bakery (along with Grandma Alice, Aunt Nancy, Uncle Burt, and Great Aunt Meatball). I remember that she would bring home lots of donuts and breads. My favorite was the famous Trenary Toast; it was so yummy. It consisted of white sub sandwich bread that was sliced, painted with a milky mixture, rubbed in a sugar and cinnamon mix, and baked in a big oven. I liked it best when I would visit mom at work: she would give the toast to me right off of the table, before it was even baked. It was so soft and tasted so good. I remember it like yesterday.

My Great Aunt Meatball.

Although my mom spent a lot of time in the bars and left us kids at home, I wasn't often bored. She left me with Great Aunt Meatball a lot. She helped me to forget about the problems in my life and with my family. We would talk for hours and play Yahtzee or card games. Even if Mom was home, I would go talk with Aunt Meatball. So did my brothers and our cousins who lived nearby.

One reason was that when she made her oatmeal cookies, you could smell them a mile away. She really loved to bake for us kids. I think she loved our smiling faces and all of the compliments she'd get for her yummy cookies. She didn't have children, so she spoiled all of us. And my mom always knew where to find us.

Aunt Meatball and I talked about everything, including God and Jesus. She liked to read books, and she loved God. She even wrote a few books of her own. Grandma had sparked my interest in learning about God, so talking to Aunt Meatball about Him was nice. She told me how He had created all the beautiful things that I enjoyed while sitting outside in my tree fort.

There was a painting on Aunt Meatball's wall of two horses; a mother and her colt. She named them, and every time I came over, she would ask me, "Do you remember their names?" She was always trying to stump me, and she did a good job most of the time.

I would say, "Yes! The baby is Goldie, and the mother is … is … is … I can't remember."

The mother horse was Matilda. That name was hard for me to remember, but Aunt Meatball always gave me helpful hints.

Many years later, I went to visit her, and Aunt Gen told me that when she passed away, she would leave everything to Aunt Nancy (they were very close; Aunt Nancy was like the daughter Great Aunt Meatball never had). Then she asked me if there was anything I wanted of hers.

I told her, "The picture of the mother and colt."

She got up, took it off of the wall, and put it on the table. Then she said to me, "I can't believe you remember this."

We chatted about all the times we had sat in her big chair talking about that picture, and how many times she had stumped me on the name Matilda.

That day, as I sat at my great aunt's table, my past rolled into my memory as if it were yesterday. I was once again that little girl, listening to her tell me stories about horses or God or whatever else I shared from my little thoughts.

Aunt Meatball was always there to listen and make me feel very loved and wanted. She will always have a special place in my heart. Every time I look at that picture, I remember our time together. They are memories I will hold dear to my heart for many years to come.

Some days it makes me cry to think that those days are gone. It is funny how you can sit in a chair with an elderly woman, and it seems like nothing else matters around you; only that moment in time when you can live in a story with someone you love.

CHAPTER 3
Attention

It was hard to grow up with two older brothers. I did stupid things to get my mom's attention, which just made her and my brothers mad. I also started fights with my siblings, then lied to Mom about what happened to get them into trouble.

In particular, Scott and I had a lot of run-ins, and my brattiness drove him crazy. We never really had a good relationship growing up. Mom once told me about the day she had brought me home from the hospital: Scott told her to take me back where I came from. He did give me my nickname, though. He couldn't say Michelle very well, so he called me Mickey instead. To this day my family knows me as Mickey or Mick.

One morning I was playing with my brother Robin's truck in the kitchen of our trailer. Scott came out and told me that he wanted it. I said, "No, Robin said I could play with it."

Well, that didn't sit well with my brother. He grabbed my arm and body-slammed me on the kitchen floor. I ran screaming into my bedroom and lay on my bed, sobbing in pain. My mother came in to check on me; she told me to get up, and that everything would be fine.

I wouldn't get up, so she left the room. A few minutes later, I tried to move but could not sit up. I lay there for a while, pondering how I was going to move and why I couldn't. Finally I yelled for my mother.

She returned, and I told her that I couldn't move.

She said, "You're just looking for attention. Enough is enough: just get up." When I still didn't move, she left the room, very angry.

I didn't know what to do. I lay there with silent tears rolling down my cheeks, thoughts whirling in my head: *My mom doesn't believe I am hurt. What will I do? How will I get up? Is she ever going to come back and believe me?*

After two hours, Mom came back in the room with a concerned look on her face. She had finally realized that I was not faking.

> I lay there with silent tears rolling down my cheeks, thoughts whirling in my head: My mom doesn't believe I am hurt.

You see, when we cry wolf too many times, no one will believe us when we are really in trouble. I had done that so often that it was hard for my mother to believe me when I told her the truth.

In the end my mother took me to the hospital, where she found out that I had a fractured collarbone. Scott felt bad about what he had done and told me he was sorry.

But that didn't stop me from seeking attention. Now I really was hurt, and I milked it for all it was worth. Since I couldn't get up if I lay down, other people had to help me into a sitting or standing position. I loved all the attention, but Scott was not amused. His nice attitude toward me left rather quickly.

Another time, I made Scott so mad that he shot me with his BB gun at close range, right in the shoulder. Of course I went crying to Mother, and after she pulled the BB out, he got into big trouble. I smugly teased him afterward.

I was not a very nice child, even though I talked to my guardian angel, spent time in nature, and inquired about God. As I look back at how we grew up, I feel bad for both of my brothers. They weren't always angels, but I know that most of the fights we got into were my fault.

The attention I got was never enough. I would get into trouble at school on purpose, just so that Mother would have to come and get me. Even though it was bad time, I still looked at it as time spent with her. Some days I felt like I drove her to drinking.

When my mom's fiancé, Jerry, died, she turned to alcohol even more. As time passed, she spent more time in bars. I lost my mother to alcohol, and she lost herself in it, so that she wouldn't have to feel the hurt of losing another man she loved to the grave.

Mom and Robert

Before Jerry my mother had been married to a man named Robert. They had called him Bob or Bobby. Bob was my brothers' father, but he died of diabetes when Scott was only five and Robin was four.

Mother once told me the story about how sick Bob became in the sixth year of their marriage. They had to put him in the hospital, and she spent a lot of time with Bob during his last days. She was there when he passed on; she had closed his eyes and said goodbye to him.

I couldn't even imagine the pain she must have been feeling. Mother knew who God was but was struggling in this world of sin and emotions, and she didn't turn to God with her grief. She turned to alcohol to numb the pain instead.

She also told me that my brothers took their father's death very hard. Robin and Scott didn't understand why their father had to be taken from them. They struggled to find reassurance in Mother, but when she looked at them with love and saw their pain, she also saw their father looking up at her.

Her own pain was so great that she would escape to the bars in town to try and drown her sorrows in a can of beer. That was where she met my father, Franz, and nine months later I was born.

My mom said that she never loved my dad, and that was why she didn't marry him. But it was hard for me to not have a father while I was growing up.

I once told my mother about a childhood memory. I said, "I remember going into a bar and seeing a man on the left side, sitting down and playing a harmonica. Then he sat down at a table with you, and you ordered me French fries. Then another man came in and sat with us. He smiled at me and shared my fries. Then he took me to the back room where all the games were, and we played foosball. He put me up on a stool because I was too little to reach the table."

My mother looked at me in shock. She said, "You were only two years old! That bar was our old tavern, called the Long Branch, that is now closed down. The man playing the harmonica was known as The Tennessee Kid. The other man that was sitting and playing with you was your father, Franz."

Today, I can look back and think of what a blessing it was that God gave me one memory of my real father.

I found out at age eleven that he died of lung cancer. I never knew my father, and I struggled throughout my teens with a burden on my heart. Why did my dad never want to see me? Or have a relationship with me? It was a hard, hurt period in my life. I had lots of family, but none of them could take the place of a father.

After Bob died, Uncle Dean moved in with my mother and helped her raise the boys. I came along a year later, so he stayed and helped raise me, too. He was always Uncle Dean; we never called him Dad. But we loved him. He was the closest thing we did have to a father growing up.

Later in life I realized I had a father who loved me more than I could possibly imagine: my heavenly Father. When I started to understand the kind of love He has for me, and how He carried me through all of my bad days and would continue to carry me through the rest of my days to come—even as I worried and doubted how my life would turn out, feeling as if I were a mistake from a past affair—my heart broke.

Matt. 6:25, 26:

Therefore I say to you, do not worry about your life, what you will eat or what you will drink; nor about your body, what you will put on. Is not life more than food and the body more than clothing? Look at the birds of the air, for they neither sow nor reap nor gather into barns; yet your heavenly Father feeds them. Are you not of more value than they?

I realized I was of great value to the Lord; to my Father; my heavenly Father.

The concept of having a father was exciting, but knowing that God was my heavenly Father made it even more exciting to me. That was when I would truly start to understand the meaning of a father's love for his child.

CHAPTER 4
Vacation Bible School

When Uncle Kent married Aunt Bell, they came to live with us in The Yard. Aunt Bell already had Misty and Donna.

Donna was one year younger than her sister and my best friend. She was a year older than me, but that didn't matter to us. We were very close. I said earlier that we all lived in The Yard, but what I didn't say was how you could walk out one door and into the next house in just a few steps (or so it seemed).

It was so much fun to have a friend. Donna and I could play together every day. I was a leader, and she was a follower. We got into a lot of trouble at times, but we stuck together without fail and took the blame as a team.

One day a lady by the name of Lucille came by the house and asked if we kids could go to VBS (that is, Vacation Bible School). This would be the beginning of my journey of getting to know who God really is, and that memory will stay fresh in my mind for the rest of my life.

I remember how much Donna and I begged to go. Each day we couldn't wait until Lucille came to get us. We would run to her car as she pulled into our driveway. She just smiled and welcomed us into her car. When we were all buckled in, she would drive us into town.

When she pulled into the parking lot of our school (where they were holding VBS), Donna and I raced through the front doors and into the gym. We were captivated by all of the decorations: homemade quilts on the walls and chairs set up in front of the stage; flags up front in their stands, a piano, and a table with music boards and two very well-decorated boxes. The back of the gym was also very exciting. That's where all of our lunchroom tables set were up, with lots of crafts on them. It was so exciting for two little girls to look around and see all the things we would be doing.

We heard Lucille calling us back to the front doors. We turned around and ran back up the steps to see what she wanted us to do. She gave each of us a nametag with a number on it; they were yellow squares with little children sitting on Jesus' lap and all around Him. They pinned the nametags to our shirts.

Our names were right below the picture, and in the bottom corner was our number. Since we were two of the first children through the door, I was three and Donna was four. Those numbers didn't mean much to us at the time, but we were told that there was something big behind the numbers. If we wanted to find out what that was, we had to wear our tags to VBS every day.

More and more kids piled through the doors into the gym, with the same amazement Donna and I had felt. The two of us decided to go up to the front of the room and get the closest seats to the front that we could. Before long we were joined by our friends; Karen, Jeanna, Melanie, and Renee.

Donna and I looked around and saw many more kids we knew from school, then we looked at each other, smiling. "This is going to be so much fun," we said to each other. Then we just giggled and talked with our friends as little girls do.

We thought it couldn't get any more exciting, but then Lucille walked up and asked if we wanted to carry the flags to the front when the music started playing. Donna was too shy to say yes, but I was far from shy. I jumped up and down and said, "I'll do it! I'll do it!"

Karen, who was sitting next to me, was just as excited, saying, "Me too, me too."

Lucille said, with a big smile, "Okay, Karen and Michelle, come with me, and I will show you what you need to do."

At this point I could hardly contain my excitement. I wanted to jump up and down and yell, "Yippee, yahoo, yes, yes! I get to carry a flag!"

I didn't understand the real meaning of carrying the flags or their significance to a free country until I helped with Vacation Bible School when I was older. I felt more honored after I married my ex-husband, who served in the military for many years. Being married today to a wonderful man who is retired from the Army, I now look back at those times and feel very honored to have had the opportunity to carry the flags.

When my ex used to come home from war zones like Iraq, I comprehended what those two flags meant, as his unit marched in, carrying an American flag in honor of our freedom in the United States and another honoring the deaths of all the soldiers who were lost to war.

It brings tears to my eyes now, as I remember "God Bless America" playing, while all the soldiers marched around the gym for their families, friends, and fellow soldiers to see. We all cried at that sight, realizing that freedom isn't really free.

Think about it! We are not free without a cost. Many men and women from all around the world died for their countries in hopes of having freedom. To think of the sacrifice our soldiers made for each and every one of us here in America brings respect and love into my heart for those families that have lost a loved one to war.

I never thought that carrying the flags for VBS as a child would have such a profound effect on me, even as an adult. However, this freedom that we fight for does not compare to the freedom that Jesus offers to us through His death on the cross.

Can you imagine dying from a broken heart? Jesus didn't only die for my sins on that cross, He died for the whole world's sins. In essence, He carried the weight of the world, and it broke His heart. God let this happen so that we would have a chance to live in Heaven with Him.

Now we have the choice to choose whom we will serve this day. When we have a longing to live for Jesus, and understand the sacrifice He made on the cross, we will follow the straight and narrow path, clinging to the Word of God.

Once I truly understood how real freedom in Jesus can change your whole outlook on life, then I realized I could never have had eternal life without Jesus. He sets us free from sin. We become a new creation and old things pass away; all things become new (2 Cor. 5:17). When we surrender all to Jesus, we will then be able to understand *true* freedom in Christ.

CHAPTER 5

VBS Impact

The first day of VBS was so much fun. We soon found out what the half-finished quilts on the wall were for. There was one for each class; Kindergarten, Primary, Juniors, and Teens. In crafts all of us had to draw a picture of what we thought Heaven would look like on a square, white piece of fabric. When we finished, they were collected and given to Lucille, who took them home and sewed the drawings from each class into their quilt.

At the end of the week, on parents' night, they pulled a name out of a box for each class; that person was the lucky winner of a handmade, beautiful quilt. I didn't win one in my first year of VBS, but my friend Karen did. A few years later, I finally won one; I loved it. I went home, put it on my bed, and slept with that quilt for many years, until it wore right out and I had to throw it away.

I bet you're still wondering what the numbers were for on our name tags. At the beginning and end of each day of VBS, Carol or her daughter Randy drew a slip out of one of those nicely-decorated boxes on the front tables. The other box was full of prizes.

All eyes focused on the front, and it was totally quiet during the prize-drawing times. It was great, but waiting as they pulled a number was nerve racking; if yours hadn't been called yet, you were hoping you were next. Once your number had been called you were happy, and your nerves calmed down. Then you longed to see who would be next. Carol and Randy made sure that every number was pulled by the end of the week, so that no one was left out. They always made all of us feel special when we won a prize.

> *I miss those days of being a little girl and the anticipation of waiting for my number to be drawn.*

I miss those days of being a little girl and the anticipation of waiting for my number to be drawn. Now I look forward to the days that I have with the Lord. They are joyous, like those of a child whose number was just called. Every day with God should be that exciting.

We kids grew to love Lucille, who had first invited us and brought us to VBS. We loved her so much that we started calling her Aunt Lu. Even though today she is sleeping and waiting for Jesus to come and take us home, we all still refer to her as Aunt Lu.

She was an amazing messenger of God. Even on her death, bed she was witnessing and reciting Scripture. She truly loved the Lord. I still look to her today as a good example of what I need to be like in my walk with God. As you read on, you will see the big impact she made in my life and my family's lives. She brought many of us to the Word and prayed for us to accept Jesus as our personal Savior and King.

God sent her to show me the right path to take. She never gave up on me, not even when I gave up on myself. She always prayed for me with unconditional love; a love that in a lifetime I will never forget. She showed me just how solid God's rock is to stand on, especially when you feel like you are on that rock alone.

Aunt Lu will always have a place in my heart. I can't wait to go to Heaven and see her again in her new form. I picture us on streets of gold, arm-in-arm, walking in the gardens and visiting with old and new friends. Having special time like that will be even more precious than when I attended VBS. Heaven isn't that far away, and I intend to be ready when Jesus comes to take us home.

There is another family that made a big impact on my life and my walk with God, which I will always remember and with whom I look forward to walking the streets of gold.

Carol, who drew the numbers for our prizes, and her husband Chuck lived half a mile down the road from us with their two girls. Randy was my brother's age, and Dalucee was a year younger than me. We played together from time to time. I remember being at their house and thinking that it was different. They didn't do things we were allowed to do, and Carol often corrected me in a very loving way.

One Friday Dalucee asked me to spend the night and go to church with her on Saturday. I asked my mother, and she said it was okay. We had a wonderful time. I didn't understand fully about the Sabbath, but Carol was sweet and told me about God's holy day, which He had created for us to spend just with Him.

When it was time to go to bed, Dalucee and I giggled and laughed until we fell asleep. We awoke the next morning, and I talked her into going downstairs and watching Saturday morning cartoons. She told me that they were not allowed to watch TV on Sabbath mornings, but I kept telling her how much fun they were to watch. She gave in, and we went downstairs and turned on the TV.

Carol came in and scolded us both, but Dalucee got in bigger trouble because she knew better (as Carol explained). I remember thinking, *What a weird family. They don't watch cartoons on Saturday mornings?*

There was so much that I learned from them. I remember that they prayed a lot and thanked God, talked about church and how much they loved the Lord. Carol taught me to be aware of what is right and wrong, to remember God's values, and to never think badly of myself or that I can't do something which is put in front of me; for if I look to God, He will give me the strength to do anything that I think is hard. And she was so right. I guess that you never realize how people will affect your life while you are growing up.

Carol was not only my neighbor but also the assistant Special Education Teacher when I was in high school. During that later phase in my life, she would always say things to me to help me realize that God was watching me and loved me. She always told me that whenever I had a problem, I could go to God with it, and He would answer.

Whenever I saw Carol's family, I longed to be with them. It was because they had something that mine didn't: God. Isn't it amazing how God places people in your life to help you find your way? Praise God for His love and goodness, that He sends to us through other people.

Time went on, and I got too old to attend VBS. I was a teenager now, and as you know, teens have a tendency to do what they think is right in life (even when, most of the time, those decisions are not good or thought through).

I was set in my ways, and I grew more and more rebellious. I swore all the time, even, shamefully, at my own family. My mother had a lot to deal with, and I never made it easy on her.

She still went to bars and drank. Most of the time she came home late, so we hardly saw her. If we did, it was close to bedtime, so it was never for very long.

My mother was a very happy drunk. This didn't make it right, but it did make it easier on us children. Since then I have witnessed abusive alcoholics; the harm that they cause to their families and others is not a pretty sight. In fact, it scares me greatly. So I praise God that I had a happy, alcoholic mother, because it was a blessing to not get beaten or verbally abused. God saved us from that, and He saved my mother from having to repent of it later, after she found Him.

Most of the time when she was not drinking, Mother was sad or quiet. Drinking let her forget her trials. I found out later that she was lonely. She felt that God had taken all her happiness away by taking the men she truly loved from her; especially Bob.

To this day my mother still mourns his death. Every year, on the anniversary of his passing, she cries and just wants to be left alone to sit in her little apartment and grieve her lost love. She never remarried. The closest she came was Jerry, but when he died, she gave up on men and the thought of a relationship. Many men have asked her out, but she always says she is not interested. She is happy to be their friend but not anything more. Mom's heart still lies with a man whom she fell in love with on October 1st, 1965, then married on April 23rd, 1966.

CHAPTER 6

Moving

When I was about nine years old, we moved a mile down the road. It was exciting and sad at once: sad that we were leaving the family yard, and exciting because we were moving into a *house*.

But there was a downside: it only had two bedrooms. Yes, you guessed it; we were back to the same sleeping arrangements we had had in the trailer. The house wasn't even much bigger than our trailer had been; it was just set up differently. The kitchen, living room, and bathroom were all downstairs. There were two bedrooms upstairs: one small, the other medium-sized.

Mother and I took the small bedroom, which was even smaller than our bedroom had been in the trailer. There was space for our beds and a couple of dressers, but we had no closet. The other bedroom, where Uncle Dean and Robin set up, was the same width as ours, only longer. It was hard for them to put up the bunk beds due to the slant of the A-frame roof, and that is why Scott wound up sleeping at the top of the stairs. He had his own room, in a way, but no privacy. There was just enough room for a dresser and a twin bed, which Scott set up under the slope of the ceiling. I remember thinking, *I hope he doesn't wake up fast and hit his head.* I don't know if he ever did, but I do know it would have hurt.

We didn't live there for very long. A little over a year later, we moved across town into a big, gray farmhouse. At least I thought it was big at the time. These days, I look at the old farmhouse every time I go home, and I think to myself, *Wow, that house is small.*

> After living with five people, first in a two-bedroom trailer and then a two-bedroom house, that farmhouse was like living in a mansion.

But back then, any house we moved into that had five potential bedrooms was big, even if the rooms were small. After living with five people, first in a two-bedroom trailer and then a two-bedroom house, that farmhouse was like living in a mansion.

It was farther away from our family but still in Trenary. It was located on the outskirts, on Highway 41, along the way to Rapid River. It sat on a little hill at the end of a long driveway. There was a big yard with lots of buildings: a barn, a chicken coop, a pole barn, an older house (that was falling apart), and a sauna.

The sauna was my favorite place to go and take a bath (we only had a shower in the house, there was not a bathtub). When I went into the sauna with my mother, we would throw water on the rocks and get it really hot in there. Then I would run out and jump in the snowbank to cool off. Then it was back into the sauna again. It was very refreshing.

If Mother and Uncle Dean didn't feel like lighting the sauna, I had to take a shower. Otherwise I could take a bath in an old, metal washtub. That was fun. I would fill it up, get my little dolls, and take my bath. I had to sit Indian style because the tub was round; but when you're nine or ten years of age, that's fun. You really don't seem to mind how small it is.

Like the last house, this one had an A-frame rooftop; but the home was nicer on the inside: all hardwood flooring, wood and propane heat, a basement, and an upstairs. It also had a mudroom as you walked in the back door. I always called it the shed or the porch. There was a line of hooks to hang jackets on just at the top of three steps as you entered the mudroom, and to the left was a set of stairs that went to the basement.

I remember those hooks on the wall very well. Whenever I irritated my brothers and their friends (Scooter, Skip, Tim, and Byron), who were over at the house a lot, they hung me up by my belt loops until just before Mother or Uncle Dean got home from work. I deserved to hang there most of the time. I gave Scott and Robin and their friends such a hard time and never left them alone. Sometimes, if they didn't use the hooks in the mudroom, they would hang me out on the clothesline or lock me in the little walk-in closet which I had in this home. Luckily for them, I was small and skinny.

One day I had made my brothers mad enough to hang me on the clothesline. I had only been there for a little while when Uncle Dean pulled up. He busted out laughing when he got out of his car.

I, on the other hand, was not amused. I crossed my arms, and as he laughed, I got so hurt and mad that I yelled, "It's not funny. Just get me down, Uncle Dean."

He laughed all the more and asked what I had done to annoy the boys this time, then he let me down. Today, I can also look back and laugh. I was a handful, and my poor brothers had a whole lot to put up with.

More about the house: if you passed through the mudroom door, you were in the kitchen. To the left was the bathroom and the door to the upstairs. Straight ahead was the living room, which led to the front door and my mom's bedroom. Upstairs there were only two bedrooms, but at the top of the stairs were two open spaces (to the left and the right) which we made into a bedroom and a sitting room. That is how we got five bedroom out of the house.

It worked out great. We could all have our own bedrooms. Robin chose to share with Uncle Dean, Scott took another, and that left me with the open space at the top of the stairs to the left. I was so happy I had my own room that I didn't care that it was open. Mother and Uncle Dean put up a curtain so I could have privacy, and that made it all the better.

When you go from having very little to having something better, you are always grateful. Most people have had their own room, but for those of us who never have, a space with a curtain for a door is just as good as a real bedroom.

It is a true blessing when you can look at the good things that God gives to you. It reminds me of a song I used to sing with my kids when they were all little. Even now we sometimes sing it. It is called "The Thankfulness Song." When you have God in your heart, you are thankful for all that you have and all that He gives you. It may not seem like much to some, but to others it is a treasure. Still, our true treasures should be laid up in Heaven. God tells us in Matt. 6:19-21:

> Do not lay up for yourselves treasures on earth, where moth and rust destroy and where thieves break in and steal; but lay up for yourselves treasures in heaven, where neither moth nor rust destroys and where thieves do not break in and steal. For where your treasure is, there your heart will be also.

God sure does know how to humble our hearts, doesn't He?

CHAPTER 7

The Old Gray House

After moving into the old gray house, my brothers and I made more friends. However, some of them were not a good influence on us. In my teenage years, I would make a lot of bad choices because of the people I chose to hang around with. Now, don't misunderstand: I still had good friends. But I didn't always choose to hang around them. I was always looking for excitement in my life.

I still talked with my cousin Donna, and we went to each other's houses when we could, but it wasn't like when we lived next door to each other and could walk over to visit. Being miles apart made it hard to spend time together. Now we had to ask for rides, and that didn't always work out. Our parents were not too keen on driving us to see each other every day because of gas, work, their nightlife, and not enough money.

We talked on the phone, but Donna and I mainly saw each other at school. We drifted apart a little, and as we got into high school, we each found our own new group of friends. We tried to talk at school, but we only had one class together freshmen year, and every year after that was the same: just one or two classes together, until graduation. Still, we were always there for each other.

I loved that old gray farmhouse, though. I loved going out to sit in the old house that was falling apart. My mother worried that I would get hurt, but I snuck in there anyhow, on account of the fact that my cat kept her kittens there, in a big box of clothes that someone before us had left behind.

I had the most beautiful calico cat. I called her Mitt Mitts, because she had four white paws that looked like mittens. I loved her so much, and we played together every day.

When I got off the bus, there she was, waiting for me at the end of the driveway. My mother used to laugh at the way that cat just knew when it was time for me to get home from school. Mitt Mitts would walk up to the house with me. Of course I would sneak her in for a treat of meat or some milk. Mother yelled at me at first, but after a while I caught her giving Mitt Mitts treats, too. She never was a cat lover, but she didn't mind them much as long as they were not in her house.

After a treat, Mitt Mitts and I would head outside to the barn or the old chicken coop to sit and talk. She was a great listener. If she had a litter, she would lead me right to the old house that was falling apart and then to the box of clothes where her kittens were. To get in I had to squeeze through a door that only opened about a foot, due to all the junk behind it. Then I would get inside that old box with Mitt Mitts and her kittens and sing to them for hours. All the while my cat would purr, wanting me to praise her for being a good mother.

After a while I usually heard my mother or Uncle Dean yelling for me; then I would scamper out of there as fast as I could. They acted like they didn't know where I was, but later I found out that my mom had asked if the building was stable enough for me to be in it. It was, to her surprise.

She snuck out from time to time to see if I was okay. I never knew at the time that she was listening to me sing to the kittens. She told me this after I was grown and married. I thought I was being very sneaky, but Mother always knew where to find me. As long as I was safe, she just left me to my hiding places to sing and play. It goes to show that parents know more than we think they do.

CHAPTER 8

Don't Blackmail

As I mentioned, as time went on, I changed from the sweet little girl that hid and sang into an unbearable preteen. I would torment my brothers so bad that they would shoot rubber bands at me, lock me in my closet until I peed my pants, or (sometimes) give me a well-deserved punch in the arm or the leg.

I used to do a lot of things I shouldn't have done. The boys sometimes caught me in the act, like when I would sneak into the junk food that Mother got for us on occasion, when she could afford it. They would threaten to tell on me to Mother, so I would threaten to tell Mom how they snuck out to party with their friends. That only worked until they figured out that I was bluffing (I didn't want to get into trouble for knowing and not telling Mother in the first place).

One time I was going to tell on them for being mean. They did the usual, hanging me in the mudroom by my belt loop. They left me there until Uncle Dean got home from work almost three hours later. But I did not learn my lesson: while I was hanging there, I figured I needed to come up with better blackmailing skills than just saying I would tell Mother.

My bottom could not handle being hung on those hooks many more times. Not to mention that as I got bigger, some of my pants couldn't hold my weight; sometimes they would rip and I would fall three feet to the floor. Whenever that happened, I was glad to be free, but then I had to come up with a good story to tell Mother about why that pair of pants had a torn-off belt loop. It was hard to make up stories about the same thing over and over again, and Mom was catching on (she told me later that she figured it out—I believe that Uncle Dean told her—but she also said that if I was not willing to tell her the truth, she would let me hang on a hook).

> *It was hard to make up stories about the same thing over and over again, and Mom was catching on*

One day Scott and Robin got sick of me pestering them, so they locked me in my closet and forgot about me for many hours. Mother came home from work early that day, at 2:00 or 3:00 p.m. (she had decided not to go to the bar that afternoon). She saw the boys playing out in the yard with their friends. Then she came in the house and called for me.

When I didn't answer, she yelled, then she heard me faintly calling back, "Mom, I'm up here. The boys locked me in the closet."

Mom came upstairs into my room, opened the closet door, and saw that I had peed in my pants. I looked up and saw that she was really mad. She knew that I must have been in that closet for a long time. Everything was going to hit the fan; all the secrets were going to come out. Between gritted teeth, she said, "Go wash up and change your clothes, while I call the boys in."

I ran as fast as I could to the bathroom and took my time cleaning up and changing. I knew that the belt was coming out. Mother never used it on us unless we made her really mad, and that took a lot. I could feel it already. I shook just thinking of the pain that was coming like a freight train for my backside.

Sure enough, all our little secrets came out, and we all got into big trouble. My mother is only 4' 8" tall, but I think the U.S. Army must have issued her a pair of boots for that day. I'm sad to say we all learned a hard lesson: *don't blackmail.*

But it still didn't end there. My brothers found other ways to get back at me for not leaving them and their friends alone.

I learned something from all of this later in life. A wise man will listen, but a fool despises wisdom. "The fear of the Lord is the beginning of knowledge, but fools despise wisdom and instruction" (Prov. 1:7). I realized that I was a fool.

CHAPTER 9

Out of Control. The Solution? 4H

My mother was just about at her wits end with me causing problems with my brothers, always trying to talk her down, and getting into trouble at school (the principal often called her at work; it was a good thing that she only worked a few blocks away). She thought it would be best for her and me to get counseling, so she found a counselor by the name of Mrs. Stark.

I really liked her. So did my mother. Mrs. Stark was a big help to her in dealing with the death of the two men she had loved so dearly. However, I did not always take the counseling seriously.

One day the school called Mom to come and pick me up because I hurt another student. When she got there, she was shocked to find out that it was a boy. He had been teasing me, and I got mad at him, grabbed his arm, and flipped him over my shoulder into a mud puddle. I think he was more embarrassed than hurt. Nonetheless, this was grounds for me to be sent home for the rest of the day. My mother was not happy.

She struggled with me so much, but she also worried about me, because on top of being out of control at times, I had epilepsy.

I never understood the problems that my brain had. Mother once tried to explain to me what was wrong. She said that the soft spot on top of my head hadn't healed until I was eight or nine years old, where normally it closed up by age five. I had what Doctor Matthews called "petit mal seizures." I was diagnosed at age four, and he put me on some medications to help with the seizures.

My brothers used to say I was a space cadet. I would stare at nothing and not be conscious of those around me. It would be seconds in my mind (I remember just looking at an object and being fixated on it), but in reality I would do this for up to a minute or more.

It was so embarrassing to have a seizure in class. All the children knew when I had one. I would wake up at my desk and the other kids would be doing math, while I still had my reading or spelling out. After I came out of it, I would be really tired and could not stay awake.

The other kids teased me terribly and called me a teacher's pet, because our teacher would just smile at me as if nothing had happened and help me get to the lesson that the class was on. They constantly called me names when the teacher was not listening.

> The other kids constantly called me names when the teacher was not listening.

I just didn't understand why they had to be so mean. I decided that I was not going to take it anymore. If they could dish it out, so could I; but I would do it with anger and physical contact. This was an ongoing problem with me through all of elementary school and into junior high.

My poor mother had a lot to deal with. I took her away from work and from my brothers. We would go to counseling, things would get better for a while, then they would plummet again.

By the time I turned thirteen, I thought that I knew it all (I had a very rude awakening ahead of me). I would tell my mother where I was going instead of asking her. If I did ask and she said, "No," I would talk her down until she told me, "Go. Do what you want. You will, anyway!"

It seemed much easier to Mother to give in than to actually stick to her decision, because I would make her life a living nightmare, so to speak. I was spoiled and inconsiderate, to put it mildly.

Even though she knew I was wrong, she had no patience to deal with my overbearing attitude. Mother let me do what I wanted so she could have peace. A lot of that peace was at the bars, drinking with her friends and family.

Alcohol was a way for her to deal with all of her life problems. I just happened to be one of the biggest ones she had to deal with. She was not right for giving in to me, but when I look back, I realize that she was hurting and I was not helping her. If anything, I made her want to drink more.

Mother thought that if she found something which interested me, I would stop getting into so much trouble. She talked over a few things I liked to do with our counselor. They knew I loved horses, so they encouraged me to join a local 4H Club.

When mother first approached me with the idea, I told her, "I don't think I want to join." But when she mentioned that it was a *horse* 4H Club, I changed my mind right away.

Melinda was our 4H teacher, and she had a lot of horses on her farm. She was a great, inspirational lady whom I will never forget as long as I live.

She eventually trained us to ride Western style, but we learned basic stuff at first: how to care for the tack and the horses, how to groom them, and how to bridle and saddle them. Shoveling stalls was not fun, but feeding and watering the horses was a real treat.

I looked forward to those times. I even offered to feed and water the horses on days when we didn't have meetings. I sang to them, and we had the best conversations (horses are very good listeners, just like cats). It was like they really understood the hurt and pain that I was feeling. It brought a peace into my heart and a longing to always be in that peaceful place.

Before Melinda would let us ride, we also had to learn the parts of a horse. I looked at her as if she was crazy when she told us that there was a part of a horse called the "frog."

She picked up a hoof pick, then the foot of one of the horses, and started showing us how to clean their hooves. She told us that the hoof itself was like our fingernails, just a lot thicker. I watched intently so I could master this task and move on to the riding part (if it was something I was interested in, I always had the goal ahead of me and worked hard to get there).

As Melinda cleaned the hoof, she stayed to the sides, never going down the middle. The middle of the hoof, she said, had the "frog": this was like a pad on the bottom of the horse's feet. It was a little hard, but not like the hoof itself. Melinda explained what happened when a rock got stuck between the crease of the frog and the hoof, and how much pain it could cause the horse if not removed.

I remember her telling us how important it was for us to care for the horses because they were a living, breathing creature of God. She taught us the concept, "treat others as you wish to be treated." For example, if we were uncomfortable with rocks in our shoes, so were horses. At the same time, we had to learn to respect the horses or they would not respect us. What a lesson!

I never realized that Melinda was teaching me or that her lessons were impacting my whole attitude. My mother noticed a big change in me, though, and it made her very happy.

I paid very close attention to all that Melinda taught us, and soon the time came when we all got to learn how to ride. As she assigned us to the horses we would be riding and working with, I couldn't help but smile from ear to ear. I could hardly wait. The day I had been waiting for was finally here, as all the work I had put in paid off.

I was put with a horse called Bridget. She was owned by Sandy, a girl my age who lived out of town and boarded her horse at Melinda's house. Sandy had given permission for the 4H club to use Bridget. When she was there, then of course she would be riding her horse, in which case I rode another one called Fort.

Those two horses were totally different in every way. Bridget was 13½ hands, where Fort stood about 16 hands tall (they don't measure horses in inches or centimeters; instead they measure them in hands, where one hand equals four inches). Fort was dark brown, with a black mane and a lot of attitude. Bridget was shorter and light brown in color, with a white blaze down her face and a tan mane and tail. She was very beautiful and sassy. Because she was shorter than a horse but taller than a pony, Bridget could be shown as either at the shows (when it came time, I chose to show her in the horse shows, because that was where all my friends were competing).

After we were saddled and given last minute instructions, Melinda took us out on a trail ride, where she taught us how to always be in control of our horses. The way we sat, the motions we made, the noises we made with our mouths; all of these affected the horses and how they would react to us. If you sat deep, your horse would stop. If they didn't, you pulled back on the reins and said, "Whoa." We also learned how to hold the reins, and how much slack the horse needed so that you didn't hurt its mouth with the bit or give them wrong cue (like to back up).

In order to prepare us for the 4H horse shows, Melinda additionally taught us showmanship, barrel racing, jumping, halter showmanship, pleasure class, and much more.

I loved training the horses. There was a lot to learn, and I worked hard to master it all. So did my friend Tory, who lived down the road from my house and loved horses just as much as I did. We had joined 4H together, and she also rode Fort. Soon Tory and I were riding like pros.

We always did our best to learn and master the events as we practiced in the small riding arena at Melinda's house. The Alger County horseshow was coming up, and we all wanted to be ready to do our very best.

Before that show, Melinda set up a few practice ones at her arena. At the first one, we didn't receive any ribbons or trophies; it was just to get us ready for the real shows. The second one was also for practice but it was also a 4H club competition. Tory and I could hardly wait, and we invited all of our family and friends.

The day came, and I was confident that I was ready. Both Tory's family and mine came to watch us ride. Even Aunt Gwyn came, since she was not only Uncle Burt's wife but also Tory's sister. She was proud of both of us for our accomplishments in learning all about horses. (Later, Aunt Gwyn started helping out with 4H and working with the children. She even bought Fort a few years later, and he became a great horse for her.)

Grandma Alice came with Uncle Dean and my mother. My mother was so proud of me; it was written all over her face. It made me feel good to do something that made her proud. This was a feeling I had never sensed from my mother before.

Mother has been happy with some of my choices and accomplishments throughout my life, but I have never felt it as strongly as I did that day. What I needed the most in that moment was to know that I made my mother proud.

CHAPTER 10

The Horse Shows

During training at Melinda's, Sandy decided to share Bridget with me at the shows. When she wasn't showing her, I was, or else we would take turns in the same event. When one of us was done, she would jump off and let the other on to compete. It worked out great.

At the Alger County Horse Show, which was open to anyone (not just our club), the first class in the 4H horse show was halter class. I walked out into the arena with Bridget and prayed that no one would see how nervous I really was. I focused on the show and on what I had learned. I told myself that this was no different than the practice runs I had done the day before.

I kept my eyes on what the judges signaled us to do, but my nerves took over. I messed up a few times and got upset. I kept telling myself, "I know this! How come I am messing up?"

Then I regained control of my feelings and moved forward. Finally, the judges had us line up and face them. Bridget fell into place and stood with her feet and head perfect. I could hardly believe my eyes. I just smiled and said under my breath, "Thank you, Lord."

The judges looked over the horses, then dismissed us from the arena. They got together, and a few moments later they called in the fourth place winner. Then they called third place.

All of a sudden someone nudged me and said, "Michelle, that is you." I was in shock: they had called Bridget and I for third place!

I walked into the arena and accepted my ribbon. I led Bridget over and circled her to stand next to the fourth place winner, while the judges called the second and first place winners into the arena to pick up their ribbons. Then we all stood together as they presented the winners of halter class to the audience. I was in a daze as they applauded.

> My heart was overwhelmed with joy. She is proud of me, I thought. My mother is really proud of me.

Then I looked to where my family sat and saw Grandma, Uncle Dean, and my mother. They stood clapping with the biggest smiles on their faces. My attention focused on Mother, and I saw how proud she was of me in that moment. My heart was overwhelmed with joy. *She is proud of me*, I thought. *My mother is really proud of me.*

My confidence grew as the show went on, and I won many ribbons. Bridget and I competed in an obstacle course that involved jumping, barrels, and a black mat with logs on both sides that the horse had to step over and across. Most horses were afraid of the black mat. They would stop in front of it, sniff and snort nervously, then refuse to go over it. But not Bridget. She went through the obstacle like we were riding trails in the woods.

The fastest times won the ribbons. I was shocked to hear our names called for first place.

As I received each ribbon, I would run it over to my mother. She gave me a smile as I handed her each one.

I won eight all together at two horse shows at Melinda's arena: first place for the obstacle course, three second place ribbons for trail, barrel racing, and pleasure class, and two third places for halter class and an egg and spoon race (a neat race they came up with where you had an egg on a spoon while you were on your horse, and you had to race around a barrel in the middle of the arena and back to the finish line without dropping the egg). Finally, I won two fourth place ribbons, in horsemanship and showmanship.

I competed again about a month later, at the Alger County horse show, where I won several more ribbons. That horse show was special. About halfway through, Sandy came up to me (as she normally did) and handed Bridget to me. As I took the reins from her and patted Bridget lovingly, I realized something. I looked at Sandy funny, then said, "I don't show for two more events!"

Sandy looked down and then up at me with a weak smile. She said, "I know," and walked away. I watched her go, puzzled.

It was my turn to enter the arena again. My event was the obstacle course, and I ran through it smoothly. As I left the arena, the judge announced, "That was Michelle Brisson, riding Bridget. What a great run! Bridget is a Welsh Quarter Horse and has just come up for sale. For more information, contact … ."

That was all I heard, as I processed the words, "Bridget is for sale." *What?* I thought. My mind was awhirl. *Sandy can't be selling her.*

I would never be able to ride Bridget again. I never thought I would ever be without her. I loved that horse; I just couldn't let anyone have her. *What am I going to do?* I thought. *I am going to have to ask mother to buy Bridget. That is all there is to it.*

With this in mind, I ran over to where my family was sitting. I said, "Mom, can you buy Bridget for me? Please, Mom? I will never ask for another thing again."

Isn't that what most children say when they want something which they think is so important that they just can't live without it? I had run and asked Mother on a whim. I didn't think it through at all; I was just desperate.

Mom listened. She seemed to understand how lost and alone I sometimes felt. With a sad look, she said, "Sis, we can't afford a horse." (Sis was one of the nicknames my mother called me.) "Do you know how much it is to feed one?" she continued. "Not to mention the cost of putting up a fence."

"But Mom, I just can't lose her!"

"Sis," Mother said, "I will think about it. In the meantime, 4H doesn't cost that much money. There is only a signup fee and little things here and there. You ride the horses for free at Melinda's! It is a lot of money to have a horse, but as I said I will think about it."

Usually, when Mother said she would think about it, it meant no. Sad, I walked away, going over to Bridget and wrapping my arms around her neck. I told her that I loved her.

I loved riding Bridget.

Sandy came over and said she was sorry that she hadn't told me about selling her. She hadn't had the heart for it. I told her it was okay and asked how much she was selling Bridget for. She told me $450.

I knew that this was a lot of money. It would have taken three of my mother's paychecks to come up with that kind of cash. My heart was broken, and I couldn't think of anything else to do, so I prayed.

"Dear God," I said, "You could help me get Bridget, couldn't You? God, You know how much I love her. Please God, can You help me?"

I won some ribbons and a mini trophy, and I was still very unhappy. I was ungrateful for the day I had just had with Bridget.

I never realized that I needed an everyday relationship with God. I didn't hear God's voice, and I didn't feel any better about the situation.

I left that day feeling hurt and frustrated. There was nothing I could do. I realized only later that I had little faith in the prayer I had sent up. I didn't remember the verse that Aunt Lu taught us at VBS when I was praying, "Therefore I say to you, whatever things you ask when you pray, believe that you receive them, and you will have them" (Mark 11:24). Had I remembered this verse, I would have had more hope and faith in the Lord.

But God was still a gracious and giving God, even though I was ungrateful and had little faith. You see, Grandma Alice came to all my horse shows, so she was with my mother when I asked for the horse. My grandma had a talk with my mother that day; a talk that upon later reflection would show me how great and mighty a God we serve.

He cares about the littlest things in our lives that we love. It says in Psalm 37:4, "Delight yourself also in the Lord, and He shall give you the desires of your heart."

CHAPTER 11

A Gift

A week or so after the horse show, I was still sulking and feeling sorry for myself. I was thinking about quitting the 4H club and giving up riding. Mother knew this.

She got off the phone one afternoon, walked up to me, and said, "Sis, I bet you won't guess who I just talked to."

I was not really interested, but something about the tone of her voice and the excitement she was showing got my attention. I asked, "Who?"

"Your Grandmother," was her response.

"Oh?" I said, looking at her with curiosity.

With a big smile, Mother told me, "Your Grandmother just bought a really big gift for you by the name of Bridget."

I could not contain my excitement at all. I smiled from ear to ear and kept asking my

> With a big smile, Mother told me, "Your Grandmother just bought a really big gift for you by the name of Bridget."

mother, over and over, "Are you serious? This is for real? Grandma really bought me Bridget?"

It turned out that at the show, when I had begged for Bridget, Grandma had told Mom she would buy me the horse. She called Sandy's mother, and they settled on an amount. My grandma got Bridget for $300, along with her saddle, bridle, saddle blanket, and all the rest of Bridget's horse tack.

Sandy's family knew how much I loved Bridget. They lowered the price for my grandma so that she could afford to buy her for me. It's also why they threw in the tack, which was not originally part of the deal.

I called my grandma and told her how grateful I was and that I loved her. She told me to take good care of Bridget and to keep riding.

When I got off the phone, Mother said, "Michelle."

Oh no, I thought, *she used my name, not Sis. There has to be a catch to this somewhere, because she has a very serious look on her face.*

Mother proceeded to tell me that I was responsible for taking care of this horse. That meant cleaning out the barn so she that had shelter, helping put up the fence, stacking hay, feeding her every day, and making sure all her needs were met before I went anywhere.

When she finished telling me this, she added, "If you do not take care of this horse, we are selling her and giving your grandmother back her money. Do you understand?"

I was happy to comply with anything she wanted me to do. I was getting a horse! And not just any horse; I was getting Bridget.

God had opened a door for me to have a horse; and not just any horse, but one whom I loved and had bonded with.

And He didn't just answer my prayer about buying Bridget; He provided much more that I didn't think about. Uncle Dean and Uncle Dale worked at a sawmill and got logs for the fence. Mom called our landlords, who gave permission for my uncles to build the fence and connect it to the barn. I have no idea how they got the other fencing materials. Uncle Dean also bought the hay for my horse for the winter.

The day I got that news is a day I will never forget. But it is also a day which I look back on wishing that I could have learned the lessons God was trying to teach me.

I was grateful the whole time that I was putting up the fence, hauling the hay, and getting ready for my horse to come home. I did all that I was asked. But I don't ever remember thanking God for answering my prayer. I was being selfish because I got what I wanted. That was all that mattered to me at the time.

Sometimes we overlook the lessons God is trying to teach us. When we let Satan block those lessons with our own selfish motives, we end up serving the wrong master. "No servant can serve two masters; for either he will hate the one and love the other, or else he will be loyal to the one and despise the other. You cannot serve God and mammon" (Luke 16:13).

In other words, you can't serve God and Satan. When we serve self, we serve Satan, because when we look to our own needs, we lose track of God's needs in and for our lives. That is what Satan wants: for us to lose track of God so that we do not trust in Him or lean on His everlasting arms. I long to be in the Savior's loving arms, protected and safe from all harm. Don't you?

The very last horse show that I competed in was Alger County Fair's. This time I rode my own horse. I remember it well, because I won the grand prize trophy for the entire show, along with a first place trophy and a first place ribbon in the pop race.

The pop race was a little like the egg and spoon, except that you didn't carry anything. You raced to the end of the arena, where you circled a barrel. But before you circled it, you stopped, jumped off your horse, chugged a soda, then jumped back on your horse and rode as fast as you could to the finish line.

I remember that race well, because Tory competed with me. Our times were really close until right before the finish line, when her saddle slid to the side of her horse and she fell off. She was so mad that she started slapping her horse and yelling at it. Then she came over to me and said, "You know that was my ribbon. I would have won, had my saddle not fallen off. My time was faster."

I was really hurt. I thought Tory was my friend, and friends didn't treat each other like that. But God was teaching me a great lesson at that very moment. He wanted me to see that *I* didn't always treat others with respect and love. "Therefore, whatever you want men to do to you, do also to them" (Matt. 7:12a).

Tory was still my friend. She had just had a bad day at the show and was having a hard time dealing with her frustration. She apologized to me later, and I accepted. We had many more adventures together later.

I left the horse show with the biggest trophy I had ever won, plus a bunch more ribbons. I was so happy that I didn't think about all the work everyone had to put into the horse shows for me. Melinda tailored my horse and drove her to the shows. My mother made sure I had the proper dress attire and all my tack to care for Bridget at the show. They and others did so much, but I didn't pay much attention. As long as I got to the shows, I was happy.

There was my selfish side coming though again. Today I wish I could go back and tell them all thank you for all the hard work they did for me; but I can't, because some of them are no longer living. They are resting, waiting for Jesus to come take us home.

Later on my grand prize trophy broke. All I have left today is the horse from the very top. I do still have all of my ribbons and my little trophy in an old, metal lockbox.

That memory box from childhood holds many little trinkets to remind me of my life growing up in Trenary. But the best memories I have are still the ones I hold dear in my heart, of times past and lessons I have learned.

CHAPTER 12
Answered Prayer

Because we were a poor family, for my mother to allow my grandma to buy me a horse was a big deal. Mother's check went to the bills, and what little she had left she kept for herself to go out to the bars with my aunts and uncles.

We had little food at times. Mother would go to the Trenary Co-op and charge what she could. She paid toward the bill every payday, but it grew too large and the co-op refused to let her charge anymore until she had paid off the previous bill. Mother knew that things were getting rough, and she stopped going to the bars so much. She began to drink more at home.

We were living off of rice, macaroni, canned tomatoes, eggs from the farm down the road, and whatever meat my brothers brought home from hunting. Even when hunting season was over, Mother send Scott and Robin out to hunt rabbit, partridge, and deer. We never worried about getting caught, because the DNR knew how poor we were and acted like they knew nothing.

My brothers both worked at a locker plant that processed meat, so when they killed a deer, the owner would let them bring in the carcass and process it to bring home. Then mother would freeze the meat. The deer would last us a while, but eventually it ran out. Then we would be eating goulashes, fried oatmeal, or fried corn meal mush.

Meanwhile, we still had a few months to go before Bridget could graze. I went out to feed her one morning and opened the door to the chicken coop where we stored her hay (the hay was easier for me to get to here, and anyway we didn't have a tractor to put hay in the loft of the barn). I stood there and looked at the last of what we had. There were only about twenty square bales left, and I knew that wasn't going to get Bridget through until summer.

My heart broke. I didn't want to lose my horse; not now! I had just gotten her two summers earlier.

I spent a lot of time in the barn and in the field with Bridget while she grazed. She was the best listener I ever knew besides Mitt Mitts, and she always knew how to make me feel better. I would tell her my deepest desires and secrets, knowing that she would never tell anyone else. Not that she could have; she was a horse. But the bond we had was so strong that, even if she could talk, I knew my secrets were safe with her.

She would nudge me and nuzzle her nose into my jacket so that I would pet her. If I walked away, she would follow. But if I wasn't around, sometimes she would take off back to Melinda's house to be with the other horses. I can't tell you how many times I had to go get her and ride her home.

After thinking of all the good times we had had, I grabbed a bale and threw it over the fence, then jumped in and cut the strings. I patted Bridget on the neck. Tears started to run down my face. I didn't want to lose her. I jumped on her back and lay down on her, hugging her neck while she ate. She had no idea what might happen soon; how our friendship might end.

After a while I jumped off and walked slowly back to the house. I looked at Mother and said, "Mom, we are low on hay. We only have about twenty bales left."

I think Mother was watching me through the window that morning. She looked at me with a worried face and in a low, sad voice said, "I know, Sis. I know."

I went upstairs to my bedroom and lay on my bed. "God," I prayed, "if you can hear me, I have a favor to ask. I really love Bridget, and I don't want to have to sell her, but we can't afford to feed her. Can you please help?" I lay there on my bed and cried for a long time. Even though I prayed, I didn't see how God could save my horse when we had very little food, even in the house.

I never thought about it back then, but we never completely ran out of food. We always had something in the house. My mother's family or friends in the neighborhood would always bring us food. It wasn't a lot, but every little bit helped. The bakery let Mom take home bread and cinnamon toast; once in a while they even had leftover donuts. Grandma Alice always made sure she brought some sort of food over. Never did we go hungry. We may not have had the best meals, but they filled our bellies.

The next morning my mother went to work. The local farmer who made a weekly stop to pick up bread ends popped in to see if they had a load for him. My mother happened to wait on him.

She got to talking to him and asked what he used the bread ends for. He told her that he fed them to his cows, because it saved him money on buying grain.

This gave my mother a great idea. She thought, *Cows are not much different than a horse.* The next week she came home from work with a lot of fifty-pound bags of bread ends. When I asked her what they were for, she said, "To feed the horse."

I looked at her funny. I thought she was losing her mind. "Horses eat hay, Mom, not bread!"

Uncle Dean and I helped her unload the bread and put it in the chicken coop. Then Uncle Dean grabbed a few pieces, walked over to the fence, and held them out to Bridget in the palm of his hand. She sniffed it and then took it. She loved it!

I never realized until that day just how much my mother cared about me or how much my horse meant to me. I knew Mom thought horses were pretty, and nice to watch running in the field or in the riding arena, but I also knew that she was afraid of them. For her to do this for me was a great act of kindness, because she was not a horse lover.

We started to give Bridget hay and bread mixed together to help stretch the hay out over a longer period. I learned later that it is not good to feed horses like that, but at the time it helped to feed her, and I didn't have to sell her.

One day when I was at school and my mother came home from work early, Bridget got out of her corral. Oh, how I wish I could have been there to see the whole thing play out.

At first my mother sat at the kitchen table to do crosswords, by a window that looked out at her favorite lilac bush.

As you may know, lilacs only bloom at a certain time of the year and don't stay too long. We had a very big bush with many flowers on it. When they came into bloom, my mother was very happy; she loved the smell of them, their color, and how beautiful they looked. If you were coming up the driveway and the wind blew just right, you caught that beautiful scent and felt the peacefulness of nature.

So you see, this was a very important bush to my mother. And that day she happened to look up and saw Bridget tasting her lilacs: biting them, pulling them off, and stomping on them.

"No, no, no!" Mother yelled. She ran outside and tried to get the horse away from the lilac bushes. She pulled on her mane and yelled at her to get out of the flowers. Bridget didn't move. Mother pushed on her neck, also to no avail. She gave up and angrily turned around. As she started to walk away, Bridget pushed my 4' 8" mother with her head, knocking her face-first into the dirt.

When I got off the bus and walked up the driveway, it was a sight to see: my mother, standing there with her hands on her hips, telling me to go and get my stubborn horse and put her back in her pen.

Of course I made the mistake of asking what had happened. She yelled at me that the horse was eating her lilac bushes. I gave her my backpack, ran, and grabbed Bridget by the mane, leading her back to her corral.

As we walked, I remember asking her, "Bridget, you getting into trouble again? You know Mom loves those bushes. Why can't you just eat the grass like a normal horse?"

I put her in her corral, fixed the fence, and headed back to the house to find out more about what happened. Uncle Dean was now home and was cracking up at my mother. She didn't look amused.

I asked again what happened, and Uncle Dean told me that I had better wait until later to get that answer, "After she has time to cool down," he said.

I just knew the story had to be funny, so I waited till I could get a moment alone with Uncle Dean. When he told me what happened, I cracked up laughing, too.

CHAPTER 13

The Loss, and Turning to Rebellion

---—◦—---

One day Mother and Uncle Dean told me that the landlords raised the rent. Also, fuel to heat the house had gone up, gas prices had gone up, and so had food prices. They ended with, "So we just can't afford to feed your horse for another year."

My heart sank. I went to my room and plopped on my bed. I began to cry, and instead of turning to God, I decided I was going to be tough about this and find all the good in not having my horse around. *I don't have to feed her*, I thought. *I don't have to water her, and I don't have to clean the horse manure out of the barn. Yeah, this will be great not having a horse. No more chores.*

If I had turned to God in my time of need, I know that He would have found a way to help us keep Bridget. But my faith in God was not very strong; "O ye of little faith."

Sandy talked to her mom, and they bought Bridget back. I later found out that they sold her to a farm that did trail riding for the disabled. Bridget would one day die on that farm after living (I believe) to be twenty-eight years old.

I would cry the day when I found out that Bridget died. She was a big part of my childhood. Caring for her taught me many responsibilities and helped to refine me into a better person later in life.

After selling my horse, I went back to my old ways and many other bad habits. To think that God was watching me as I was an unbearable child to my mother makes me very sad today. I had learned a lot at VBS and at 4H Club, and I should have carried it with me, but as a teenager I thought nothing of others. I only thought about myself.

Most teens focus on themselves, but most were not as bad as I was. I kept going out and doing what I wanted, not thinking of how my mother felt or how it affected her as a single parent.

I thought, *if my mother can drink whenever she wants, then so can I.* I felt like drinking was fun, but it wasn't enough, so I also started smoking behind my mother's back (I would steal cigarettes from Robin, who was old enough to buy them).

Don't get me wrong. I was not ungrateful and selfish all the time. I did chores for my mother around the house, and I loved to help other people. I did have a loving heart; to see someone smile because of something I did for them was nice and very rewarding.

Sometimes, though, that was hard for me to do. Most people didn't want me around them or their children because of my foul language. Recall that my family liked to drink and hang out at the bars, so their language was not very Christian; and my brothers and I picked up their bad habits.

So while swearing was normal to me, it limited my friends. Unless my mother was friends with their parents, I was considered disrespectful and adults would discourage their children from spending any time with me.

It hurt my feelings a lot. I didn't understand until later on in life why those parents made that decision. Today I look back and think, *If those were my children, I would do the same thing.* As a matter of fact, I direct my children to have Christian friends and be a witness to those in need. I encourage them to be around Godly people so they can learn and grow in the ways of the Lord rather than the ways of the world. I want them to make good decisions when they are older.

Back then, though, I did not have God in my heart to help me see what was right and wrong. I knew God; I even knew that He heard and saw everything I did. But it just wasn't as real to me in my heart as I now wish it would have been. I didn't always feel that what I did was wrong; not until later.

One day my friend Melanie came over to spend the night, and we both ran out of smokes. She had this bright idea to steal cigarettes from my brother Robin.

> She had this bright idea to steal cigarettes from my brother Robin.

I told her, "If we take a lot, he will know, and he will come after us to get them back."

She didn't think we would get caught. Melanie used to take five or six at a time from her mother and never got caught (what she didn't understand was that her mother was usually drinking at the time and just thought she, Melanie's mother, had smoked them all). She kept insisting that Robin would never know, until I finally said, "Okay! Let's try it."

We snuck downstairs and looked around. Good: no one was there. Robin's cigarettes were on the counter. We walked over quietly, and I took one. I said, "Let's go before he sees us."

Melanie said, "No! Let's take a few more; he will never know."

Again, I tried to talk her out of it. "Melanie, look; he has a full pack with only one or two taken out. He will know if we take more!" She disagreed and persisted until I gave in and said, "Okay."

Melanie grabbed several more cigarettes, and we walked out of the house as quickly and quietly as we could. Then we ran to the sauna, went in quickly, and shut and locked the door behind us.

We looked around and realized that we couldn't smoke in the dressing area, or it would smell badly. We decided to go into the actual sauna and sit on the top bench, where there was a one-foot-square wooden window. We opened it and lit up our smokes.

Melanie said, "See, I told you we would get away with it."

I was shocked and relieved at the same time. I told her that she was right; it had worked.

We sat there laughing and talking about what we were going to do for the rest of that day and evening. Then I heard my brother Robin yelling.

"Open this door right now," he said. "Open it, or I will break it in."

Melanie and I looked at each other. If Robin found us with his smokes, we were dead meat. We threw them all out of the wooden window, both lit and unlit, and shut it. Just then we heard him break down the door, and he stormed in.

I was scared, but I knew I had to be calm. He started yelling and threatening to do us bodily harm unless we gave him back his cigarettes. Of course we lied through our teeth and told him we didn't have them, even though you could smell the smoke in the sauna. I said; "Go ahead: search us."

Believe me, he did; then he searched the whole sauna. But he found nothing. He figured we had thrown them down the drain.

Melanie and I let out a sigh of relief when Robin left. We waited a while, and when we knew the coast was clear, we ran out to the back of the building to find our smokes. We grabbed the ones that were still lit and put them out (it was lucky that we hadn't started a fire). We put the unlit cigarettes in our pockets, then ran and hid them in the chicken coop.

I knew that Robin was telling Mother and that she would be checking out the situation soon. Once again, of course, we lied, telling her that we never took any of his smokes. We said we were just talking in the sauna and didn't want the boys in there, so we locked the door. As for the smoke smell? We said it was like that when we went in.

Mother and Robin searched in the sauna and all around the outside of it, but they found nothing. Finally, Mom told Robin that Uncle Dean probably took them before he went to work. Melanie and I sighed with relief. We never again took anything from Robin; we both knew that he was on to us.

God must have been so grieved by my lying, stealing, and disobedience to Him. I look back at those days and cringe to think of all of the sinful stuff I did.

God tells us, "And you shall know the truth, and the truth shall make you free" (John 8:32). In Exodus 20:15, He says, "You shall not steal." Just a few verses earlier, God says, "Honor your father and your mother, that your days may be long upon the land which the Lord your God is giving you" (Exod. 20:12). And in 1 Peter 1:13-21, we read:

> Therefore gird up the loins of your mind, be sober, and rest your hope fully upon the grace that is to be brought to you at the revelation of Jesus Christ; as obedient children, not conforming yourselves to the former lusts, as in your ignorance; but as He who called you is holy, you also be holy in all your conduct, because it is written, "Be holy, for I am holy."

And if you call on the Father, who without partiality judges according to each one's work, conduct yourselves throughout the time of your stay here in fear; knowing that you were not redeemed with corruptible things, like silver or gold, from your aimless conduct received by tradition from your fathers, but with the precious blood of Christ, as of a lamb without blemish and without spot. He indeed was foreordained before the foundation of the world, but was manifest in these last times for you who through Him believe in God, who raised Him from the dead and gave Him glory, so that your faith and hope are in God.

I followed none of these promises and commandments from God in my young life. I realize today that I could have had a better life if I had. But God let me go through those hard times to learn and be refined, so that I could warn others of the danger of losing one's salvation to the lusts of the world.

Had I given my life to the Lord and listened to the still, small voice which I heard telling me that I was wrong, I could have been a good example of Christ-like character to my friends. Instead, I lived for the world and whatever I could get out of it that made me feel better.

Even then, I noticed that I only felt better for a little while and then always wanted more. That is Satan's snare to pull us in.

When God gives us His love, it never changes. We don't have to long for more of His love for us to be happy, because He pours it out abundantly onto us from Heaven. We never have to crave more, because our cup is so full that we can't contain the joy. We want to share the goodness of our Lord and Savior Jesus Christ.

Satan, on the other hand, only gives you a little pleasure at a time, trying to suck you into his evil plans to cause others pain and hurt, while you think you are living the good life. It is painful to think about, but so true.

CHAPTER 14
The Bible Study

One day when I came home from school, I passed by the kitchen window and saw Aunt Lu sitting at our table with my mother. I couldn't believe it. I ran in and gave her a big hug, and as I looked into her smiling eyes, I remembered my times at VBS.

It was like the love of God was pouring out from her and into my heart. When others looked at me, I would feel judged or belittled. I would sometimes feel like crawling in a hole and hiding, because I knew they saw some of the ungodly things I had said and done. Aunt Lu, on the other hand, saw some of my bad choices, and heard a lot more about the bad things I had done, but it was like I had never done them when she looked at me.

She treated me with love, kindness, and a tender touch. She always had a big smile and a loving voice when she spoke to me. She made me feel like I really mattered and was a beautiful child of God, even though I was stained with sin. I felt goodness inside me and a love I didn't want to let go of.

I realized later that this was Jesus working through her to show me how much He loved me. Aunt Lu was a true disciple for Christ; one I will never forget as long as I live.

In my excitement, I didn't see what my mother had in front of her. When I looked down at the table, I didn't know what to say. It was a Bible. Not a beer? I looked again just to make sure. Sure enough, it was a Bible. I slowly asked, "What are you guys doing?"

> *I didn't know what to say. It was a Bible. Not a beer?*

Aunt Lu looked up at me with the most angelic smile and said, "Studying the Lord's Word! Would you like to join us?"

I didn't know what to think or say at that moment, so I nodded my head yes and sat down. I don't remember what the lesson was about, but I do recall Aunt Lu telling Mother and me how much God loved us and wanted us in His kingdom. When she prayed for us, it was so heartwarming that we could feel the presence of the Holy Spirit surrounding us; like the angels were so close, even though we could not see them. When she finished, she looked up at me and asked if I would like to do more Bible studies, too.

I felt the Lord tugging at my heart, so I told her, "Yes."

After Aunt Lu left, I looked at my mother and smiled. "I really like her, Mom. She is always happy and smiling."

My mother agreed, then went to the refrigerator and grabbed a beer. I noticed it was an open can. She tasted it, then walked to the sink, spit it out, and mumbled something about a waste of money and hating the taste of flat beer. Then, to my surprise, she tipped the can over into the sink.

Mother never wasted beer. Because we were poor, when she got beer and put it in the fridge, we didn't touch it. We knew it was hers.

Now I sat there amazed, listening to it run down the drain. I thought it best not to say a word, so I changed the subject, telling her I had homework to do and that I would be up in my room.

Every time Aunt Lu came over, she would ask my mother if she could put the beer she was drinking in the refrigerator while they did Bible study. My mother cooperated, but she was not willing to give it up or waste it, so she decided to drink on the days Aunt Lu was not coming over.

But then Aunt Lu began to just pop in randomly and say, "I am here to study with you, Ruth."

Mother would tell her it was not their Bible study day, but Aunt Lu would just smile and say, "I know, but I was in the neighborhood. I thought today was as good as any to study with Ruth." Then she would put my mother's open beer in the fridge.

Finally one day my mother told her, "Lu, every time you come over, you put my beer in the fridge, and it goes stale. I don't like stale beer, you know! I always end up putting it down the kitchen sink."

With the biggest smile, Aunt Lu said, "Well then, let's clean the pipes of your sink and not the pipes of your body, because it is not healthy for your pipes." And she dumped the beer down the sink. Mother could not get angry at her because of that smile and happy-go-lucky attitude. Aunt Lu really did have the Lord leading her, as she helped my mother to find God and to live a good, Godly life. That day was the beginning of my mother seeing how much she really drank. I know it was the Lord intervening then, and my mother knows it, too.

The Bible studies with Aunt Lu continued, and Uncle Dean started to join us. It was an interesting time, and we learned a lot, but when the studies were done, we still didn't attend the Seventh-day Adventist Church very much. Actually, we rarely went.

Grandma Alice was different. She did Bible studies with Aunt Lu before we did, since she and Aunt Lu were good friends. Before long my grandma was attending the Seventh-day Adventist Church regularly. She wanted us to go with her, and when we didn't, she was sad and would pray for us.

Satan was strong in our household, and the temptations that he laid out before us were very great. To be honest, our flesh was very weak. This was because we did not trust in God enough to take away our temptations. "And the world is passing away, and the lust of it; but he who does the will of God abides forever" (1 John 2:17).

Still, the Lord was touching my mother's heart. She went from drinking at home all the time to just on the weekends, because of Aunt Lu's visits and Bible studies.

And though I never saw it until later in life (because I was so wrapped up in myself and the fun the world had to offer), when Aunt Lu was there, I felt different. I longed to be better.

But my faith was weak, and I didn't trust the Lord the way I needed to. When the Bible studies ended, so did my desire to be a Christian. However, the Lord did not give up on me.

CHAPTER 15
Rivalries

We had a nice little school in Trenary that was kindergarten through twelfth grade. The classes were not very big; about six to fifteen children each.

I was in junior high. I loved eighth grade and thought it was a blast. I had my own locker and hung out with the high school kids, which was the cool thing to do because it meant you were in the "in-crowd." Yes! Even in small schools, there were still an in-crowd and an out-crowd.

I think I was in the in-crowd only because Robin, who was a senior, was very popular. So was Scott, who had graduated the year before. I was therefore known as Scott and Robin's little sister. I thought this was cool, because I looked up to my brothers. Even though I didn't always do the right thing and even if I annoyed them a lot, if being their little sister got me into the cool crowd, it was all worth it. Or so I thought.

Everything was going well until one day it slipped out that Trenary was going to downsize and consolidate with Eben High, our rival. It was said that our school was in the red and could no longer afford all of its students. They were going to send the high schoolers to Eben the following year and become only an elementary and middle school. If that didn't work out, they would send the junior high students over, too.

The news spread like wildfire throughout the school, and I can't remember one person who was happy about the consolidation. The Trenary Comets and Eben Eagles had been rivals in basketball for years. We were sheer enemies and expressed it often. How could they make us go to school with those kids? We were all mad.

I was in on the rivalry with Eben because my brothers and I played basketball. I was also a cheerleader, so I attended all the games. You see, because our school was so small, it was hard to have sports teams and cheerleader squads without bringing up younger students to help out. For that reason they put junior high students in junior varsity cheerleader positions, and JV students on the varsity cheerleading squad with the juniors and seniors. I loved it, because it made me feel more grown up to be on the JV squad (even though this also drew me into the rivalry).

We kids were very wrong for being rivals with each other. As a young adult, you just don't think things through the right way. Self and feelings come first, and we forget that God is there, ready to help us through the tough choices in our lives.

But back then, when I found out we were going to consolidate, I was angry, and I didn't care who knew. The more I thought about it, the angrier I got. Then I recalled a girls' basketball game we had played one night at our school against the Eben Eagles.

Afterward we had been upset because we lost. Actually, we got slaughtered; we had never lost to them that badly before. Everyone had gone to the locker rooms to shower and change. The visiting team was using the boys' locker room, since it was available.

Because our school was so small, the locker rooms were right across the hall from each other on the upper level. There were two ways to get to them. You could get to the boys' locker room either from the gym or from the second floor, up by the balcony. The girls' locker room was on the other side of a staircase in the middle of the second floor. If you went through that locker room, it came out on the other side of the balcony.

That night, for some reason, when we were done showering and coming out to go home, we emerged on the staircase side, instead of going out on the balcony side, where we could have just gone down the steps and out the door to the parking lot. So when we walked out, we came out facing the boys locker room. Meanwhile the Eben Eagles also decided to come out upstairs instead of going out through the gym.

At first I became angry when I saw them, because we had lost the game. I wanted to say something to express my unhappiness about that. Then I realized I was wrong for my selfish thoughts, and I decided it would be best to express a gesture of good sportsmanship to the girls.

So when we walked out and met the Eben Eagles, I put my hand out to shake one of their hands and said, "Good game! You played well." In my mind, she was going to shake my hand, smile, and say, "Thanks! You played well, too." Not a chance.

She balled up her fist and slugged me, then said, "That's only because you stink and can't play ball to save your life."

I looked her right in the face.

She had hoped that I would hit the floor, she said, so that she could spit on me while I looked up at her. Instead she taunted me about being a tough girl.

I *never* fell to the ground. With two older brothers who pushed me around and punched me on a regular basis, I had learned to brace myself for impact.

I didn't realize that I had my own fist balled up, ready to take that blond-haired, blue-eyed girl out. Putting her in her place was all that was on my mind, but just as I was getting ready to swing, Karen grabbed my arm and said, "Come on, Michelle, it is not worth it. She is not worth it. Let's go."

I looked into my friend's eyes and knew that she was right. I was going to do the right thing. I put my fist down and started to walk away.

Then the blond girl pushed me from behind, and I stumbled forward into Karen. Karen turned and said, "Maybe it *was* worth it!" She stepped in front of me, ready to fight the Eben girl for me. Of course, that didn't go over well.

The blond-haired girl said, "Oh, now your friends have to fight your battles for you, too? Can't play basketball, and you can't fight your own battles!"

I was ready to plow her into next week. I looked at Karen, she looked at me, and we both started swinging.

The fight was on: their team versus ours right in the middle of the hallway. But just as fast as it started, it ended, as the balcony doors opened up and a few of the guys from our school saw what was going on.

They came to our rescue, or it seemed so at the time. In reality they just broke up the fight and told the other girls to get going. If they didn't, they said, the boys would either go and get their coach or else hold them there (those girls would have a long walk back home if they missed their bus).

The fight was over; the Eben Eagle girls were gone. I prayed silently, "How can people be so rude, God? I thought you wanted me to say 'good game' and shake their hands, even if I was angry because we lost. There has to be a reason we lost this game, Lord."

But I heard no answer at the time, probably because I couldn't hear God talking to me over the anger in my heart. I had let Satan in and didn't even know it.

How often we this and not even realize we don't have our armor on anymore? In order to put it on, we first need to remember what James 4:7 says: "Therefore submit to God. Resist the devil and he will flee from you." We need to submit to God before we can truly understand His Word.

Then we need to do as Paul says: "Put on the whole armor of God, that you may be able to stand against the wiles of the devil" (Eph. 6:11). That just sums it up. I truly recommend that you read the whole Scripture.

CHAPTER 16

New School

―――⊃o⊂―――

At the beginning of September in 1987, I stood at the end of the driveway of the old gray house we lived in and waited for the bus to pick me up. I was so nervous. This was my freshman year, and I was starting out my high school days with kids I had grown to hate.

The bus stopped and the door opened. Aunt Gwyn, who was our bus driver, said, "This is the first day at your new school, Mick. How do you feel about that?"

I looked at her smiling face and said, "I am not sure I am going to like it at all."

She told me to try and give it a chance. Aunt Gwyn was always trying to help me to look at the good side of things.

I went to the back of the bus and sat down. I was one of the first kids to be picked up, so I watched as the other kids from Trenary got on. I noticed that they didn't look so happy about their first day, either. Usually I loved to talk and laugh with my friends every time we got together, but this particular morning was different. No one said much on the way to school.

Aunt Gwyn couldn't stand our long faces anymore. Looking in her mirror, she told us, "Be positive, and don't judge your first day of school before you even get to experience it. If you think your day will be bad, then it will. Even though you may not see it now, you all are going to make new friends. Things will become normal for you again."

Most of us groaned, and she sighed. But I began to think that maybe this wouldn't be so bad, after all.

When we arrived, Karen and I walked into the school and looked at each other with half-smiles. Then I said, "Where do we go?"

"I don't know," said Karen, "but I am sure someone will help us out."

We saw that there were teachers and staff waiting to help us as we walked farther in. We discovered that all of them were nice. We got a tour of the school and were shown where our classes were.

I was still very nervous and scared. Karen was a grade ahead of me, so we had none of the same classes. My cousin Donna and I had a few classes together, and some classmates from Trenary were with me, too, but for the most part, I was on my own. As I looked around the room in my first class, I realized that most of the Eben kids were just as nervous as we were.

However, some kids from both schools were already exchanging words that were not so nice. Later, when I walked down the hallway to my locker, I heard some Eben girls saying to some older Trenary girls, "You're on our turf now. Better watch your step."

I sighed, shoved my new books into my locker, and got my notepad ready for my next class. I thought, *This is going to be a long year.* But the weeks passed, and most of us made new friends. We got along a lot better than any of us thought we would.

When the try-out sheets came out for basketball and cheerleading, we Trenary teens looked at each other with amazement. We had never had to try out before. At our school, anyone who had wanted to play was automatically on the team. This was a new experience for us.

Most of us tried out, and a lot of kids from both schools made the cut. It ended up being a mixture for boys' basketball and cheerleading, while the girls' basketball teams ended up being mostly Eben girls.

The teachers and coaches were determined to get us working together, but I felt bad for them when we first started. There was a lot of competition about who would be captains and who the best players were. Trenary and

Eben had really good players for the boys' teams, so for those coaches it was a dream team in the making. But on the girls' team, those of us who were only average players became benchwarmers, and I was one of them.

It bothered me. At Trenary I had been captain one year and co-captain the next. I had never thought about why everyone got moved up. Now there were sixty-five students in my class alone. This was a new ballgame, in more ways than one. When I got tired of sitting the bench most of the time, I tried out for the cheerleading squad. I made that team with flying colors. I also joined track. I did well in both of those sports.

I finished my first year of basketball, but I was not sure that I wanted to sit the bench again the next year. They had played me a little; when they knew our opponent was a team we could beat with our eyes closed, they sat out the popular players and played the rest of us. That didn't make us feel any better, though.

Still, when given the opportunity, I would play my best to prove a point. Competition was what I was all about in high school. My anger welled up, and jealousy raged inside. I wanted to be noticed; I wanted to be the center of attention. I thought, *Why can't I be the best ballplayer? Then they will all look at me and look up to me.* Deep in my heart, I never forgot what was taught to me about the Lord and His love. I just let my selfish pride get in the way, and that blocked the wisdom the Lord was trying to give me.

I think I was always trying to prove myself because I was not very smart when it came to learning. I had a hard time with spelling, reading, and remembering what I read.

> *I think I was always trying to prove myself because I was not very smart when it came to learning.*

Being in special education classes was fun while you were with the other students that struggled like you, but when you were back in the regular classroom with the rest of your peers, it was hard. They made fun of us and called us names like "retard," "slow learner," "dumb," "gifted dorks," and "special idiots." The list went on. They were all hurtful and always made us feel bad.

Donna was in special education classes with me, and she got hurt too; but she dealt with it differently than I did. She just ignored them and loved the friends she did have, who were mostly way younger than her.

I, on the other hand, did all I could to prove I was not a special ed kid. On several occasions Carol addressed my pride issue with me and tried to get me to look to the Lord for answers (as I mentioned earlier in the story, she was the assistant special education teacher). Nevertheless, I joined all sorts of activities in school to prove that I was not stupid and could do everything that the others did. On top of all kinds of sports, I signed up for a gym class and a media class. I did all of it to fit in.

What was wrong with this picture? I was trying to please people and be noticed. That is not what God wants from us. As teenagers, I think we close our ears to anything we don't want to hear. We are selfish, and we want our way no matter what the cost, until the cost comes to us full force, as mine did.

Recently I read a saying in our quarterly study that hit home for me. I added a few things to it according to how the Lord moved me to view it, and how He wanted me to make changes in my own life. It goes like this:

> The concept of flattery picks up on the theme of pleasing people; a poor basis for evangelism. We should not be motivated by what other people think of us, but should stay focused on the only motivation that really matters: *pleasing God!*

I was not very pleasing to God at that point in my teenage life. When I realized this later, I could not go back and change what I had done and said to other people. It is not a good feeling to look back and be ashamed of what you have done in your life.

But when I run into some of my old classmates, they comment to me on how I have changed. It makes me feel better to know that I have made a difference; helping someone else to see that there really is hope for the broken, bruised, and battered, through our Lord and Savior, Jesus Christ.

CHAPTER 17

A Lesson Learned the Hard Way

As time passed, my efforts to get people's attention got worse. I started partying with my brothers pretty heavily while Mother was at the bar. Sometimes she even stayed home and partied with us. Our house became the place where everyone wanted to be.

When Mother was there, she always took the car keys away from all of the kids so that they wouldn't drink and drive. She was not right for letting us all drink or for buying us the beer, but she felt that we would go out and do it somewhere else if not here; so why not her house, where she could keep an eye on us? Most of the parents in town knew where their kids were and what my mother was doing, but they agreed about keeping us off the streets and safe.

I look back now and realize that most of those people were my mother's drinking buddies. Because our town was so small, almost everyone thought the only thing to do in Trenary was to sit in the bars or party at someone's house. I know now that this was not true.

When I take my children to the Trenary area today, we go for hikes in the woods and to the park. We like to walk by the river and see family and friends. When we went to church in that area, we would spend the day with our church family and have picnics and fellowship. Then we usually went for a hike or did something special together, like going to the ice caves and waterfalls in the middle of winter. It is a beautiful sight to see the snow and the ice. It makes me think of the purity of God and the beauty He gives us.

So going to a bar or drinking is clearly not the only thing you can do when you live in a small town. Being in nature with God is far more enjoyable. I never understood that back then.

Partying at the house with all our friends was fun at first, but I wanted more excitement. I felt like it was getting boring because I was not the center of attention. I got pushed aside a lot and teased by my brothers' friends (and I deserved every bit of it, I am very sure of that).

I had a crush on one of them; his name was Stan. He was tall, handsome, and funny. I couldn't stop thinking about him. I even wrote him a letter and put some of my perfume on the paper.

Stan was the second crush I had ever had, but it turned out to be a very embarrassing, uncomfortable situation that I just wanted to run away from. He was about five years older than I was, so I was just a little girl in his eyes. That really hurt my feelings. He and my brothers' other friends loved me like a sister, and that was all I would ever be to them.

I became really angry at Stan and the others for teasing me about my crush. I decided to move on in life and show them I was not a little girl any more. And I hid my feelings of hurt and anger from my mother, because I didn't trust her to help me fix them. She was never around long enough to have a conversation with, anyway.

There was a really cute guy named Bradley (everyone called him Brad) whom I had met the prior Fourth of July. He lived thirty miles away, in Munising, Michigan. I decided that I was going to go see him. I told Mother I was going out with my friends and would be back later. What I didn't tell her was that I was going out of town to see a boy she did not know, and that I had no idea what time I would be home.

> I was angry, I was going to change my life, and I didn't need any interruptions. I thought I knew what was best.

I was angry, I was going to change my life, and I didn't need any interruptions. I thought I knew what was best.

I caught a ride into town with Mother as she headed to the bar. There I met up with my friend Casey. I talked him into heading out to Munising by telling him there were some really good parties out that way. I used my friend because he had a car and I wanted something I couldn't get without a driver. That was not very good friend behavior, was it? I was not being very Christ-like.

In my search for Brad, I had gotten the address to his house. We went there to find him (I told Casey this guy knew where all the parties were). His parents told us he was at a friend's house. We asked for that address and were on our way again.

We drove about six miles out into the country where there were very few houses that were close together. We finally found the address in the middle of nowhere. Casey and I saw all the cars, looked at each other, and decided that this was the place.

We walked up to the door and heard loud music playing. Casey was bobbing his head to the music and smiling. I knocked on the door loudly (there was no way they were going to hear me otherwise), and some young guy answered. I asked for Brad.

The guy smiled, and said, "Yeah, he's here! Come on in and join the party." Casey's smile got bigger, and we walked in. He went to get a beer with the guy who answered the door. I was left standing alone.

As I looked around, I saw my crush. I went over and started talking to Brad, and asked if he knew who I was. I couldn't believe it when he remembered me. He expressed how interested in me he was, and said that he would love to get to know me better.

We talked for a long time. I found out that he was nineteen years old. I thought it was so cool that a nineteen-year-old boy was interested in me, a fourteen-year-old woman. Well, that was what I wanted to believe I was. In reality, I was a confused and hurting young lady seeking love wherever I could find it.

After a while, he invited me to play some drinking games with the rest of the group. I motioned for Casey to come over. Before I knew it, Casey was completely drunk and passed out on the sofa.

I looked at the time. It was 1:30 a.m. The bars closed at 2:00 a.m. I knew I had to get home before my mother. I shook Casey. "We gotta go," I said. "My mom is going to kill me if we don't get home before her." He just groaned and rolled over.

I was in panic mode now. My thoughts were just racing. I had never before pulled a stunt like this with my mother, and I knew that she would not be happy with me. *Think, Michelle, think!* Then I had it.

I would ask the guy who owned the house if I could use his phone (we didn't have cell phones back then, only land lines). I would call home and leave a message for Mother that I was spending the night at Karen's house. Everything was going to work out. I just needed to find the owner in this mob of people and get everyone to be quiet while I made the call. It was possible, wasn't it? *Yes! It is possible,* I thought. I was trying to convince myself this would work.

I finally found the man I was looking for. He was older, in his late 40's, medium height, with long, brown hair and a long beard, both streaked with gray. I asked him if I could use his phone. I told him that I would make it short and pay for the call.

My heart sank as he told me that he wouldn't mind if I used it, but unfortunately he hadn't been able to afford to pay the bill last month, so it was shut off.

I immediately went back into panic mode. I kept thinking, *What am I going to do?* This was a problem.

Brad then came over to me and said, "There is nothing you can do about it tonight. Come on: let's go play some more drinking games to take your mind off of it."

I decided that this might help and went over to the table with those who had not passed out yet. I was still very upset and could not stop thinking about what my mother was going to do to me. Then I thought about how worried she would be. I started to feel really guilty for the decision I had made. What had I been thinking?

Then Brad grabbed me and sat me on his lap. He kept telling me, "Everything will be just fine. I hear your mom is really cool."

I thought to myself, *If you only knew how uncool she is going to be when she finds out I went out drinking, and that I stayed out all night with a guy she has never met*

A photo of me, taken as a high school underclassman.

and who is five years older than I am. I knew I was in big trouble, and there was no way out of it.

Satan uses other people that he has ensnared to try and convince us that what we are doing is okay. When we follow the crowd and listen to the calling of the devil, we break the heart of our Lord and Savior, Jesus Christ. Luke 21:34-36 says:

> But take heed to yourselves, lest your hearts be weighed down with carousing, drunkenness, and cares of this life, and that Day come on you unexpectedly. For it will come as a snare on all those who dwell on the face of the whole earth. Watch therefore, and pray always that you may be counted worthy to escape all these things that will come to pass, and to stand before the Son of Man.

I sat on pins and needles the whole night. Brad passed out at about 2:00 a.m., but I was wide awake, wondering what my mother and Uncle Dean would do to me when I got home. Finally, after many hours, I fell asleep, sitting up at the end of the sofa. The next thing I knew Casey was waking me, saying, "We've got to go before my mom and dad get up, or my dad is going to whoop my backside!"

I looked at my watch and said, "Too late; it's 9:30."

He mumbled about how he was going to feel after today. I felt sorry for him, but I knew I was going to be in trouble as well. I jumped up and grabbed my jacket. We hoped to get home, sneak in, and not be noticed.

As we ran out the door, we didn't say goodbye to anyone. They wouldn't have noticed anyway, for they were all passed out on the floors, chairs, tables, and beds. It was a sight I would never forget and never wanted to be a part of again.

By the time we got back to Trenary, Casey was very nervous. He didn't look forward to the pain he would be in or the grounding that was to follow. As he drove me home, he explained that he was not going to pull into the driveway: his hope was that my mother would not see him drop me off. He knew that if she did, he would get yelled at by her and might never be welcome over at our house again. What he didn't know until later was that she was watching out the window as he dropped me off.

He pulled up to the end of the drive.

I said, "I will see you at school on Monday!"

He looked at me and said, "If I live that long."

I felt bad as I watched him pull away. Then I realized I still had to deal with the consequences of my own actions. I turned around and looked at our long driveway. That day it was not long enough. Then I looked at the house and saw my mother watching through the window. I knew that this Sunday morning I was not going to be going to church. I decided I was going to be bold and tell my mother she had nothing to worry about. Really, though, deep inside, I felt terrible for the heartache I had caused her.

I walked up to the front door and walked in. Mother was sitting and waiting for me. She looked as if she had not slept at all. Her face was creased with worry, and she had a stern look on her face. I was about to tell her I was sorry for making her worry and that I would never do it again, but before I could open my mouth, she started yelling at me.

"Where have you been? What makes you think you can stay out all night without calling me and letting me know where you are?"

My thoughts of sympathy and regret turned to anger. How dare she yell at me when I was feeling bad for what I had done? She didn't know I had tried to call home and that there was no telephone where I was. How dare she think I didn't care enough to want to call? I got angrier and angrier until I started yelling back at my mother. I tried to justify what I had done as being no big deal. I told her that she was worried over nothing.

We screamed at each other until Uncle Dean stepped in. "You are a spoiled, little brat, with no respect for your mother or her feelings," he said. "You have no concept of right or wrong, and you're so selfish you don't think of how you make other people feel. This person gave birth to you and deserves respect."

I was still so angry that I started yelling at him, too, telling him to shut up and stay out of it. I realized after it came out that I should have just stayed quiet and taken the punishment.

He raised his hand and slapped me. He told me to shut my mouth, listen, and respect my elders. As much as I wanted to yell back at him again, I knew better. It wouldn't be my face that would get slapped next; it would be my backside.

I stood there and took the punishment in silence with tears in my eyes. I knew I was wrong; I just didn't want to admit it. I got grounded that day for a very long time.

It was one of the first times in my life I got grounded for any length of time, and also the first time I had ever seen my mother this upset with me. Later she explained to me that she had been sitting and worrying about whether I was lying in a ditch somewhere, hurt or dead. She wondered where I was and if I was okay. She kept waiting for the police to come knocking on the door to give her the bad news.

I felt very sad then that I had not realized the extent of her worry. My heart broke because I knew I was wrong, but I didn't know how to make it better. I had messed up bad, and there was no taking back what I'd done.

Just a few years ago, while I started making notes for this book, I recalled this event and many others in my life, and they brought tears to my eyes. I dropped to my knees and asked God to forgive me. I then got up, went to the phone, and called my mother. I cried as I told her I was sorry for the ways I treated her while she was raising me. I finally understood what I had put her through.

I said, "Mom, I can't fix what I did to you in the past, but I ask for your forgiveness now."

She was very shocked that I had called her to apologize for actions from many years ago, but she expressed how much she appreciated my call. She told me some things about my life while I was growing up that had made her laugh. I was happy that my mother didn't just remember all the bad things I had done.

We laughed and cried together for hours that day over many memories. God is good.

CHAPTER 18

A Big Mistake

A few months passed. I had learned my lesson about going out of town without permission, but I kept on going to parties and hanging out with my friends. We all agreed it was only fun to drink until we were silly and giggly. In reality we just wanted to be noticed by the older guys.

Meanwhile, my attitude did not change. I was still selfish and rude to many people. The sad part was that I didn't realize it. I was so caught up in what I wanted that I never stopped to think of how it would affect the people around me.

One Friday evening I was sitting at home with my family. My mother was getting ready to go to the bar when she happened to look out the window. She asked who was walking up the driveway. I jumped up to look and could not believe my eyes: it was Brad.

I ran to the door and opened it as he walked up. I asked what he was doing there, and he said he had come to see me. I stepped out of the way and told him to come on in.

I introduced him to my mother and Uncle Dean. Mother didn't ask me how old he was, and I know why: he was short and skinny for his age and looked like he was only fifteen or sixteen years old. She did ask where he was from and how he had got there. He told her he had hitchhiked to our house from Shingleton. She then asked if his parents knew where he was, and he said yes.

Mother left for the bar, while Uncle Dean, Brad, and I continued to visit at the kitchen table. When she got home, it was late and she was drunk. Brad, Uncle Dean, and I were still up talking. Mother again asked Brad where he lived and if he had a ride home.

He told her where he lived again and that he did not have a ride. "I was just planning on hitchhiking," was his reply.

My mother, being the person that she was, told him that he could spend the night and that she would drive him home the next day. I was shocked. Mother was letting a boy stay the night? This was the beginning of a big mistake on our part.

Scott had moved out, and Robin was in lower Michigan, living with our aunt and uncle for the summer and working to earn some money to live on his own. Brad was put in the spare bedroom.

She drove him home the next day as she had promised. When she met his parents and found out that he was nineteen, she was not mad at all. She liked them and approved of us dating if it was okay with his parents, too.

So every weekend, for many months, he would hitchhike to our house, or Uncle Dean or Mother would go get him and bring him to spend the weekend with us. As time passed, they frequently left us alone. This was another big mistake.

Brad became comfortable with the way things were going and wanted a more intimate relationship. I said no many times, but he did not accept my answer. He kept pushing me to do what he wanted until I gave in. Later I refused to have intimate relations with him anymore, and at that point he threatened to have his friends come and gang rape me. I was stuck and scared, and I had nowhere to turn.

While all of this was going on, Mother and Uncle Dean decided the old gray house was too big for the three of us. Therefore my mother and I moved in with Grandma Alice, while Uncle Dean moved in with Scott and his roommate Zack. I started going to my brother and uncle's house to get away from Brad, but he finally found me.

He asked Uncle Dean if he could stay the weekend. My heart sank when my uncle said yes. I didn't want Brad there; I wanted him to go away. I felt very violated and dirty; also, my body was feeling very funny. I had missed my period for two months, and I hoped I was not pregnant.

That night he insisted that we be intimate. I said, "NO!" He became angry and threatened me. I told him, "Go ahead! Do what you have to, but I am going to tell my brother everything, and then you can deal with him. If you even try and touch me, I will scream. I think it is time for you to go home and never come back again."

Brad got up, left, and never came back to Trenary. I had called his bluff.

It had taken me a long time to build up the courage to tell him to go. I wish I had relied on God so that I would not have been in that mess to begin with, but it was too late. What was done, was done: I was, in fact, pregnant.

I got scared and didn't know what to do, so I hid it for many months. It was easy at first because no one noticed. I watched people to see if they were looking at my stomach. I became very paranoid and uneasy around others, thinking that they might find out. I felt guilty, unclean, unworthy, and very judged, even though no one knew yet. I didn't *want* anyone to know. I worried that the ones I loved would stop loving me and cast me out for the mistake I had made.

I wished I would have stood strong when I first told Brad "no." But I didn't, and I could not go back and change that now. How could I have let this happen to me? What had I been thinking? I acted tough all the time; so why couldn't I have been tough when I most needed to? All these thoughts and many more went through my mind. I felt unworthy to live and became very depressed. This is when my friends finally started to notice.

Let me tell you about my personality. I was, and am to this day, a very happy, go-lucky, always-smiling type of person. So when I became depressed and looked sad all the time, my friends started to question me about what was wrong.

I would tell them, "Nothing, I'm just down today."

They believed that only for a little while; and Karen could see right through me. She kept asking what was wrong, and when I told her nothing, she would laugh at me sarcastically and say, "Yeah! Right! Now tell me what is wrong."

At last one Sunday afternoon, I went to visit Karen. When she asked me what was wrong, this time I told her I thought I was pregnant. Her mouth dropped open, and she asked me what I was going to do. I was scared, so it felt good to tell someone what was going on with me. I started to cry and told her I had no idea.

She did what any best friend would do. She took me in her arms and said, "Everything is going to be okay. We will figure something out."

I look back now at our friendship, from elementary all the way up to high school, and I realize that Karen was there for me no matter how many hateful, sinful, unholy things I did. She never left me. Even when we got into disagreements, we never stayed mad at each other for long. She was always there in the end.

I also realize when I look back that God wanted me to rely on Him. When I was going to my friend, He wanted me to be coming to Him instead and laying my sins at the foot of the cross, where He shed His blood for me. He would have carried me through; all I had to do was ask. In God's Word, it tells us that He will never leave us nor forsake us (Heb. 13:5b).

I could not see past my pain to let God in. I wish I had let Him into my heart back then, but I cannot change the past. However, I can help those who may be struggling with similar events in their lives to see that God is always there, waiting for us to surrender everything to Him. "Ask, and it will be given to you; seek, and you will find; knock, and it will be opened to you. For everyone who asks receives, and he who seeks finds, and to him who knocks it will be opened." (Matt. 7:7,8).

Don't get me wrong; friends are good. They help lift us up and give us love and assurance when we need it. But we should never put our friends before God. We should be lifting up our friends to God and telling them to seek His guidance.

I believe Karen had the best intentions in her heart to help me during the time of trouble I was in. I also truly believe that God brought Karen and me together for a reason, since we understood each other and were always there for each other when one of us needed a friend, no questions asked.

But if you think about it, isn't that how God is with us? He is there for us no matter what is happening in our lives. If we seek Him and ask for forgiveness, if we pray in faith, if we surrender all, does not God grant us forgiveness and embrace us in His loving arms? Yes, He does, if we are sincere in our pleas to Him and willing to have an open heart to receive His wisdom, in order that we can walk in this life with Him as our guide.

God knows we make many mistakes in life. He is all knowing, all seeing, and all-loving. "The Lord looks from heaven; He sees all the sons of men" (Ps. 33:13). "Before I formed you in the womb I knew you; Before you were born I sanctified you" (Jer. 1:5a). "And had no need that anyone should testify of man, for He knew what was in man" (John 2:25).

After telling Karen about my pregnancy, we tried to figure out how to get me out of the situation without getting me into trouble. We came up with many ideas; abortion was first on the list.

I had actually thought about this and checked out information on abortion, but I just didn't think I could go through with it. I told Karen, "First of all, I am too far along, and second, I don't think I can kill the baby. What else can I do?"

Adoption! As I mulled this over in my head, I thought it could work. I started to think of who could adopt my baby, and on the same day that I talked to Karen, I decided to confide in my cousins Misty and Donna.

Misty was a senior that year and had a boyfriend, Eddy, whom she was planning on marrying. She told me that they would take the baby and raise him. Eddy was going to enter the Armed Forces, and the baby would have a good home.

I thought that this was the solution to my problem. Now how I was going to pull off being pregnant without anyone finding out?

Misty told me there was no way that was going to happen. I needed to tell someone so that I could get the proper help, or else I might hurt the baby and myself.

I decided she was right, and I knew just the person I needed to confide in. The very next day at school, I ran to Mrs. Chenail's office. She was the high school counselor and also our home economics teacher. When I got to her office, she was not there. I heard the bell ring and knew I was late for class, but I decided it was now or never. I needed to do what was right.

I went to the main office and asked the secretary where Mrs. Chenail was. She told me she was teaching home economics. I thanked her, then ran through the halls of the old school building into the new addition. It seemed like it took forever to get there.

As I started to knock on the door, fear overwhelmed me. I loved Mrs. Chenail. Would she look at me differently after I told her? Would she treat me like I didn't matter or even exist? I asked God to give me the strength to make the right choice.

I slowly turned the doorknob and peeked in. She was already teaching. I was just about to shut the door when a student pointed to me and said, "Mrs. Chenail, someone is at the door."

She looked in my direction with a big smile, then came over to the door. "What can I do for you today, Michelle?"

The fact that she was smiling at me the whole time made it even harder to tell her, but I mustered up the strength to say that I really needed to talk to her, and that it was important.

She asked me if I could come back after class, but I knew that if I left, I would never tell her. I needed to tell her now. I said, "No, I need to talk to you now." Then, in a soft, low voice, with my eyes on the floor in front of me, I said, "Because I think I am pregnant."

Mrs. Chenail's smile faded to a serious look. She called the teacher's aide over and informed her that she had to leave. She needed her aide to take over the class, and she would be back as soon as she could.

Walking down the hallway with her was scary. It hit me that an adult now knew my ugly secret. Tears started to form in my eyes, and I could not stop them from flowing. I was scared again. What was going to happen now? How would I face all the kids in school? Everyone would know, and I would be looked down on.

Thoughts kept whirling through my head, and I couldn't stop them. Mrs. Chenail was a step or two ahead of me, so she didn't see me crying. I knew I needed to be adult about this, so I wiped my eyes with the sleeve of my shirt and composed myself the best that I could.

We finally reached her office. She unlocked the door and asked me to step in, then she motioned for me to sit down in the chair in front of her desk. I slowly sat and looked around. For some reason her office looked different. I had been here many times, to talk with her or just to say hi in passing, but today it seemed to close in around me. It felt almost like the room knew my secret already. I started to regret telling her, when she interrupted my thoughts.

"Michelle, why do you think you're pregnant?" she asked.

I told her that I hadn't had my period for four or five months and that my belly felt weird, like I had a ball inside of it. She continued to look at me with a serious face and asked me for the details.

I was scared so I didn't tell her everything. I was embarrassed about what had happened to me, and I didn't want people to know.

Mrs. Chenail talked with me for two hours about the responsibilities of being a mother, and how I needed to tell my own mother that I was pregnant so that she could be there to help me through the hard times that lay ahead. She made arrangements for someone else to teach her last class, then she called my mother and told her it would be best if she came and picked me up today, because I needed to talk to her about something important. Of course my mother was worried and left work early to drive to the school.

> *I remember being so scared. What was my mother going to think of me? Would she still love me?*

I remember being so scared as I waited in Mrs. Chenail's office. What was my mother going to think of me? Would she still love me? I knew I couldn't stop what was to come in the future. *I was going to have a baby.*

These words kept repeating over and over in my head, and I became overwhelmed. I started to cry again, and Mrs. Chenail walked around her desk, hugged me, and kept telling me, "Everything is going to be alright."

When my mom walked into the room, she had a worried look on her face. It broke my heart, for I knew I now had to tell her my dark secret. Rather than ceasing, the worry of her heart would greatly increase at the news she was about to receive.

Mrs. Chenail asked her to have a seat. My mother sat down and looked from me to Mrs. Chenail. She finally asked if everything was okay.

I had missed a lot of school due to morning sickness, but my mother thought I was just getting tired of school and becoming lazy, like most normal teenagers at my age. She assumed I was going to get expelled from school or have to repeat the same grade the following year. If that wasn't what this was about, then she figured I had gotten into a fight and was getting suspended.

Mother knew that I never backed down from anyone. What she didn't realize was that I was a very happy and social person with everyone at school. I didn't belong to one group of people; I talked to everyone: smart kids, geeks, athletes, social groups, druggies, special education kids, preppies, and the popular groups. I was really liked by most of the students because I always had a smile and treated them all the same. There were some who didn't like me, and I didn't care for them either, but I never started fights with them; I just left them alone and usually they left me alone.

As these thoughts went through my head, my mother waited to learn what was really going on. Mrs. Chenail gave me a smile of encouragement, then she looked at my mother and said, "Ruth, Michelle has something very important to tell you. She will need you to listen and not say anything until she is done talking."

My mother gave her another worried look, and my heart sank in my chest, because I now had to tell her that I was going to have a baby at fifteen years old.

I looked at the floor and slowly started to speak. "Mom, I, um, well, I am pregnant." I said it so fast that I didn't know if she heard me or not. I slowly looked up and saw that her face was pale and even more worried than before.

She didn't say anything for a few minutes, so Mrs. Chenail asked her if she was okay. Mother nodded her head yes. Then she slowly turned and looked back at me. With tears in her eyes she said, "We will make it through this together."

She got up out of her chair and hugged me close. It felt like when she hugged me when I was little, and I used to run down the stairs in the middle of the night, because I had had a bad dream. I would climb into bed with her, and she would wrap her arms around me and say, "Had another bad dream?" I would say yes, and she would hold me close to her until I fell asleep.

My mother hadn't hugged me this way in a long time. Often she was so frustrated with me that she would say very hurtful things, like, "I wish I would have had all boys!" or, "You were a mistake from a bar fling!" or,

"Boys are easier to raise!" Those comments would push me farther away from my mother, because I always felt like I was in the way of her happiness.

So now, when my mother hugged me, my heart was overwhelmed with love. Tears rolled down my cheeks. *My mother still loves me! She really loves me!* My fear of her rejection faded away, and peace came over me.

Mrs. Chenail got up, came over, and hugged us both. She offered to be there for me throughout the whole pregnancy and afterward. She then looked my mother straight in the eye and, with a smile, said, "I will be here for you, too, Ruth."

My mother thanked her, and they hugged again.

On the car ride home, I told my mother of the adoption plans I was making with Misty. She took her eyes off the road long enough to look me square in the eyes and say, "No! Not my first grandchild." She looked back at the road. "We will make it through this together. I will help you through this, Sis. I will be there for you, and so will our family.

"Misty isn't going to adopt this baby," she continued. "Besides, she has a lot of growing up to do yet. Her life will just be starting, since she graduates this year. That would be way too much responsibility for her at this time in her life, whether she realizes it or not.

"We will make it through this together," she repeated. "That is what we will do."

I sat there looking at my mother as she drove us home. I couldn't make sense of what she was thinking. I had already been scared, and now she wanted me to keep this baby? Now I was horrified. How was I, a fifteen-year-old girl, going to take care of a baby, go to school, play in sports, hang out with my friends, and work in the summer? It seemed like my life was going to be over. My mother told me later that she saw the worry on my face as the stress of the situation took over.

She worried about me through my whole pregnancy. I became very depressed, and she saw it. The bigger I got, the more I wanted to eat. I would sit down for dinner and in one sitting eat two fully-loaded pizzas by myself. I had begun to hide my pain behind food instead of giving it in prayer to God. I just couldn't understand why I had to go through this or why people were so mean.

CHAPTER 19
Pregnant and Depressed

The bus rides to school were not very enjoyable for me. We had moved out of my grandma's house and into a trailer in town, so I no longer had my Aunt Gwyn as a bus driver. Plus there was a boy a year older than me who rode the same bus. He always made fun of me when I got on. I usually ignored him, but one morning he said something that really hurt my feelings.

As I was walking to my assigned seat in the back, I heard, "You're getting so fat you need to walk to school." I didn't say anything. I just sat and looked out the window while tears rolled down my face. For the whole eleven-mile ride to school, I kept thinking, *How can people be so mean?*

He kept taunting me until the bus driver told him to sit down and be quiet, or *he* would be walking to school for a week. He sat and didn't say another word. I was very grateful for the new bus driver standing up for me, even though it didn't stop the pain of the hurtful words.

Looking back at this event in my life makes me think of how I need to be careful about what I say to people and uplift others in their time of trials. Thoughts that come from the enemy can bring great pain to those around us. When we say hurtful words to others, it cuts deep into their hearts and brings them down. We in turn become a stumbling block to our brothers and sisters. The Bible leads us in this way:

> But why do you judge your brother? Or why do you show contempt for your brother? For we shall all stand before the judgment seat of Christ. So then each of us shall give account of himself to God. Therefore let us not judge one another anymore, but rather resolve this, not to put a stumbling block or a cause to fall in our brother's way. (Rom. 14:10,12,13)

We need to be careful what we say to others. Do we not praise God with the same tongue? Again the Bible guides us:

> But no man can tame the tongue. It is an unruly evil, full of deadly poison. With it we bless our God and Father, and with it we curse men, who have been made in the similitude of God. Out of the same mouth proceed blessing and cursing. My brethren, these things ought not to be so … But the wisdom that is from above is first pure, then peaceable, gentle, willing to yield, full of mercy and good fruits, without partiality and without hypocrisy. Now the fruit of righteousness is sown in peace by those who make peace. (James 3:8-10,17-18)

> *I would come home, then just watch television and eat, sinking lower and lower into depression.*

The boy's comments really made an impact on how I felt about myself. I would come home, sit on the floor Indian style with a plate of food, then just watch television and eat, sinking lower and lower into depression.

My mother saw this and decided to take me to see a counselor. All I remember about that man was that he didn't understand how I was feeling. He said to me, "You're just a child having a child!"

I told Mother I never wanted to go back and see him again. After a few sessions, she realized that all I did was yell at him and that it wasn't helping me or the baby; it was just putting stress on us both.

Later, as an adult, I read a quote that I wish I could have seen back then:

> We are prone to look to our fellow men for sympathy and uplifting, instead of looking to Jesus. In His mercy and faithfulness God often permits those in whom we place confidence to fail us, in order that we may learn the folly of trusting in man and making flesh our arm. Let us trust fully, humbly, unselfishly in God ... When all things seem dark and unexplainable, remember the words of Christ, "What I do thou knowest not now; but thou shalt know hereafter." John 13:7 (White, *The Ministry of Healing*, p. 486)

My mother and I were looking to people for help with my depression, when all we really needed was to look to God in prayer and trust in His Son, Jesus. It sounds so simple, yet people today do not trust whole-heartedly in our Lord and Savior, Jesus Christ, just as my mother and I never fully trusted in Him back then.

A few weeks later, I happened to stay at my Grandma's house and got on the bus from there. When we reached that boy's house and he got on, there was a very visible handprint across his left cheek. His dad had slapped him so hard that the mark remained for a few days. He didn't say much and kept looking down in embarrassment.

It was not enjoyable. In fact, I felt bad for him. Yes, he had been mean to me and caused me a lot of hurt and pain, but still my heart broke. I knew what it was like to be teased and come to school with your body not looking normal.

I never told him I felt, but I think he saw it written all over my face. I had had an opportunity to get him back but instead I had felt sorry for him. He didn't tease me anymore after that day.

In Matthew 7:12, Jesus tells us, "Therefore, whatever you want men to do to you, do also to them ...." I just could not be mean to that boy, no matter how mean he had been to me.

CHAPTER 20

The Birth

I was getting tired of going to school, and it got harder and harder for me to stay awake in class. Walking all over the school and doing homework at night was very exhausting.

As time went by, my belly got so big that Uncle Dean told me I was waddling like a duck. He would smile as he said it, then laugh. Then he would tell me to "hurry up and get that baby out." I couldn't help but smile back at him. I was way past ready for that to happen. Almost everyone at school made me smile or laugh as well, which kept me in good spirits.

One day I was walking down the hall and saw my friend Ben, who was like a brother to me, talking with his girlfriend. I stopped to chat with them for a minute. We joked about whether the baby would be a boy or a girl. I made Ben a deal: if it was a boy, I would name it after him.

He smiled from ear to ear and said, "*Really?*"

I smiled back and said, "Really!" We all laughed as we went to class.

A week later I told my mother I was hurting and that the pain was coming and going. She knew I was in labor and called Uncle Kent.

The Birth

He showed up very quickly with Ethel, a good friend of my mom's (who was also Tracy's mother). The three of them got me into the car, then headed for the hospital. Every time I had a contraction, Uncle Kent drove faster, passing all the traffic in front of us.

He pulled up in front of the emergency room doors. They got me out of the car and into a wheelchair. Uncle Kent pushed me in while my mother went to tell them I was in labor. I was moved to labor and delivery quickly, where I was put in a hospital gown. Grandma Alice showed up a few hours later, after she got off of work.

I was a scared, fifteen-year-old girl sitting in a hospital room and waiting to get the nightmare over with. I was glad that my mother and grandmother were with me to see me through this difficult time. I needed their help. I was so appreciative of every kind look and gesture they made toward me. I knew that they were worried about me and that they loved me.

Every time I had a contraction, I grabbed the arms of the chair I was sitting in and squeezed as hard as I could. Between the pains, my thoughts spun with confusion and depression. *What's going to happen to me? I feel like I'm dying. I should have gotten an abortion. This baby is going to take all my fun away. I'm not going to have time to act like a teenager ... I'm going to be too busy acting like an adult and a mother!*

Another contraction came, and I clenched my fists and squeezed. "Michelle!" my mother said, "Your hands are bleeding! Why didn't you cut your nails?"

In my pain, I didn't realize that my fingernails had cut into my palms.

"I'll get the nurse," Mother said, and ran out of the room.

I tried to tell her that all she had to do was press the little red button, but it was too late: she was already gone.

My grandmother sat by my side, coaching me through the contractions. "Try to think about something else honey. It might ease the pain."

"Thanks, Grandma," I said, "I'm trying."

"Michelle, honey," she said, "it might help if you say the Lord's Prayer when you start to feel the pain. You know God will always be there to help you."

I didn't feel like getting a sermon. Annoyed, I wanted to say, "Not now, Grandma! I'm in pain, not church." But the concern on her face caused me to swallow my words. I appreciated her being there, and I didn't want to hurt her feelings. I tried to smile through the pain, and murmured, "Thanks for the advice, Grandma."

"You're welcome. And I know you think I'm crazy for telling you to say the Lord's Prayer, but I said it when *I* was pregnant with all of *my* children, when they were on their way into this world. So trust me this time. I'm not crazy." Her protest and encouraging smile seemed to tell me it would be over soon.

When the nurse arrived with my mother, she wiped my hands and wrapped them in bandages. Then she put two wooden dowels in my hands and brought me into the labor room to see how far dilated I was. I was only about four centimeters, and I had already been in labor for eighteen and a half hours. How much longer could this go on? I wondered. How much longer could I endure it? I just wanted it to be over. Hadn't I suffered enough?

The nurse was concerned, so she stayed on for a second shift. She wanted to see me through the delivery. "Michelle, would you like a shot?" she asked. "It might help you sleep, but it also might not do anything. It reacts differently on different people."

"Yes, please!" I pleaded, exhausted. "Just give me anything. It hurts so badly." But then, ten minutes after the shot, I hollered, "Nurse! My water—it just broke." Was this it?

She checked again to see how far I was dilated. "Nine centimeters, now. I'll get the doctor."

I was burning up. My fever was so high that even when they put ice cubes on my forehead, I didn't feel the coolness. But in my delirious, foggy state, I felt something change. "Nurse," I said, "the baby—it's coming out! It's coming out!"

"Don't push yet, Michelle. Try to hold it if you can, okay?"

I couldn't believe this. Were they crazy? Hold it? After all these hours? *No!* "What? I can't hold it! It's coming out right now, whether you're ready or not."

Two nurses pushed my bed into the delivery room, picked me up, and transferred me onto another table. The doctor put my legs on the upper bars and strapped them there. One of the nurses placed *my* hands on bars to either side of me.

Then all I could hear was the doctor: "Push when you have a contraction. Alright, you're doing fine ... the baby's coming through the birth canal ... I can see the baby's head!"

When the baby was halfway out, something happened; it was like it got sucked back in. My mother turned white and started to panic. This was dangerous: she could lose her daughter and grandchild.

"Michelle, the baby has gone back up inside of you," the doctor said calmly. "I want you to stay calm and start again. When you have another contraction," he directed, "I want you to push."

Then I felt the incision. He had given me two shots in my inner thighs, but they weren't working; I still felt the pain of the cut. If I could have moved my legs, I would have kicked that doctor.

Finally, when I thought I couldn't bear any more, it was over. The doctor had pulled the baby out with a forceps and was stitching me up. The nurse had to lead my mother out of the room. I looked up as she left, and saw her pale face. She kept saying, "So much blood!"

I didn't pay much attention to her comment because I was drifting in and out of consciousness. I was so out of it that I didn't even know I had had a boy until after they had moved me to my room. Because I was so weak, they wouldn't let me hold my son until the next day. Even then, I didn't want to hold this baby who caused me such great pain.

In total, I spent two days—forty-eight hours—in labor. My total time of hard labor was nineteen hours and twenty minutes. It was the longest labor out of all four children I would eventually give birth to. (One daughter, Bethany Ann, doesn't appear in this book; she was stillborn two months before her due date, some years later).

The doctor and nurses were very worried about the amount of blood I had lost. I could barely move without passing out. They decided to keep me in the hospital for a week to monitor me.

The day after I gave birth, a nurse came in to help me to the bathroom. After I sat up, all I remember was opening my eyes again and seeing the floor before me. The nurse did then get me into the bathroom, where things started going fine. She decided to put me into the tub to help soothe the pain below and to clean me up. But after a few minutes in the bathtub, I passed out again.

Two nurses got me out, dried me off, and put a new gown on me. One of them got a wheelchair and rolled it in. They helped me into the chair and brought me to my bed. As they were helping me up, I passed out yet again. When I opened my eyes, I was once more on the floor, leaning on one of the nurses, while the other one talked to me. They helped me up slowly, successfully got me into the bed, and covered me up. For the next few hours, they kept a close eye on me.

My mother stayed with me the whole time; during labor and after the baby was born. She and my grandmother were the first two to hold my boy. My mother asked several times if I wanted to hold him, but I said no. I would not even look at him.

She went to the doctor and asked him why I didn't want to hold my son. He told her to just give me time and that I was suffering from depression. My mother was sad for me. She and my grandmother started praying that God would help my depression.

When the nurse came in the next day, she asked, "Would you like to hold your baby?"

I was reluctant at first, but when the other nurse wheeled him in, I took one look at him and my maternal feelings started to kick in. The nurse gently placed my baby boy in my arms. As I held him for the first time, I looked down at him and whispered, "Ben-Oni!"

As I looked at this tiny little being, I realized that all the pain was worth it. This special, loving boy I held in my arms was mine to love and to receive love from in return. I remembered my grandmother's words and whispered. "Thank you, Lord. You did see me through."

My mother called the school to let them know I had had my baby. The secretary took all the information down, then she got on the loudspeaker and announced, "Michelle Brisson had a healthy baby boy, weighing seven pounds, thirteen ounces. He was twenty-one-and-a-half inches long." I was told later by several people that you could hear my friend Ben yelling, "Yahoo!" in most of the surrounding classrooms. He was jumping up and down with the biggest smile.

CHAPTER 21

The Accident, and A Vision from God

After a week in the hospital, I was given permission to go home. Uncle Kent and my mother came to pick me up. It was nice to finally be back. A lot of my friends stopped by to see the baby and me. It was good to have so much company. But after a while, it died down and it was back to just me and my mother.

For the first few nights, my mother got up with the baby to let me rest. But when she saw that I was taking advantage of her by letting her get up and do the feedings, she told me it was my baby and that I needed to take responsibility for him. I was mad at her for not helping me anymore, but I was also very grateful that she taught me that lesson (even though I didn't want to do it).

I was still a spoiled and selfish teenager. I hadn't changed much, and when I got mad at her it was worse. Sometimes I think I acted more like I was nine or ten than fifteen.

My poor mother suffered through a lot with my attitude. Our relationship was like a roller-coaster of emotions, and the love that we both needed was not always there. She had often told me that she never thought she was cut out to be a mother. She always thought she was too picky to have children. My attitude and harsh words would remind her of those thoughts.

As time went on, I did take responsibility for my baby, and I eventually fell in love with my little boy. He brought joy to my heart. His was the cutest little smile I ever did see. When he giggled, I had to laugh at him. It was a warmth I will never forget. I often wondered if I ever brought joy like this to my mother, or if for her I would always be the child that was a mistake.

Soon Ben was four months old. He was growing fast, and he continued to bring me joy, but I also still wanted to be a teenager who could go out and have fun. From time to time, my mother let me go out with my friends, but it had been about three weeks since my last break, and I was getting antsy.

That weekend my friend Stephanie asked me if I wanted to go to a dance club in Marquette with her. I was so excited: I would get to go out with my friends and see my boyfriend, Brian.

Brian was a really great guy whom I had met one time when Katie and I went roller skating in Marquette. We had exchanged phone numbers and gotten to know each other. Katie and I went up to the roller rink a few more times, and Brian and I hit it off. We loved each other's company and started to date.

That weekend I couldn't wait to see him. He usually drove down to see me once a week (unless he had a few days off of work, in which case I could see him more). To have this opportunity to go and see *him* was exciting.

I ran to the phone and gave him a call. He said he had to work but that he would see me at the club afterward, if my mother would let me go.

I asked Mother if she would babysit Ben. She agreed and said that I needed to be home at a decent hour. I was so excited. I called Brian back, then Stephanie, and let them know that I could go. Then I ran to my bedroom and started getting ready for my night out on the town. I thought this was going to be the greatest night ever.

I came out quickly when Mother yelled that my ride was there. I figured I had better not change again; this outfit would have to do. I walked into the living room and grabbed my jacket and purse. Before I left, I picked up Ben to give him a hug and kiss, but the strangest thing happened.

He wouldn't give me a kiss. He was acting so strangely. Ben kept wanting *my* mother to hold him, and would not stay with me. I was

The Accident, and A Vision from God

hurt, but I thought that maybe he was mad that I was leaving for the night, so I brushed off my feelings and went out the door with my girlfriend. We hopped into her parents' new Blazer, put on our seatbelts, and headed out.

"Stephanie, aren't we going the wrong way?" I asked.

"No, Darlene and Brittney are coming with us. They are at Darlene's house, so we are going to pick them up first and then head out."

"Really? That is great!" I was excited that two more people were going out dancing with us. The more friends, the more fun!

We turned down Darlene's dirt road. It was three or four miles to her house. The road was like a washboard from all the rain and gravel, so we bounced around as we drove. Stephanie was going a little fast, but that was normal for us, and I didn't worry about a thing.

She asked me to grab her purse out of the backseat and hand it to her. I took off my seatbelt, reached back, and got her purse.

The next thing I remembered was waking up and seeing that Stephanie was gone, and I was in the Blazer by myself. I climbed out of the smashed vehicle and staggered down the road in a daze.

I must have fallen on the ground. Next I faintly remember seeing a vehicle coming down the road. It stopped, and Mr. Simon got out and ran up to me. He covered me up with his coat because I was shaking.

I don't remember too much after that; only bits and pieces. I told Mr. Simon that I was cold, but it was not cold out. He was worried; he figured I was in shock and must be bleeding internally.

Then he saw the Blazer and all the damage to the road and the trees, extending for about an eighth of a mile. He knew I needed help.

It turned out that the Blazer had rolled several times, back and forth from one side of the road to the other, then smashed into the trees like a pinball. Mr. Smith could not believe I had lived through the accident.

What he didn't know was that there were two of us in that Blazer. Knowing I was badly injured, Stephanie had run to the nearest house for help, where the owners called the paramedics and the police. They now arrived at the scene.

I looked up and saw all these people around me, grabbing things out of the paramedics' ambulance. Someone knelt down beside me and started checking my vitals. I said, "I know you!"

It was Stan, my brothers' friend whom I had had a crush on a few years earlier! He looked very worried about me. I drifted in and out of consciousness, and that scared him.

Many people were there, and I heard even more sirens coming. It was the Marquette ambulance. The next thing I knew, I was being put inside it with Stephanie and her mother. Stephanie had a few cuts and bruises and had hit her head, so they wanted to make sure she didn't have a concussion.

I heard my mother. She was upset because Stephanie was awake, alert, and talking, and her mother was riding in the ambulance. Mother felt that she should be in there too, with me. I heard arguing, then someone telling her that they would give her a ride to the hospital. I fell unconscious again.

I awoke at the hospital to a bright light shining above me. I saw a man holding a mask, getting ready to put it over my face. He told me to count to ten with him. Mr. Simon had been right: I was bleeding internally. My spleen was punctured.

After surgery, the doctor came out and talked to my mother while they brought me to the ICU to monitor me. He explained to her that it had been touch and go. "Your daughter had to be resuscitated," he said. "We almost lost her when her heart stopped, but she is stable for now.

"This was a rough surgery," he stated. "Time will tell if your daughter will make it."

I had lost a lot of blood and had to have many transfusions. They kept checking my vitals while they waited for me to wake up. To the doctor's disappointment (as well as my family and friends), I did not. I was in a coma.

The doctor informed my mother that just the previous week, they had lost a girl from a car accident to the same surgery. He wanted her to know that there was a possibility that I wasn't going to wake up.

She struggled with the fact that she might lose me. It didn't help that everyone kept calling her to find out how I was doing. Mother came back and forth to the hospital every day. She was stressed and beginning to lose hope. She started thinking of the funeral arrangements that would need to be made.

After about a week, I awoke in the ICU with my mother sitting at my side. She looked very worried. I slowly looked around the room, and then my eyes fell back upon Mother. In a soft, weak voice, I said, "God ... He talked to me. He told me I needed to stay here and take care of Ben. Mom! God spoke to me.

I continued, "He was in a really bright circle of light, with lots of angels, and He said it was not my time to sleep. He told me it was time to wake up."

My mother looked at me in surprise but did not have time to respond. I was still very weak. I became tired right away, and my eyes felt really heavy. I fell unconscious once more.

She went right to the nurse's station and told them that I had awoken and talked for a few minutes before falling unconscious again. They called the doctor and he raced into the room. He checked my vitals again and asked my mother to repeat what had happened. Then he told her this was a good sign.

They monitored me even more closely over the next few days. I was in and out of consciousness, never staying awake for more than a minute or two. When I was coherent enough, I would tell my mother how God was talking to me. Then I would drift off again.

After about the third day of this, I woke up alert and confused. I looked around the room. My mother and Brian were there with worried expressions on their faces. I looked at Mother with a puzzled look. "What happened, Mom?"

She looked confused too, and said, "Don't you remember? You were in a really bad car accident. You were bleeding internally, and they had to remove most of your spleen."

Then Brian said, "You scared the life out of us; that is what happened. I almost cut my fingers off at work slicing meat when I got the news. You're in big trouble when you get better, Missy!"

I tried to laugh, but my stomach hurt so bad that I had to stop.

The doctors and nurses checked me over many times during the next few days. I was still not able to stay awake for long periods. After twenty minutes to half an hour, I would have to sleep for a while again.

During my recovery, Mother and Robin came up with a plan to get me to sell my Honda three-wheeler to him. He called the hospital one day, and they woke me up to tell me my brother was on the phone.

"Hello," I said.

"Hi, Mickey!" Robin said. "How are you feeling?"

"Tired and sore," I said.

"I won't keep you long. I will let you rest. I just wanted to know if I could buy your three-wheeler from you."

"Sure! You can have it," I said, half-asleep.

"You get better," he said. "We will see you soon. Goodbye!"

I said goodbye to him and was asleep before the phone was hung up.

Let me explain why my mother decided to trick me like this. You see, my grandmother had bought the three-wheeler for me about four months after she bought me Bridget. She knew I really wanted one and figured it would keep me out of trouble when I wasn't riding my horse.

The problem was that I rode it with no fear. I would go up big hills, and it would flip. I would get up, flip it back over, and ride again. This happened a lot. My mother thought I was going to kill myself on that machine. She had tried to get me to sell it for a long time, and I had always told her no.

Her fears (and my fearlessness) dated back to when I first got the three-wheeler. I was out in the yard, and it was almost dark. I was pulling the starter string really hard, but all I heard was a rumbling sound; the engine would not start. Finally, I said a prayer. "Lord, if you will start this three-wheeler, I will just ride around the yard with it, I promise."

I pulled the string, and it started. I was so happy! I started riding around. After a while I got really bored, and I decided to ride out into the big field.

My mother was watching me from the kitchen window. She had instructed me not to ride in the big field behind the house, because it was getting dark, and I had told her I would stay in the yard, but I had just disobeyed … plus I had forgotten the promise I made to the Lord. The sun was down, but I rode out into the field because the three-wheeler had a headlight. As long as I could see, I was not afraid.

I was a good distance out when all of a sudden my three-wheeler stalled out and would not start again. I tried over and over without success. I began to get really scared, fearing that there might be wild animals in the field. Then I hear the sound of coyotes yipping and calling to one another.

That was when my prayer came back to me, and I realized what I had done; I had disobeyed God and my mom. I did the only thing I knew to do: I ran back to the house as fast as my legs could go, in fear that wild animals would attack me.

God convicted my heart, and I will never forget the lesson He taught me that day: promises are not meant to be broken. Obey thy father and thy mother. Don't pray for things that you will not follow through with. God was molding my character, but it would be several years before I fully understood what He was trying to teach me.

God answers prayer, but it is up to us to follow His laws and walk in His ways. He has given us free will. We can follow Him or the world. If we choose Him, He will give us salvation through His Son, Jesus Christ, and a wonderful life with Him in Heaven. If we follow the world, we are following Satan, and our lives will be filled with sorrow and hurt.

Our fun will only give us pleasure for so long. Then we will have to find more fun, more excitement, in order to stay happy. The Bible tells us that Jesus Christ is the same yesterday, today, and forever (Heb. 13:8). He stands for truth and righteousness. What do we stand for, when we do not follow His Laws or stand in His truth?

CHAPTER 22

Visit from Aunt Lu

---◦◦◦---

Once they moved me out of the ICU, many people came to visit me, including Stephanie and many of my other friends from school. I never realized how many people loved and cared about me. I had so many visitors coming in and out that it was hard to rest. The nurses had to limit my guests; otherwise my room would be full and it would disturb the other patients.

Visitors told me many stories of what had happened after the accident. Stephanie once asked if I remembered the fire extinguisher that sprayed all over the inside of the ambulance on the way to the hospital. I only vaguely remembered, since I had been fading in and out of consciousness.

> *I realized at that moment just how much God had protected me from instant death.*

"No one knows how we survived that accident," Stephanie stated. "Many people have told me that we both should not be here." I looked at pictures of the accident and listened while she told me how we had bounced off trees and rolled several times. I realized at that moment just how much God had protected me from instant death. The Blazer was totaled, but we two girls were alive to tell the story.

Even though I knew it was because of God that we survived, I didn't know how to tell Stephanie that. We never talked about the Lord; only worldly things. I was afraid to tell other people, too. I was more worried about what they would think of me than about my own salvation through Jesus.

While in the hospital, I learned that the police were not happy about the accident. My mother was really good friends with a lot of the officers in the surrounding area, and they told her they were doing an investigation at the scene. They were determined to get to the bottom of what really happened.

I found out that the person who had brought my mother to the hospital was her good friend, Trooper Carlson. He had helped her with my brothers during their wild partying days, keeping them out of jail as much as possible (Scott and Robin had their share of illegal fun, but that is another story).

Trooper Carlson was very irate about the whole situation, and one day he made a big scene at the hospital. He yelled at everyone, asking why my mother had not been in the ambulance, especially when there was nothing wrong with the other girl (except for the need for an attitude adjustment and some discipline, which he would be happy to administer). "Meanwhile her daughter," he said while pointing to my mother, "was lying in there dying."

My mother had to calm him down. The doctors had already asked him to leave several times and were about to kick him out. Mother finally got him to sit. Through clenched teeth, he told her, "I will get to the bottom of this, Ruth! You can count on that!"

He held true to his word. Stephanie was fined for reckless driving and speeding. He tried for more, but I do not recall the outcome. What I do remember is that Stephanie and I stayed friends. She visited me in the hospital and was sorry for what had happened. We remained close all through high school.

There was one visitor to my hospital room whom I will never forget. It was early afternoon one day when Aunt Lu came walking in with a huge smile, a bouquet of flowers, and a stuffed white duck with a pretty blue bonnet on its head and a blue apron. "How is my beautiful Michelle feeling today?" she asked me. "I brought something to cheer you up." I looked up at her and smiled as she pulled up a chair. She told me about all the prayers that had gone up for me.

While she spoke of how much God loved me and how He must have a mighty work for me to do for Him, I just looked at her with amazement as the Lord brought back to my mind the vision He had given to me while I was in a coma. I had seen a bright circle of light, made out of angels and with Jesus in the middle, then I heard the words, "Follow after Me. Do not let sin in. It will take you over, and Heaven will be blocked from your view. Cling to Me."

In the vision I had resisted Him, and dark demons had started to engulf the light, blocking it from my sight. Darkness and evil were all around me. I was scared, unable to move or speak. It was like I had been wrapped in sin, and the demons would not let me go no matter how much I struggled.

Aunt Lu stayed only for a short time. She prayed with me and told me she would continue to pray for a speedy recovery. Then she hugged and kissed me goodbye.

I lay there with tears flowing down my face after she left. I shivered at the memory of the vision. I knew I needed to know God better, but I didn't know how to start. I was scared of both God and Satan, and very confused.

I recovered, and a week after I was released from the hospital, I went back to school. Everyone welcomed me. They even announced it over the loudspeaker, saying how grateful all the staff was that I had returned. It felt really good to know that everyone cared about me and missed me.

CHAPTER 23

Learning to Drive, and Breaking the Rules

After a few weeks, everything had gone back to normal. I was back to my old self and my old ways. I blocked out the visions God had given to me and the words He spoke. They scared me too much. I am sure He was looking down on me with tears in His eyes while I decided to just live my life.

When I got my learner's permit to drive, I was so happy that I had passed the test despite how nervous I had been. I wanted my mother to be proud of me. As I came into the house to tell her, I ran into streamers. I stepped in between them, ran right up to her, and said, "Look, Mom! I got my student driver's permit."

I then looked around at the party and asked everyone, "what is this all about?"

They said, "It's a 'Congratulations, you got your permit and also happy sixteenth birthday' party!" Katie and Brian had decided to surprise me. In the worry of getting my permit, I had forgotten about my birthday! We had a wonderful time that day (even though they were disappointed that I hadn't broken the streamers when I came in).

Once during driving practice with my mother, I asked her if I could get a car., I told her I would pay for it since I had worked all summer. She agreed and co-signed for a $500 loan to buy a car from a schoolmate down the road.

It was a blue 1978 Maverick. Karen went with me to pick it up. I was super excited. As I handed the guy the money, it felt good to know that this was my car.

I jumped in and backed down his driveway. When I got to the end, I put on my blinker to prepare to turn out into the street. Karen asked me what I was doing. She told me I didn't need my turn signal on when backing out of a driveway. The guy I had bought the car from was still standing in the driveway, also watching me with a puzzled look. I turned beet red and turned off the blinker.

I drove Karen home and then went back to my house to show my mother the new car. She was excited, too: her car was broken down, and this would be transportation for both of us. Plus, even though I still only had my learner's permit, because it was Trenary and because my mother knew the entire police force, I was able to drive all over without anyone in the car with me.

One night my mother wanted the car to go to a dance at the community building, but I wanted to go to Escanaba with my friends to see a movie. We argued, and finally I said to her, "It is my car." She got mad and told me to take it and go, so I left.

I picked up my friends and Donna. Even though she was a year older than me, she did not have her license, either. So there I was in my new car, driving to Escanaba to go to the movies, with a bunch of friends who did not have a license or permit.

On the way into town, I got irritated with a driver that was not going the speed limit. I started to pass him, but then he picked up speed until he was matching the limit. At the time, I didn't know that I could drive a few miles per hour faster to pass him, so we remained side by side. A whole line of cars backed up behind me in the passing lane (I made many people angry that night). At one point I looked in my rearview mirror and saw that everyone was moving to the right. Then I saw him: a sheriff.

He pulled up behind me with his lights on. I got scared and said, "What do I do, guys?"

My friend Tobi said, "Just act like you don't see him and keep driving. Maybe he will go away."

Not knowing much about policemen, I listened to her advice. But after a quarter of a mile, he hit his siren and I knew I needed to pull over. As he came up to the car, he asked me the famous question, "Do you know why I pulled you over?"

"No," I said.

He proceeded to tell me that he had received a call to go to a crime scene, and that is why he had his lights on. This was a signal to drivers that they needed to move over and let him by. But I hadn't moved out of the way. He got suspicious, and that was why he pulled me over.

The sheriff asked for my license and registration. I told him I forgot my license at home and that I was on my way to the movies. He took down my information and told me to move over the next time emergency vehicles were coming through with their lights on. I thanked him, and we all let out a sigh of relief as we continued on our way to town.

As we passed the movie theater, we looked to see what was playing and decided to go to the late show. Donna knew a friend in town who was having a party, and she wanted to stop in for a little while to say hello to some old friends.

We went looking for her friend's place, but we must have turned down the wrong alleyway or just didn't see the house. We decided instead to go to Ludington Park and wait for the second showing of the movie to start. When we parked by the lake, a bunch of friends who we knew from Rapid River School pulled up. We were laughing and having a good time when the same sheriff from before drove up behind me.

I knew I was in trouble this time, and I was scared. The sheriff told me that he had looked for me at the movies, so I told him we'd decided to go to the late show. He then said that he knew I had been lying before.

He wrote out a ticket, then told me I was not allowed to drive my car home; someone else who was a licensed driver had better drive it, he said. I was not happy but knew I had no other choice after he said, "I am on patrol all night, and I will be watching. If I see you driving, I will arrest you."

I asked my friend Andy from Rapid River if he would drive my car home, and could his friends follow us. He agreed. Then he said, "Hey, we are all here anyway, right? Let's go see the movie and then go home."

The movie was *Jaws*. It was a scary movie about a great white shark that kills people. When it was about halfway through, the vision God had given me at the hospital flashed before me once again. I saw the circle of light, with lots of angels and Jesus in the center, then very quickly the demons came and covered the circle. In the theater, I turned pale and was shaking. I could feel the demons all around me and was scared. I had to get out of there, so I stood up and walked out.

Andy came and asked if I was okay. I lied and told him that I was just a little scared of the movie so that he would comfort me and not make fun. He stayed outside with me, and we talked while waiting for the others to come out. When the movie was over, he drove us home in my car, and his friends followed to pick him up. I thanked him and went into the house.

> My mother was there and did not look very happy. The sheriff had stopped by our house and told her the whole story.

My mother was there and did not look very happy. The sheriff had stopped by our house and told her the whole story. My car was taken away for a few weeks, and I was grounded from going out of town for the next month. I was not happy with my mother. I yelled some very ungrateful, unkind words at her. But in my heart, I knew I was wrong.

That night stayed in my mind for quite some time for another reason. Why did God keep letting the demons block Him from me? I just couldn't understand. Wasn't He supposed to be stronger than Satan?

I finished my punishment, and my mother took me to apply for my license. I couldn't wait. She went up to the counter with me. I was nervous while the man asked us a bunch of questions, then gave me a test.

I passed it. This was it! I was getting my license. Then the man behind the counter asked, "Have you ever had, or do you still have, any medical conditions that could prevent you from driving?"

I said, "No, not that I am aware of."

He asked, "No blindness, times of blacking out, fainting, or seizures?"

I froze.

I mentioned earlier that I had been diagnosed with epilepsy at age four. Mrs. Buckles, my teacher in Head Start, had first noticed how I would stare as if in a trance, and no one could get my attention. It was as if I was looking through them. She had informed my mother, and both of them were very concerned about me.

That's when Mother first took me to see Doctor Matthews. He was a wonderful, caring, loving doctor who would take really good care of me for many years. I loved him very much because he always made me feel special and happy, even while I underwent tests such as EEGs and blood panels.

The blood tests were my least favorite. I would scream and cry. It usually took two people to hold me down and one to draw the blood. It was a terrible time for such a little girl. As I got older, I would be braver, holding my arm up and telling them which arm gave the best blood.

For the EEGs, I remember lying on the bed as they put glue on my head and attached the wires to a little pad. I had to lie really still for a long time. That was the hardest thing for a little girl to do. They had to redo several tests because I would not sit still.

When all the tests results came back in, Dr. Matthews explained the diagnosis to my mother.

"Ruth, your daughter has epilepsy. This is what is causing her to have petit mal seizures. These are referred to as absence seizures, because the child will blank out for a period of time.

"When she is at school or at home," he continued, "she may stop and stare for several seconds. If she was in the middle of an activity or schoolwork, she will pick up what she was doing without skipping a beat. She will not even be aware she is having a seizure unless she is playing a game that involves active moving.

"This will not affect her growth. However, it is common for children with this form of epilepsy to have learning disabilities and trouble with schoolwork."

He continued, "There are many types of seizures. Michelle has a mild case of epilepsy. However, it could lead to grand mal seizures if they are not taken care of. So we are going to put her on some medications that will hopefully help her to function like a normal child and reduce her seizure activity. I am prescribing Zarontin. I will see her back here regularly for checkups and tests, to make sure she is doing well on the medication. Do you have any questions for me?"

My mother asked several, then we left. I saw how worried she was, but being a child, I just tried to make her smile. When we got home, she told me I had to take medicine to help my brain feel better. The liquid tasted gross; I didn't like taking it.

As I got older, Dr. Matthews would change my prescription. My seizures had not lessened the way he wanted, so he told my mother he was going to add a new medication and see how the two worked together. The liquid Zarontin was put in pill form, and I received a new medication called Tegretol. Dr. Matthews hoped this would lessen or eliminate the seizures.

I hated swallowing those pills. For a week, I would hide them in the vents of our trailer. My teacher at school would call my mother and tell her my seizures were happening frequently and that I would come out of them exhausted, falling asleep at my desk. Uncle Dean found the pills I had hidden and told Mother. After that they made me stick out my tongue to be sure I swallowed them.

As time went on and I was on medications regularly, my seizure activity slowed way down, then stopped. At the age of ten, my mother brought me back to the doctor's office, where Dr. Matthews told her, after several tests and an EEG, that I had normal brain activity.

From that moment on, I was seizure free! That didn't mean that my learning disability was gone, though. I would still have to work harder than the average student. Mother knew this, but she left the office with a smile on her face. That evening she took me out for dinner at Trenary Tavern to celebrate.

Now a teenager, waiting and hoping to get my driver's license, what would happen? My mother told the man at the counter that I had a history of epilepsy but had been seizure-free for about six years.

He told us that we needed to go back to the doctor's office and get a paper stating this and that I was able to drive without restrictions.

My heart sank. I worried whether I would be able to get my license at all, because Dr. Matthews was no longer practicing medicine.

"Don't worry about it, Sis," my mother said encouragingly. "I will make a few phone calls, and we will figure this out. I am sure I can get you in to see a doctor."

She scheduled an appointment with a new doctor. When he was done evaluating me, he smiled and wrote me a letter stating I had no restrictions for driving. We drove back to the Secretary of State the next day and got my license.

It was one of the happiest days of my teenage years. I believe today that God was testing me. I needed to learn to trust in Him and lean on Him through all my trials and tribulations. "Trust in the Lord with all your heart, and lean not on your own understanding; in all your ways acknowledge Him, and He shall direct your paths" (Prov. 3:5,6).

CHAPTER 24

Going to College, and Moving On

As the years passed, I decided that the visions God had given me were too hard to understand, so I blocked them out of my mind. Besides, the demons still scared me. Every once in a while, I would have a flashback of the dream, but I immediately pushed it away.

I was happier when I wasn't thinking about that. In truth, I was happier because I was not dealing with my sin. If I didn't think about God's visions, I could do whatever I wanted, and all I wanted was to have fun and live for myself.

I just barely graduated high school with a GPA of 1.75. I had done only what I had to in order to pass my classes. I was glad when it was over, but I didn't know what I was going to do with my life.

I quickly realized that I had better figure that out, or else what I read in our yearbook might come true: *Michelle can now be found at home with her son and grandson.*

This was printed on a page that contained supposed prophecies of where my classmates and I would be in ten years. It would be reviewed at our first class reunion, when my son Ben would be twelve years old.

When I read it, my heart sank. I was very hurt that they would write such a mean and hurtful thing in the yearbook, and I felt like a failure. But I really started to reflect on what I was doing with my life.

I decided it was time to grow up, be a mother, and take care of my son and myself. I got a summer job as a waitress and rented our old two-bedroom house that was down the road from my grandmother (the one where Scott had slept at the top of the stairs). My mother watched Ben for me while I worked.

Scott and his wife Annie, along with my nephew Jordan, moved in with me a few months later. Jordan was just a baby, and they needed a place to stay. I gladly opened my door to them. They were a lot of fun to have around, until a few months later when they moved into their own place. I soon missed the company and adult conversation.

Being a single mother was lonely. I had broken up with Brian only a few months after the accident and was not interested in the guys from our little town. They were not interested in a girl like me, either. I had made a name for myself, and it was not a good name.

I really was trying to do what was right, now. My problem was still my selfish attitude. I just could not get past *me*; I wanted attention and fun. I set a very bad example for my son.

Yet God was working on my heart once again, because Aunt Lu never gave up on me. She would come to visit and pray with me often. She counseled me on good behavior and always did so in a very loving, Christ-like manner. Each time she left, I felt so much better about myself. I even started to pray again.

One evening, I asked God what I could do with my life. "God," I said to Him, "I just don't want to be stuck in this town. There is nothing here for me, and most people don't really care for me. What can I do to make myself better?"

Then it came to me: *go to college*. That was it! I would go to school and make something of myself. I would show all of those people I could be somebody.

I told my mother what I was planning to do. She said, "Sis, that is a great idea. I think college would do you good."

"Thanks, Mom," I said, "Me too! I think I am going to try and find a place to live up in Escanaba. Otherwise the driving will be too much for me, and I won't be able to afford the gas."

"You will need someone to watch Ben while you are at school, won't you?" she asked.

"Yes, Mom, I will."

"Well," Mother said, "Why don't I move up there with you? See if you can find a three-bedroom apartment, and I will help you out with Ben. The state will pay me to babysit him while you are in classes, and that will help out with the household expenses."

I began looking for apartments in the newspaper. In the meantime, I applied at Bay de Noc Community College and was accepted. I started working on a major in counseling and social work. I was determined to better myself.

As I had guessed, driving back and forth got to be too much. I had to borrow money from Uncle Dean for gas. He always gladly gave it to me, though, and I always tried to pay him back right away. One day I said a little prayer that God would help me find a place to live, then I opened the newspaper again. My eyes fell upon an ad for an apartment in Escanaba which read, *Three-bedroom upper apartment for rent, $350 a month, plus security deposit.*

I called the number right away and set an appointment with the man to come and see the apartment. I called and told Mother; she was excited.

The next day we went there. The man really liked my mother and me. He even played with Ben for a long time. We told him we would love to have the apartment, and asked when he needed the money. He responded that he would love to have us as renters, then asked how soon we could get it to him. Mother and I had very little, so we asked for a few days and said we would call him when we had it. He agreed, and we left for home.

We told our family what was happening, and Uncle Dean offered to help us out. We also found out about a program called HUD which could pay a good portion of our rent. I applied, they came and looked over the apartment, and it passed their inspection. HUD agreed to pay all of our rent except for $23 a month, which I was responsible to get to my landlord. Mother and I were excited. My uncles, Uncle Kent especially, helped us move. We were very grateful. I could now focus more on college, which was a new world for me.

I talked to my English professor about how I had barely passed high school, explaining that I struggled with reading and spelling. I had a hard time keeping up, and this made me really not want to do the work.

After correcting some of my papers, she and one of my other professors realized that I had a learning disability and needed some guidance. Together they sent me to a special place in the library for testing.

There they used a machine that had a light on it. I had to follow it with my eyes and read as fast as it went across the words on a page. I had to answer questions when I was finished. It was hard; I wasn't a very good reader at the time. They used this method with me for the whole year that I attended Bay de Noc Community College.

Later, when I decided to apply at Northern Michigan University and had to transfer my transcripts, I received a copy of my GPA. I looked at it, then looked again. I could not believe it: I had an average GPA. I looked a third time, and tears ran down my face. I thought to myself, *I did it. I am not dumb, after all.*

On the home front, while attending Bay de Noc, my mother and I did not get along very well. I always wanted to be with my friends or be at some extracurricular activity; most often volleyball.

I was on the college team at the YMCA (they took me on since I had been on my high school team). My teammates and I loved the sport and played often. But because of this extra activity in my schedule, I was gone from home a lot. My mother was not happy taking care of her grandson twenty-four seven.

I knew I was wrong, and eventually I started to feel badly about the situation, so I began taking Ben with me to my practices. He would sit on the bleachers and cheer me on. All my teammates loved and played with him.

He was very happy when he was with me. During one practice I saw him sitting on the bench, swinging his legs, with his hands on his knees and the biggest smile on his face. He never took his eyes off us.

But I never realized how much he loved me, or how I must have made him feel so unloved. I wanted to be a good mother to him, I just never knew how. I had not had anyone to show me.

Where my own mother had spent most of her time in bars while I was growing up, I was now doing the same thing to Ben, just in a different way. I did also go out to bars with my friends a lot (while my mother babysat), but I was never a heavy drinker. I just liked the excitement and attention. In both cases I put my wants before Ben's needs. It wasn't what Jesus would have done.

Meanwhile my mother had almost completely quit drinking. She had fallen one day at the Trenary Home Bakery while working (her crippling arthritis was getting worse), and her boss had told her it would be better for her not to work. Partly that was him seeing that it would be a liability for him if she fell, but he was also good friends with her and didn't want to see her get hurt.

After this accident, Mother started to realize that she needed to make some life changes concerning her health. She took her boss's advice and quit her job. She also decided to stop going to bars and buying beer for consumption at home.

She was still in contact with Aunt Lu, who prayed with and for her on a daily basis. She read her Bible more and decided to start attending the Escanaba Seventh-day Adventist Church. She asked me if I would like to go with her, because she was no longer able to drive.

What she was really doing was getting me to attend services with her. To her surprise, I enjoyed going with her, and I liked the people. We met a lot of special people, two of whom were Joe and Carol.

Carol was in her early sixties when we met her. She was an amazing woman who stood about 5' 2" tall. She was always smiling and giving encouragement to others. When she was happy, she loved to clap her hands and say, "Amen!" She taught the teen Sabbath School class for many years and loved to encourage the kids to walk in the ways of the Lord.

Whenever I walked into church, she was the first person I looked for. She always had a big hug and kiss for me and Ben. There was never a day that I saw her there without a smile. The light of Jesus always shone on her face.

Carol always made me feel special, and she loved my son Ben as if he was her own grandson. She reminded me a lot of Aunt Lu. She gave me confidence in myself when no one else would, along with great hope that I could be someone special for the Lord.

Her husband Joe was a tall man; about six foot. He was usually found by Carol's side and was also always smiling. His face glowed with the light of the Lord, and he was filled with great wisdom. They made a great team witnessing to those who came into the church. He also fell in love with Ben and took him under his wing.

My mother started doing Bible studies with Pastor Miller. Carol came with him from time to time, and if she didn't, Rick Binford (another church member who made a huge impact on our family's walk with Jesus) came. Pastor Miller and Rick tried on several occasions to get me to commit to a Bible study as well. I sat in on one with my mother, but I was being pulled so deeply by Satan that I didn't want to give up my worldly ways and make a heartfelt commitment to Jesus. I liked how I was living, and I was happy. I believed in God, but was not ready to have a relationship with Him.

My mother completed her Bible studies and decided she was ready to make a commitment to the Lord. She was very grateful for her relationship with Jesus and the love she now had in her heart. On May 30th of 1992, Mother gave her heart to Jesus as Pastor Miller baptized her in church.

Aunt Lu was there to support her decision. She had the towel ready when my mother came out of the water, and she was the first to hug her after the pastor. The smiles on both Aunt Lu's and Carol's faces were like light shining from Heaven.

As I heard my mother's testimony and watched her baptism, my heart was touched and tears ran down my face. I felt the presence of the Holy Spirit very strongly that day, and I longed to stay in the moment. God was touching my heart.

However, as in the past, this feeling of God's love for me didn't last long. I once again put God aside and started living life for me. What I didn't know was that God was not done fighting for me.

He loves us all in a very special way. He showed this great love when He sent His only Son Jesus to die a horrible death on a cross, in order to save the lost sheep that wander astray throughout the earth. The sacrifice God made for all of humanity was out of sheer love for His children.

God did not give up on me, and I am very grateful for that. He kept placing people in my path who would lead me closer to Him. I continued to go to church, even though I was out living a selfish life. Carol and Joe also never gave up on me. They continued to love me and talk to me at every opportunity.

Carol asked me one day if I had ever considered dedicating Ben to the Lord. I asked what she meant.

She explained how important it was for us to give our children back to the Lord, because they are truly His first. I told her that I thought it was a good idea, but I was scared. I asked if she and Joe would come up with my mother and me, as part of our family.

Carol jumped up and down and clapped her hands, smiling and saying, "We would love to. Amen, amen, amen!" She hugged me very tightly.

I looked over at Joe. He was nodding his head and smiling at me and his wife. He then said it would be a blessing, and echoed Carol's excitement.

So on August 15th of 1992, my mother, Carol, Joe, and I stood before the church with Pastor Miller, as he prayed and dedicated my son Ben to the Lord. It was a happy day, and I felt the presence of the Lord fall upon my family.

God impressed upon my heart that I should turn away from my sinful ways and follow after Him. I longed to do just that, but my walk was not strong enough; I did not study in God's Word or pray for His help or guidance.

God couldn't guide me if I was not willing to listen to that guidance and walk in His ways, and the temptations were too great for me to withstand on my own. The only way I could have done it was through Jesus Christ, who is today my Lord and personal Savior.

My church family didn't judge me for what I was doing, though; they just loved me where I was.

Joe and Carol used to invite us over for potluck lunches after church. After we were done eating, we would visit, and then Joe or Carol would read out of the Bible or *The Desire of Ages*. Sometimes Carol turned on 3ABN, and we watched spiritual programs. Usually it was *Kids Time*. That's a show on which kids sing, give their testimony, read Bible stories, and have "nature nuggets." Ben really liked watching it with Carol. She would sit on the floor with him and tell him that her granddaughter was on the show. Carol pointed her out and told Ben all about her. He would just smile and ask her a bunch of questions.

Those Sabbath afternoons were a delight to my family.

CHAPTER 25

Baptism: God Is Working

So now I was attending church regularly, but I was also still partying and making a mess of my life. Things started to get hard: I was making some friends angry with my selfish attitude. I no longer wanted to face them. I knew I was wrong to treat them the way that I did.

I became determined to move to Marquette to start over. I was running; that was what I did when things got messy or uncomfortable for me. Running was so much easier than having to face the problems I created.

My girlfriend Kristina lived in Marquette. She was going to NMU and wanted me to join her. I still had a few more years to go before I would complete my schooling at Bay de Noc Community College. Nevertheless, without really praying about it, I said, "Yes, I will apply to NMU." I was stepping out in faith to move, but it was not God's faith that I stepped out in.

And I was moving, but with no place to stay. I started looking into shelters and found a home called Loaves and Fishes. It was a Christian family that helped those who were down and out. I called and explained the situation I was in. I told them how I wanted to attend Northern Michigan

University and better my education. The husband and wife I talked to said they needed to pray and seek God's guidance. The next day I received a phone call from them, stating that they would love to help Ben and me. I packed our belongings and borrowed a friend's truck to move.

My mother was not happy. She decided that she would move back to my grandmother's house. She packed her stuff up with a heavy heart.

Mother was apprehensive about moving back to Trenary. She had left her drinking days behind and wasn't sure if she could resist the temptation if it presented itself. She loved the Lord and wanted to do His will, but she knew that she was not strong enough on her own. The hard part for her was to claim the victory in Jesus.

She had many other worries on her mind as well. She would miss her grandson more than anything. She had been there for him for the past three years of his life. Her thoughts for me turned to prayers. She knew that I was on a road that was that did not lead to God. Satan had a hold on my heart, and my mother could see this very clearly.

Kristina, on the other hand, was excited that I was going to be living by her. When I got to Marquette, she let me store my things in the basement of her apartment. Then we took only what Ben and I needed to the home where we were staying.

Kristina went with me to the NMU registration office to work out the details for my classes and financial aid. It was a big campus, and I was not used to that. Walking across it took more than a few minutes. But I knew I would be okay.

The couple we were staying with helped us apply for food stamps and assistance through the state. They also helped me get in contact with HUD, so that I would be able to find an apartment that suited Ben and me.

They were a really sweet couple with big hearts. One day the husband decided to make homemade pasta for Ben. It was Ben's favorite meal. I watched as he mixed the dough and let my son pour in the ingredients. The two of them rolled out the pasta and then put it through the cutter. He boiled the water and started putting in the noodles. It was the best pasta I'd ever had; it amazed me that homemade could taste that good.

The time came when I found a little one-bedroom apartment in Ishpeming. It was affordable, and the bedroom was big enough for two beds and our dressers. It had a small kitchen and living room, but a big

Baptism: God Is Working

bathroom. I was going to have to take a bus to school, and I needed daycare for Ben, but I was confident that it would all work out. Things were starting to fall into place.

I would need the bus because I didn't have a car at the time. My Maverick was gone, having broken down. More recently I had purchased a small station wagon with a four-speed on the floor (I loved driving a stick shift), but I didn't have this car anymore, either.

You see, one day I had gotten mad at my mother and punched the wall. It hurt my hand so bad that I could not shift my car. My girlfriend from college said she would stay at my house until my hand got better and drive us back and forth to school.

Once after classes I was ready to go home, but my friend wanted to stay in the dorms and visit. I got really grouchy and rude with her and said I needed to go home. She got mad, grabbed the keys, and we left the parking lot.

We got to the stop sign at US 2 and Highway 41. The roads were covered by about six inches of slippery, slushy snow. There was a lot of traffic, so we had to sit there for five minutes. My friend grew impatient, and as the car beside us went straight across, she decided to turn right onto the four-lane highway. However, the driver of the car going straight had also been tired of waiting and had gunned it across the intersection, causing the other traffic to slide. One of those cars lost control and hit us.

The police came and wrote up a report. No one got a ticket; it was considered a no-fault accident. However, my car was not in good shape. We had to inch it back to the apartment. I didn't have the money to fix it, so I ended up calling the junkyard and having them pick it up.

This was how I wound up at NMU with no transportation. It was a bit of a problem, but I managed to get to where I was going. God was watching over me and placed many loving Christian people in my path.

I loved our little apartment, but it seemed like something was missing in my life. I was alone with my son in a new town, and I didn't know many people. Kristina lived two cities over, so we didn't get to see much of each other. Plus we had different majors. She was in medicine, while I had changed my major to legal secretary. I didn't do much but go to school and come home to my son.

As I walked in the door after school one day, the phone rang. It was Aunt Lu, and she wanted to come over for a visit. Back when I was in the Loaves and Fishes home, she had tried to get me to come and live with her. Even though I had declined, she was by no means giving up on my salvation. I was excited and told her I would love to see her.

> *her smile and loving character always won over my heart*

When she stopped by, Aunt Lu prayed with me and talked about going to the Marquette Seventh-day Adventist Church. I was a little apprehensive about the idea at first, but her smile and loving character always won over my heart, so I agreed to go. She set up an appointment for me to meet the pastor. Then she found me a ride with Donovan and Dorothy, a couple who lived in Ishpeming and attended the church.

Pastor Johnston was delighted to meet with me. He asked if I would like to do Bible studies with him. I agreed, and he set up a day for us to study once a week. For our first study, he brought me a large print King James Version Bible, then told me it was mine to keep if I finished the study with him. I was thrilled to have my very own Bible.

He, his wife, and his three boys were such a blessing to me. Pastor Johnston and I studied for six or seven months. Afterward, he talked with me about giving my heart to Jesus and asked if I would consider being baptized. I accepted his request. On March 6th, 1993, I would be baptized in the Marquette Seventh-day Adventist Church.

It was too cold to do it out in Lake Superior, so they set up a portable baptistery in the back of the church and turned all the chairs around to face it. As the building filled up with loved ones and my brothers and sisters in Christ, I started to get really nervous.

While Debbie helped me get into my robe, Aunt Lu came into the room. She expressed how proud of me she was for taking a stand for Jesus and letting Him wash all my sin away. As she hugged me, I felt warm tears run down my cheeks. Aunt Lu had never given up on me. She had always prayed for me and lifted me up to Jesus. She had longed for me to be in Heaven with her, walking the streets of gold with Jesus and our Father God.

As Pastor John and I walked out to the baptistery, he smiled at all the brothers and sisters and said, "Today is a day of rejoicing. Sister Michelle has decided to give her life over to the Lord."

He talked for a while to the congregation and visitors about the love of the Lord and how important it is for us to give our hearts and lives over into the hands of the Savior. He then asked me to give my testimony.

I was nervous and scared. I don't recall all of what I said, but I do remember thanking Aunt Lu, Carol and Joe, and my mother for never giving up on me.

Then the pastor walked to the back of the baptistery, and I followed him. My heart was pounding so hard in my chest that I could hear it. He saw how nervous I was, smiled at me, and whispered, "This is a glorious day in Heaven today, Michelle. You are surrendering your life to Jesus. Are you ready?"

I nodded and entered the baptistery with him.

I had gone swimming many times, in many rivers and lakes, but when you step into the waters of baptism, you feel the presence of the Holy Spirit so strong around you that it is indescribable; feelings of love, and the cleansing feeling of all the sinful dirt being washed away from your life. Your heart is overwhelmed with a joy that you could never receive from this world; it only flows from Heaven.

Pastor John placed his hand on my back and a white cloth in my hands. He put his other hand under mine and said, "I baptize you in the name of the Father, the Son, and the Holy Spirit." He then plunged me backwards under the water and brought me back up.

Tears ran down my face as I felt the presence of God fall upon me like a downpour of rain. I was happy and at peace in my heart, knowing the Lord had just washed away my sins.

My mother was there. The smile on her face and the tears she shed that day meant so much to me. She was proud of my decision to follow Christ and accept Him as my personal Savior. Uncle Dean, Carol, and Joe were also there.

Aunt Lu gave me a copy of *The Desire of Ages*. She wrote in the book, *If you want to know Jesus better, read a chapter a day. I love you.* I still have the book, and I read her message from time to time in order to remember how much she loved me. I also read it to remind me that Jesus loves me more, wants me to be saved, and that He died on a cross to set a sinner like me free.

> But He was wounded for our transgressions, He was bruised for our iniquities; the chastisement for our peace was upon Him, and by His stripes we are healed. All we like sheep have gone astray; we have turned, every one, to his own way; and the Lord has laid on Him the iniquity of us all. (Isa. 53:5, 6)

CHAPTER 26
Unevenly Yoked

Everything was going very smoothly for me. Ben had been accepted into the Head Start program in Ishpeming at the beginning of the school year, and I was still going to college and working hard. I was also attending church every Sabbath. I was happy and moving forward in my life with Jesus as my guide.

On the transit bus back and forth to school, I met a lot of new people. One of the girls became very attached to me and often came over to visit. One day I heard her outside talking to someone. There were two young men, whom she invited into my apartment. "Michelle," she said, "this is Nate and his friend."

We visited for a while, then we all watched movies. Nate was interested in me, and I thought he was very cute, but I was clueless about how to pick good friends (let alone someone to be in a relationship with).

I always trusted in people until they hurt me, which unfortunately got me into a lot of trouble. Here was one of those times where I was going to have to learn a lesson the hard way; because I was falling for this guy.

Nate became a part of my life that night. I was so blinded by his charms that I did not seek God's guidance. He showed me the attention I so longed to have, or at least that I thought I wanted (I realize now that true love comes from God, and anyone who is filled with His love will show you the love that He has placed in their heart).

He was not a Christian; he had his own ways of doing things. We started dating and spending a lot of time together. This was my first mistake: dating him while knowing that he didn't have a relationship with Jesus.

After a few weeks of dating, he told me that he had no place to live. He said his father and stepmother had kicked him out. I had already fallen in love with Nate and didn't want to see him on the streets, so I let him move in with Ben and me. This was the second mistake I made. I was so head over heels that I could not see through his intentions, nor did I seek God's guidance and wisdom. "Do not be unequally yoked together with unbelievers. For what fellowship has righteousness with lawlessness? And what communion has light with darkness?" (2 Cor. 6:14)

Nate went to church with me for two Sabbaths in a row, then he refused to go anymore. He said it was a waste of his time. Satan was slowly pulling me away from God, and I didn't even realize it. First I went to church on my own, but before long I stopped attending altogether to spend more time with Nate.

Ben missed Sabbath School and longed to go back. I would tell him that we would go to church the following week but then never take him. Instead, Nate started taking him fishing on Saturdays. Soon Ben forgot about church and came to associate the Sabbath with fishing.

One afternoon Pastor John came to the door. When he knocked, I asked Nate, "Who is here?"

Nate looked out the window and said, "It is the pastor."

I told Nate to tell him I was not there and ran to the bathroom. Nate laughed at me, then answered the door and lied to the pastor. He came to me, still laughing, and told me the pastor was gone.

I came out feeling a huge weight of guilt. I knew God had sent the pastor to my door. I knew I was living in sin, and that I had left God and my commitment to Him. I just didn't want to face the fact of it; I was happy, and I didn't want to give it up.

I had put my needs before God's and my son's. I was losing sight of my salvation. Satan found a crack in my armor and came right into my life full force.

The devil knew that I had felt unloved for most of my life; my flesh was weak in this area. First my mom had neglected my emotional and physical needs for the sake of alcohol, because she was hurting, and now I was neglecting my son's needs, because I was seeking the love I had longed for as a child.

It was not actually just love that I was searching for. It was also assurance that someone truly cared for me and wanted to spend time doing things with me. I wanted to be cared for and loved unconditionally. I longed for a perfect relationship. I was seeking that in Nate.

If I had taken the time to really study the Bible that Pastor John had given to me, I would have had a better idea of true love. 1 John 4:18 and 19 says, "There is no fear in love; but perfect love casts out fear, because fear involves torment. But he who fears has not been made perfect in love. We love Him because He first loved us."

Perfect love can only come from God. People cannot provide it because sin lies within us. Only when we form a relationship with God do we realize what perfect, true love is. As for a companion? I should have been seeking love in Christ first, and then I would have realized that God is my husband:

> Do not fear, for you will not be ashamed; neither be disgraced, for you will not be put to shame; for you will forget the shame of your youth, and will not remember the reproach of your widowhood anymore. For your Maker is your husband, the Lord of hosts is His name; and your Redeemer is the Holy One of Israel; He is called the God of the whole earth. (Isa. 54:4, 5)

As time passed, I started to notice things about Nate: I caught him in several lies, and I realized Ben was uneasy around him. When I confronted him about the lies, he would change his story to make himself look innocent, and then tell me that I was just overreacting. I ignored the signs. I thought to myself, *Maybe he is right.*

We talked one day about having a baby. We thought we were both ready, so I had the doctor remove the birth control implant in my arm.

Around the same time, Aunt Lu was praying for me and about how she could bring me back to Jesus. She called me up, told me about Spring Retreat at Camp Sagola, and asked me to go with her. "I will pick you and Ben up. You are not too far out of my way," she said.

I felt scared and convicted of my sins; I didn't want to go. She sensed this in my voice and told me how much fun I would have and that it would cost me nothing; she was going to pay my way. After ten minutes on the phone and lots of prayer, she talked me into it.

I told Nate I was leaving in a week and a half for four days. He asked what time I would return, but didn't seem to mind that I was going. I was quite surprised at his reaction, but not knowing what to think, I dismissed it.

Thursday came, and Aunt Lu was right on time. She picked up Ben and me, said a prayer for safe travels, looked at me with a smile, and said, "We are on our way to spend the weekend with Jesus."

On the way I started to get sick to my stomach. After we arrived and put our things in the cabin, we ate supper and I began feeling better. I realized I had not had my monthly cycle and figured I was pregnant. It was less than three months since I'd had my implant removed.

The guilt of having a baby with a man I was not married to weighed heavily on my heart. I started to feel bad about being at camp. Satan was trying to make me think I had sinned so much that God could not forgive me. *Why are you here, Michelle? You know God has seen your every sin.* Thoughts like this raged through my mind. *He knows how you have disgraced Him. Isn't it better not to be reminded of your sins? You should just leave and go home. Tell Aunt Lu you are sick and want to leave.*

Aunt Lu brought me out of my thoughts. "Are you ready to go to our first meeting?" she asked.

I nodded my head and gave her a faint, nervous smile. At the meeting, when the people embraced me with hugs and love, I began to see God's mercy and grace shining through them.

I loved the meetings, but Satan kept telling me that God could never forgive me for what I had done. My spiritual walk was not strong enough to resist the devil's taunting. I did not rely on God and His Word to get me through. All I needed to do was trust Him, but I was struggling deep within my soul.

On Saturday afternoon the meeting was about to start, but I told Aunt Lu that I was not feeling well and just wanted to lie down.

She was very disappointed and looked worried. She looked over to Kristin, a fifteen-year-old from our church who was also on the retreat, and asked her if she would take Ben to his class so that I could rest. Kristin smiled at Ben, took him by the hand, and walked out of the cabin. Kristin was a positive influence on me. She was young, but her family was grounded in the Lord. They knew Aunt Lu well and also helped out with VBS and went on missionary trips.

As the cabin door shut behind them, I started to cry. I wondered how God could ever love a sinner like me. I wept and worried over this until I became physically ill. My soul was yearning for a walk with God, but I didn't understand how He could forgive my actions.

On Saturday night at the last meeting of the retreat, they had testimony time for new believers. I was so intrigued by their stories that I wanted to do what was right, too. I decided that I was going to talk to Nate about getting married. If we were going to have this baby, we needed to do it the right way.

> *I wanted to do what was right, too. I decided that I was going to talk to Nate about getting married.*

When that weekend was over, I was happy to go home. I had a new perspective on life. I told Nate that I was pregnant, and he was really excited. We talked about names and if it was going to be a boy or a girl. He told me he already had two girls from two other women, and he hoped this one would be a boy.

I asked him about those relationships, but he gave me the runaround. This bothered me and should have been a big red flag, but I did not question him further. Then I mentioned getting married, and he told me that it would be better if we waited until after the baby was born. That way, he said, I wouldn't be so fat when I walked down the aisle. I was offended but didn't say a word. He seemed to think it was funny.

A few days passed. I was cleaning the house when I heard a knock at the door. I thought it was a friend of ours, and I was excited to tell her I was pregnant. I hurried over to the door with a big smile upon my face, but when I opened it, I saw that it was a police officer.

"Good afternoon," he said. "I am looking for a Nathan Smith."

I went into the bedroom and woke Nate up. He got up and went to the door.

I stood back and watched as the police officer stated, "Nathan Smith, you are under arrest for the rape of … "

For the rape? I thought. *He raped someone?* I was in a fog. I couldn't move.

The officer was reading him his rights. "You have the right to an attorney. If you cannot afford an attorney, one will be appointed to you. Do you understand all of your rights?" Then he handcuffed Nate and put him in the back seat of the squad car.

As it drove away, I stood in the doorway, dumbfounded. Ben was on the living room floor, watching with a confused look.

Eventually I sat down in the chair by the door. I was in shock. I ran the events back through my mind and thought, *There has to be some mistake.*

When would he have had time to do such a thing? I called his sister and told her what happened. She knew many people, and called me back within a short time to tell me all of the details.

A few hours after they took him, I received a collect call from Nate telling me how it was a setup. He asked me to bail him out of jail and told me how much it was.

I had just enough money. I had been saving because I was planning on moving to New Hampshire with Donna. I went to the hiding spot that only Nate and I knew about, opened up the can, and counted. There was a lot missing.

When I told Nate, he said that one of his friends must have stolen it. I said I would get him out one way or another, then I got off the phone with him and called Uncle Dean. He helped me post bail for Nate.

After we got home, Nate told me the whole story from his point of view. He and a friend had gone over to his friend Kailey's house to visit, but she was not home. However, her fourteen-year-old cousin was there babysitting, so they stayed and visited with her for about an hour. Then they left.

I believed him that this girl was lying to get attention. I was ready to do whatever it took to keep him out of jail. He had caught me hook, line, and sinker.

The case dragged out. They had forensic evidence on him (which I didn't find out about until later), but Nate changed his court-appointed attorney, which bought him more time. While the case was at a standstill, we just lived our lives as if nothing had happened.

With the baby coming, we knew that we would need a bigger house, so we moved to Maple Street in Ishpeming. I had found us a two-bedroom house to rent at a reasonable price. I loved the bathroom; it had an old-fashioned, cast iron, claw-foot tub. I loved to take baths, so this was a blessing for me. Ben liked having his own room and told me this was his blessing. I just smiled. Nate was also happy that we moved; a little too happy.

I found out that he was doing drugs. I also learned that he had stolen money from many people who were looking for him. Moving to a new house was a way to avoid being found. This helped me to realize that he was the one who had most likely stolen my money. But I was determined to make this relationship work, because he was the father of my baby. I believed his lies when I confronted him. I did not want to believe that he was doing anything wrong.

My due date approached quickly. I longed to deliver the baby girl who was inside me. It was a rough pregnancy; the stress of Nate's lies along with the court case was wearing me out.

One evening I started feeling labor pains. I was taken to Marquette General Hospital, and they brought me right up to labor and delivery. I was in labor for twelve hours, and my beautiful baby girl, Nautasha Marrie, was born at 12:16 p.m., weighing eight pounds and measuring nineteen and a half inches long. She had a full head of jet-black hair. I could not help but stare at her beauty.

When Nautasha was one month old, Nate and I got married in the Methodist Church in Trenary, Michigan. His friend Ray was his best man, and my brothers were the groomsmen. My cousin Donna was my maid of honor, and Kristina and Dina were the bridesmaids. I wore my sister-in-law Annie's old prom dress for the wedding. We had the reception at the Trenary Tavern with a potluck meal.

Robin sat at the bar with my husband and said to him, "If you hurt my little sister, you better have some good running shoes on, because I will find you and you will be sorry."

Nate assured Robin that he would not hurt me. Scared, he avoided my brother Robin as much a possible after that encounter.

We didn't have a honeymoon because we had no money; our families had paid for the wedding. Instead we went home that night with our kids, like we did on any other normal night. The only thing that was different was my last name.

CHAPTER 27
Prison: The Truth Revealed

The attorney's office kept calling and getting more information from Nate. His court date was approaching fast, and they needed all the facts to be able to defend him. They set up an appointment for him to come in.

We went in the next week, and his attorney gave us a copy of the police report. He told Nate, "It does not look good. They have evidence with your DNA on it. There was a sweatshirt turned in to the police that went to forensics, and it tested positive: it is a perfect match." We asked the attorney what we could do. I knew Nate was guilty after reading the police report. I still did not want to believe he had done such a horrible thing, but I was starting to doubt everything he told me.

A week passed and we were sitting in the courtroom, waiting for his attorney. As he approached us and sat down, he looked Nate right in the eye. He said, "I just talked to the judge and prosecuting attorneys. The evidence against you is strong. If you do not plead guilty, and you are found guilty, you are looking at twenty years to life. If you plead guilty, they will give you five to ten years in prison with a release date after two and a half years for good behavior."

My heart sank. Was this really happening?

Nate looked at me, then back to his attorney, then said, "I will take the plea bargain."

The attorney looked at him again. "Nate, you will then have to tell the judge you are guilty of this crime. Do you understand?"

He nodded his head yes, but his face was beet red. His attorney walked back to the judge's chambers to negotiate the plea. Then Nate looked over to me. "This is such a joke. Court-appointed attorneys are all just a setup to put people in jail. They never really fight for you. It is all a scam." He was really angry. His fist were balled up, and his eyes looked so evil. I sat there dumbfounded, not knowing what to say or do.

The prosecuting attorneys came out of the judge's chambers, followed by Nate's attorney. Court went into session and lasted less than twenty minutes.

The judge sentenced Nate to five to ten years in prison. The bailiff then came over and handcuffed him. Two other officers assisted (these two would transport him to Marquette prison, where he'd stay until it was time to send him out to another prison located in upper Michigan).

As they were handcuffing him, Nate asked the judge if he could have an extension on going to prison. He said that I had just gotten out of the hospital after having a kidney infection, that we had an infant at home, and that someone would need to help take care of the baby. The judge denied his request, and he was taken away.

As I got on the transit bus to go home, I was in complete shock at what was happening in my life. I had truly just spent three days in the hospital for a kidney infection. I'd lied to the doctor and told him my back was not hurting, so he had put me on antibiotics and released me to go home. I'd lied because I knew Nate's court date was coming up, and I wanted to be there. Now I was feeling the ill effects in my body and mind.

My mother was at the house watching the kids. She stayed for two weeks while I recovered, taking care of the kids and my house. I was very grateful for her presence in my home and for her shoulder to cry on.

Mother had never wanted me to marry Nate. She had said he was not a nice guy and would never treat me the way that I deserved. She'd stated this on several occasions, but for those two weeks, she just stayed by my side and comforted me. I know she must have been praying for me. I really appreciated her not saying, "I told you so!" and instead just loving and supporting me. All I had ever wanted from her was love and a bond like a mother and daughter should have. It felt good to have that relationship with her that I had longed for, even if it was only for a short period.

After Nate went to prison, a bunch of people came and told me all the things that he had done over the last year. He had cheated on me, sold and consumed many drugs, stolen money from me and my family, abused my son Ben, and threatened that he would hurt him worse if he told me. When I learned these things, I started asking questions to people around town who knew him but didn't really know who I was. I heard similar stories wherever I went.

I decided to take Nautasha to the jail to see him. I wanted to confront him about all of the things I had found out.

"Michelle," he said, "all those people are just jealous and want to break us up. They will say anything to ruin our marriage. Don't listen to those stupid people."

He had been good at lying to me before, but by this point I'd had enough. I left the jail. He was transferred out to a prison in Lower Michigan, and I never saw him again.

CHAPTER 28

A New Job: The Casino

I started going to church again and praying for God to help me with all the hurt and pain that was in my heart. I went for about two months. During this time I knew I needed to get on with my life, and living in Ishpeming was not going to help me. Everywhere I looked there was a reminder of all the things Nate had lied about. I just wanted out; I was about to run away from the problem again.

One day Uncle Burt called and told me that they had openings at the casino where he and my aunt worked. I was excited, and he said he would put in a good word for me.

I told my mother about the conversation, and she decided to move with me to Kincheloe, Michigan, where I got a job at the casino as a waitress and bartender. While I worked, Mother watched Ben and Nautasha.

After a few months, my aunt and uncle encouraged my mother to work at the casino, too. She applied and started a part-time job in the casino deli.

I hired a babysitter from down the road for my children. They decided to call her Nana. She was a great lady and took really good care of them. She loved them like they were her own grandchildren.

A New Job: The Casino

During the process of moving and finding work, I also filed for divorce from Nate. Aunt Gwyn encouraged me to file before we had been married six months. She thought that it would go quicker and that I might be able to get it annulled. However, the attorney told me that it was not possible to divorce him quickly with an annulment, because we had a child together. Still, it only took six months for the divorce to go through (even though Nate fought it and used as many of his rights as he could while being in prison).

I gave my attorney the police report on Nate, and at the divorce trial he gave a copy to the judge. The judge called a recess, went to his chambers, and read the report. Fifteen minutes later he came back out. He granted my divorce, and I left the courtroom feeling free of a burden I had been carrying for months.

> *I left the courtroom feeling free of a burden I had been carrying for months.*

As I got used to the way the casino was run, I realized that I could make more money in a different department. I applied for a transfer to a job going around the casino selling change at the slot machines. But I got really tired of walking around yelling, "Change! Change!" Aunt Gwyn then asked why I didn't just apply to work with her as a slot attendant. So I applied for that position and was hired.

I liked working at the casino. It was so exciting. I met many famous people and turned a lot of heads. I lost a lot of weight and started to flaunt my body. I would smile and flirt with men, then walk away.

This was very dangerous. I forgot what I had learned from God's Word. I lost my connection with Him and started living a life of sin all over again. Not only this, I was also causing men to sin by lusting after me. "Do not lust after her beauty in your heart, nor let her allure you with her eyelids. For by means of a harlot a man is reduced to a crust of bread; and an adulteress will prey upon his precious life" (Prov. 6:25, 26). "The righteousness of the upright will deliver them, but the unfaithful will be caught by their lust" (Prov. 11:6).

Satan had his hands deep in my life as I indulged the sins and selfish ways of the world. My life consisted of partying and work. I made a lot of new friends at the casino who liked to have a good time. Meanwhile my children received very little of my time. Sometimes I would take them to the party houses just so that I could be there when my mother had to work (my babysitter did not watch my children after work hours).

Even while I was hooked on a life of attention and no worries, I quickly became convicted that the parties were not a place for my children to be. I found other people to babysit so I could keep going out. When I could not find someone, I stayed home. Even though I was angry and wanted to go, I made the right choice.

Then my girlfriend asked me to work with her at the Hollywood Café bar. I thought that this was the best opportunity for me to be able to party and bring in more money. I worked both jobs for a long time (I was at the bar on Fridays and Saturdays). My mother, or someone I hired, continue to babysit if I needed them to.

CHAPTER 29

The Dealer

One day as I was walking by the blackjack tables, my friend Steve asked why I didn't become a dealer. He told me how much money he made every two weeks: it was double my income. I told him I would think about it.

I talked to a few people in personnel about being a dealer. They encouraged me to apply for the position. Within a week, I was called into the office. They interviewed me and set up a date to train me on the tables. Within two weeks I was dealing blackjack.

It is illegal for a casino to teach you how to cheat at the tables. However, they have ways of getting around this. For instance, there are pit bosses who walk the pits and check on each dealer. Their job depends on making each pit run smoothly and bring in money for the casino. If a pit is not making a good profit, the pit boss gets penalized. So they intently watch the tables; the wins and losses.

As I got really good at dealing, the pit bosses took a big interest in me. During my breaks in the backroom, some of them told me how to stack the deck or change a winning table into a losing one. They brought a few decks of cards and had me practice. I listened very carefully to each step.

I knew when to throw a game based on a signal from the pit boss; likewise, I knew when they wanted me to change a winning streak to a losing one (or vice verse) to keep a player there. They would walk behind me and tap my lower back with their hand. They did this unnoticeably.

The pit boss knew when to stack the decks or when to change up the rotation of the cards. They observed how many people were at a table. If someone joined in the middle of a game, it would change the placement of the cards and whether it was a winning or losing table. They needed to watch carefully to know when to turn around a table.

I got really good at my part in this, so they trained me on many other tables. The one they liked to put me on the most was big money blackjack. Whenever they opened up that pit, I was usually transferred to work in it.

The table would start at $100, and highest bid was $1000. One time I had a gentleman sit down and I was given the signal to let him win. He was rolling in some good money when he asked to see the pit boss. I called him over, and the gentleman requested that the stakes be set higher.

My pit boss informed him that he had no authority over that. He asked for the manager to be called down. The head manager from the gaming department arrived, and she authorized the table stakes to be raised: $1,000 was the low bid, and $10,000 the highest.

The gentleman was happy; when we finished up that round, he was doing very well. But as I pulled in the cards to reshuffle, my pit boss walked behind me and tapped my lower back. I did what I was asked, and within five minutes, the gentleman lost most of his money.

Another dealer came up and tapped my shoulder, indicating that it was time for my fifteen-minute break. I left. When I returned and as I headed to the pit, I saw the same man being held at the security booth.

I asked my friend Lewy, a security guard, what had happened.

"The man lost all his money at the table and was yelling at everyone, causing a scene. He tried to go after the dealer and the pit boss. We are waiting on the tribal police to get here."

I looked at the man one more time with sadness in my heart, then went back to my table.

A few minutes later, I heard a woman yelling. "You lost all of it. All of our retirement nest egg. That is all we had to live on. What are we going to do now? You and your stupid gambling cost us everything. I have had enough of this."

I looked over to the security booth and saw the woman crying uncontrollably. The guards had to get her under control. I felt terrible. What had I done?

At that moment, I no longer wanted to be a part of the casino or gambling. I stood at my empty blackjack table, and for the first time in two years I prayed. I really, sincerely prayed: that God would take me from this awful place and guide me closer to Him. I no longer wanted to live a life of sin. I was longing once again for the relationship I had once had with God and for my church family who loved me just the way I was.

> *I looked over to the security booth and saw the woman crying uncontrollably. I felt terrible. What had I done?*

God heard my prayer, but He knew I was not grounded enough in His Word or in prayer to hear His call the way that I needed to in order to make changes in my life. I was still learning to trust Him and to have heartfelt faith in a God Whom I could not see.

God could have moved me at any time. He can move mountains. But what would I have learned if God had just granted me everything I wanted and asked for? I was not willing to give everything up to serve Him. I had not accepted Jesus back into my heart yet.

As time passed, I prayed more. I quit my waitress job at the bar, but I needed to support my family, so I felt I could not quit the casino, even though I longed to be out of it.

"Now if God so clothes the grass of the field, which today is, and tomorrow is thrown into the oven, will He not much more clothe you, O you of little faith?" (Matt. 6:30). God was waiting for me to step out in faith, knowing that He would take care of me.

Even though I was praying, my life was still deep in sin. I was not studying the Bible. I was not taking God's words of love into my heart. I still longed to have attention from men, and I wanted a relationship with someone who would love me.

My mother did the best she knew how with me, but I was not helping her walk with Jesus, either, while she lived with me and worked at the casino. She was not attending church regularly anymore, and she had a beer from time to time with the other employees.

CHAPTER 30

Lessons Still Not Learned: The Second Marriage

One of my friends was a dealer named Candy. She had the most beautiful, long blonde hair and blue eyes. She was bubbly, upbeat, and friendly to everyone. She liked to play matchmaker and was always smiling. Everyone loved to sit and talk with her. Candy was a very good blackjack dealer, as well. Like me, she was getting tired of working there, but she liked the life of the casino and did not want to quit. When Candy was given an opportunity to work for our sister casino in St. Ignace, an hour away, she decided to take a job there as a pit boss. She drove back and forth from her home in Brimley to work.

One stormy winter day, I was sitting in the breakroom and waiting for my shift to start when a friend came up to me. She said, "Have you heard?" Tears were running down her cheeks.

"Heard what?" I said with a worried expression.

"Candy was found dead this morning. She was driving home after her shift ended at 2:00 a.m., and she hit a patch of black ice. She rolled her car into the big drop in the median. She was thrown out of her car, and it landed on her.

"They said that she didn't die right away. It was so late at night that no one saw the accident. Being so far down in the median, no one could see her from other cars. A semi driver finally saw her and the car. He stopped and called 911. But by the time the ambulance and police arrived, she was dead."

I sat there in total shock as tears ran down my face. I would never see my smiling friend Candy again.

No one was in the mood to work that day in the gaming pits. We all mourned the death of our friend and coworker. All of the customers noticed that the atmosphere was gloomy. Some of the regulars asked what was going on. A few dealers told them, and they cried for the friend they had lost too.

The casino set up a memorial service for coworkers and family in one of the lounges. This was to take place after the funeral, and it would accommodate anyone who could not attend the funeral because they had to work. Many of us attended both.

A group of us, dealers and pit bosses, decided to ride over together to the funeral. As we walked in, most of us started to cry. There was not a dry eye by the time we approached the casket. I lagged behind a little. I was not taking Candy's death well.

I slowly walked up with tears staining my face. The young man standing beside it asked how I knew Candy.

I told him, "I worked with her. She was a great person."

He asked me a few more questions about work, then said, "Sorry, where are my manners? My name is Phillip, but everyone calls me Phil. I am Candy's brother. What is your name?"

With tears in my eyes, I said, "Michelle."

He looked at me a little more seriously. "Michelle who?"

As I told him my last name, his mouth dropped open, and he stared at me. I thought I might have a booger hanging out of my nose from all the crying, and I got embarrassed. I wiped my face with a Kleenex and told him it was nice to meet him. He closed his mouth and looked back at the casket. I walked away.

I sat out in the foyer to get away from all of the people and to shed my tears alone. An older woman came out, sat down on the steps, and looked at me. She comforted me and told me it was going to be okay. Then she asked how I knew Candy.

I told her that we worked together. Then it dawned on me: she was one of the night shift cooks from the employee breakroom. I worked mornings, so I only saw her for a few brief moments if I came in early to eat breakfast. I had never really gotten to know her.

As I sat in thought, Phil walked up and said, "Mom, they are ready to start the funeral. Are you? They don't want to start without you."

"Ready as I can be," she said.

Phil stuck his hand out to his mother and helped her up. She looked back to me and said, "It was nice talking to you." Then she walked back inside with her son.

I was amazed that she had lost her daughter and yet was comforting me. I was only a friend grieving over Candy. She was the mother who gave birth to that beautiful child. I sat for a few more minutes and said a short prayer for her family and all of Candy's friends. Then I got up and went in to sit with my friends for the funeral service.

Afterward we all headed back to the casino. The managers only opened up one pit with a few tables. They closed the rest so that most of the employees could attend the memorial service. Those of us who were off-duty offered to rotate work so that the working dealers could attend.

They performed a special Indian service for Candy's family, who were part-Indian. They talked about the spirit world and burned some lemongrass. They chanted over the smoke for a while and then spoke a few words of love for Candy.

The chanting and all the talk about the spirit world made me very uncomfortable. I didn't believe in this and knew it was not biblical, but I could not remember any Scripture to back this up. I sat there quietly and just listened. I didn't voice what I was feeling, for I did not want to offend anyone or bring attention to myself on a subject I could not explain. Oh, how important it is to study, know, and memorize the Word of God!

As they ended the Indian service, they announced that a meal would be served for those of us who wanted to stay. Most of the dealers stayed. Also, anyone who wanted overtime was offered a second shift after the meal. Most of us said yes (we were already in uniform from giving the dealers on shift a break earlier). The meal was grand, and we all enjoyed the food. We sat there talking and recalling good memories of Candy.

Her brother approached the table. He crouched down right next to me, but addressed us all:

"Hi! My name is Phil, and I am Candy's brother. I am in the Army and don't get home much. I was stationed overseas for a long time and didn't get to spend much time with my sister. If any of you would like to get together and tell me some stories about Candy, I would love to hear from you all." He laid his phone number in the middle of the table, said thank you, and walked away.

One of the girls at the table looked over and said, "Mmm, he sure does have a thing for you, Michelle. Did you see how he was staring?"

I looked over my shoulder at Phil, and he was looking at me. He just smiled and waved. I turned around quickly.

One of the guys looked at Phil and said, "I think he is arrogant, and it is all a show. Anyone really want this number?" No one answered. He grabbed the paper, crumpled it up, and threw it on his plate to toss on his way out the door.

My sister-in-law Annie called me over to the kitchen while everyone was getting up to leave. She had worked there while living in Kinross with Scott and their son Jordan for a long time. She and my brother had split up, though, and she was now living in Sault St. Marie with her new boyfriend. My brother had moved back to the Trenary area and then to Delta County to start a contracting business with Robin. Scott and Annie were not divorced yet, but I was still friends with her. I tried to stay out of that whole mess. I didn't want to be in the middle and hurt my brother.

Annie asked how I was doing and if my mother was okay. She didn't see us much, but mother and I had always treated her well, even though we did not like how she had hurt Scott. We chatted for a little while, then I told her I had better get moving, or else I would be late for work. We said our goodbyes, and I headed for the door.

Phil was standing there, waiting for me to leave. He stopped me and handed me the phone number to his parents' house. He said he would be home on leave for the next two weeks, because of the Thanksgiving holiday and because he wanted to be there for his family. He told me again that he would love to get together and talk about his sister.

I took the number, put it in my pocket, and smiled. I said, "Thank you. Sorry for your loss. Candy was a good friend. I have to go, or I am going to be late for work. It was nice meeting you." I turned and left the lounge. I could feel his eyes on me all the way down the hallway until I turned to enter the next part of the casino.

It was exciting to have a handsome Army man interested in me. I longed to find out more about him, but something told me it was not a good idea. I fought with that nagging feeling for a while, until I finally just called him at his parents' house.

> *I had an overwhelming feeling that this was not a good idea, but I kept pushing away that still, small voice.*

He was not home, so I left him a message to call me back with my name and number. The whole time I had an overwhelming feeling that this was not a good idea, but I kept pushing away that still, small voice. Had I listened, I would have realized it was the voice of the Lord.

Phil called, and we set up a time to meet at the Spirits Lounge in Brimley. I called up my friend Sid, who was also a dealer, and asked if he wanted to go with me. I explained that I did not want to meet this guy alone.

Sid agreed, and we went to meet up with Phil. He was there with his two cousins. We played pool and darts, drank, and laughed, while talking about Candy and the parties we had gone to. She had definitely been a witty girl with a lot of spunk, and Phil enjoyed hearing the stories.

I loved the attention Phil was giving me and wanted to spend more time with him. I felt the nagging sensation in my heart again, but once again I pushed the feeling aside and set up another date.

We continued to see each other throughout the time he was home. We went to bars together, and he met more of the dealers his sister had worked with. I thought it was going great, and I loved how he flirted with me.

Then the first red flag came. I introduced him to my friend Natalie, and he started ignoring me and flirting with her. He even went with her on a date to the movies. I was not happy.

After that he called me up and wanted me to go out to see him at his parents' house.

I had the feeling again that I should cut off the relationship and walk away. He was jumping from one woman to the next; we only acted like a couple until he saw another woman he wanted to be with.

God was showing me warning signs every time I turned around, but Phil would say some smooth words that would melt my heart, and he would give me the attention that I so longed to have.

His vacation ended, and it was time for him to go back to the military base in New York. He asked me to meet him at the airport. My girlfriend Jo Jo went with me. Phil gave me a hug and a kiss goodbye, handed me his cell phone number, and told me to call him. This gesture made me feel special. When Jo Jo and I left for home, I had tears in my eyes.

I called him several times, and we talked for hours. Then, two weeks later, he told me that he was seeing another girl—but wanted to marry me—because that girl was just a fling.

I was hurt. He kept telling me he would not see her again and that he really wanted to be with me. He told me that even in death, his sister Candy was trying to play matchmaker and set us up, and that is why he had acted the way he had when he'd asked me my name at the funeral services. That touched my heart.

I argued with him on the phone for two hours about getting married. I told him that he was not just marrying me; he was marrying my children, too. We were a package deal; a ready-made family. It would not be like raising children from infancy. Mine were two-and-a-half and seven-and-a-half years old. I told him that Ben was a handful, and so was Nautasha. He assured me that he could handle them.

I finally gave in to his pleas and said yes. We set a date to elope, deciding on January 1st. Phil had me call the Justice of the Peace and make the arrangements.

They informed me that, because it was a holiday, they were not open. However, they would be glad to marry us on the second of January instead. I told them that this would be fine, then I called Phil back and told him the date that the magistrate could marry us.

His sister and brother stood for us as maid of honor and best man. His mother and father attended, as well. We all went out to eat dinner at a restaurant to celebrate. His parents paid for the meal as a wedding gift to us.

As we ate, Phil told me that he was going to go over to his cousin's to play video games and would be home later. His mother yelled at him, telling him it was his wedding day and he should be with his wife.

Once again I was hurt. We had just gotten married, and he didn't want to spend the day with his new wife? Here was another red flag. How many did God have to show me before I would get the point?

Phil didn't come home that night until 2:00 a.m. He came into the bedroom, woke me up, and told me that he'd brought a bottle of champagne to celebrate our wedding night.

I told him, "That was yesterday! Where were you?" I rolled over to go back to sleep with tears in my eyes. He touched my shoulder and poured out apologies. Once again, as he promised to treat me better, I forgave him.

He had to go back to Fort Drum, New York, a few days after we were married. Phil needed to apply for military housing (it had a long waitlist), while I needed to contact my attorney in order to be able to move out of state with Nautasha.

Even though Nate was in prison he still had legal rights. I could not move out of state without his permission unless I brought it to court for the judge to decide. I contacted him in prison. It was not easy, but he did agree to the move. My attorney sent him the paperwork, which he signed and sent back. The process took until March of 1997.

Meanwhile, my new husband managed to get bumped up on the military housing list. He was given a duplex to look at. Phil liked the setup and signed the housing agreement in the middle of February. He moved his things from the barracks into our new apartment, then took some leave at the end of March to pack us up and move us to Fort Drum, New York. We were set to leave Kinchloe on April 2nd of that year.

CHAPTER 31

God is Still Calling Amidst the Trials, "Oh, Sinner, Come Home!"

---◦◦◦---

I was a smoker; Phil was not. He didn't like the smell in the air or on my breath after a cigarette, so I told him I would quit. He asked me when I planned on doing that and how. I told him that if he helped me, I would quit on April 2nd, the day we were moving.

He agreed and told me, "No matter what you say or how cranky you get, I will not give you a cigarette, and I will tell all of my friends who smoke not to give you one."

I agreed to his terms. Those were the hardest two weeks of my life. I struggled with getting rid of my cigarettes, so I broke down one day, went to the store on the military base, and bought a pack. Then I brought them home and hid them.

But Phil found them, broke them all in front of me, and flushed them down the toilet. I was not happy, but he was sticking to his end of the bargain. Months later I was very grateful that he had helped me to quit smoking.

I met a lot of new people from all races and countries at Fort Drum. It was exciting to learn about different cultures and to learn my way around the base. The Military had many different activities and places for families to spend time together. My children loved bowling and going to the gym, where they could swim and play racquetball. We have a lot of good memories from living in Fort Drum, but our time there with Phil was not all good memories for *me*.

After I quit smoking, I took on another bad habit: eating junk food. Chips, candy bars, sodas, and fast food. I started to gain a considerable amount of weight, and Phil was not so nice about letting me know that I looked heavier. "If you get any fatter," he once said, "I may have to divorce you. I don't like fat women."

After he said this, we engaged in a big fight. At the end of it, to smooth things over, he told me that he was just joking.

But he kept poking fun about my weight. When he wasn't doing that, he would tell our friends (in front of me), "She used to be hot to look at, but now she is just fat." He belittled me a lot in front of people.

If I tried to hold his hand while walking into a store, he would pull his out of mine and tell me, "I can't pick up chicks this way." Those words hurt me right down to the depths of my heart.

He was making me feel insecure and very depressed. I was not happy in our marriage at all. Phil left me at home a lot with the children, taking off on his motorcycle to go bar hopping. Usually he had a female on the back of his bike. He was never afraid to tell me he had some other woman with him, although he always implied that she was just a friend.

He didn't just treat me badly. He also punished my children harshly. When Phil didn't like something that Ben did, he would make him hold up Phil's bulletproof vest with his arm straight out to the side. The vest had a heavy metal plate in back and two more in the front; it must have weighed thirty or forty pounds. My son was only eight years old, and Phil would make him stand there holding it for up to fifteen minutes, depending on what he had done wrong. (as an out of shape adult, I could not even hold out the vest for that long). If Ben dropped it, he had to start over.

Just four years old, my daughter Nautasha was made to do thirty full sit ups, ten to twenty diamond pushups, and thirty flutter kicks.

I was angry and confronted Phil about all of this. He told me that he would not tolerate disobedience and that this would toughen the children up. We fought over his discipline methods all the time. He kept trying to convince me it was good for them, that he was not hitting them, and that it would make them more respectable.

I started to believe him while my children suffered greatly. They avoided him or walked quietly around him so that they would not have to perform these exercises. Sometimes it seemed as though he got pleasure out of the fear he instilled in the children.

However, I finally had enough of his behavior. After he went out one night, I called my girlfriend Breanne and told her what was going on. I was so upset. She told me I could come to her house and stay there as long as I liked.

When Phil got home that night, he called my cell phone several times, but I refused to answer. I hid my car in Breanne's garage so that he would not know I was there. When he could not find me, he called her, but she told him that she had not seen me.

Finally, after about two hours, I decided I had better call him and tell him how I felt. He was very angry that I refused to go and see him with the children and flipped the whole argument back on me. He was a smooth talker who knew how to make people feel either good or bad. When he did something that was wrong or dishonest to me in our marriage, he was good at passing the blame to me and making me feel like it was all my fault.

That night I did ultimately choose to go home to confront him. I left the children with Breanne, and she told me to call her if I needed to come back that night. Not many days later, the family was all under one roof again.

During that period, even while Phil passed blame, I was not always the best wife to him. I spoke my mind, and I was still very selfish. This led to confrontations and physical fights. Ben and Nautasha saw several of these fights during their younger years. Nautasha would cry, and Ben would hide or take his sister outside.

Many times Phil pinned me to the floor or the wall by my neck or shoulders. Once he pulled me down the stairs by my hair because I had walked away from him and said, "I am done listening to your lies."

When he got physical with me, I would start swinging to protect myself. He learned I would not back down. I was not one of the children and did not fear him. I was ready to fight for my life, and I told him this many times. I said that if he hit me, he had better make sure I didn't get up.

He would restrain me to get me to stop. In order to end a fight, I would have to promise him that I would not swing at him once he let me back up. If it kept peace between us, and I knew that he was not going to pin me down anymore, I would consent. But if I was not in agreement with him when he let me go, I'd be back to swinging at him or throwing things; whatever was within my reach.

It was not a good marriage. I knew that something had to change, or else I needed to get out.

One evening after Phil and I got into a confrontation, I went to our bedroom. I was so frustrated with him that I started talking out loud. "This has to stop! I can't take this anymore. Either he has to change or I am leaving."

I was moved to lay it all down at the foot of the cross. I got on my knees beside my bed and prayed for God's help. I don't remember the words, but I do remember asking for His help and what I should do. I felt peace when I got up, and I had a longing to attend church again. My heart started to yearn for the love that I felt whenever I was with my brothers and sisters in Christ.

The next day I grabbed the phone book and looked up Seventh-day Adventist churches in the area. I found one in Watertown, but I was not familiar with that town. I called the church's number and left a message asking for someone to call me back with instructions on how to get there. Someone called me back a few days later and explained that the easiest way to get there without getting lost was to use the main highway.

The next Saturday I woke the children up early and we got dressed for church. Phil did not have to work and was still in bed. I told him where we were going.

He looked at me funny. "On a Saturday?"

"Yes, we are going to attend the Seventh-day Adventist Church in Watertown. We will be back this afternoon. Would you like to come with us?" I waited for his response.

"No," he said.

I was sad, but I had suspected he would say that. The children and I got into my Corolla and headed for church.

When we entered, we were greeted by a young man in a light blue suit. He was very nice and had a smile that made his whole face glow. We met many new people that day and formed friendships that would last many years.

God is Still Calling Amidst the Trials, "Oh, Sinner, Come Home!" 153

As I sat through Sabbath School class and services with the children, I realized how much I missed feeling the love and presence of the Lord in my life. I longed to have a relationship with God and Jesus again. I made a commitment at that moment that I was going to come back.

After the services, we had potluck. A lady named Sheila and her friend Janice sat with us. They were both very kind and loving Christian women. They didn't judge me but rather loved me for who I was. I didn't know it then, but years later they were a prominent part in my walk with God.

I left church that day with a new outlook on life. I wanted my marriage to work, and if that was to happen, I needed to start making changes in my attitude. I knew this was going to be hard, because I was so stubborn and selfish, but I also knew that if I put my mind to it, I could accomplish it.

Once home I could not wait to tell Phil about our day and the people we had met. As I stood in the living room and told him all about church, he played a video game and responded with one-word answers. It was like I was not even there; he was acknowledging me just enough to get me to go away.

I was disappointed. I wanted him to have the same enthusiasm that I had about God and making changes in our home life. I could see that going to church was not on the top of his list, not even on a Sunday.

I was attending church again, but I still had much to learn about living a Christ-like life. We watched bad movies with the children and ate all kinds of meat and seafood. On rare occasions I still went to bars with Phil and drank.

I was trying to have a relationship with God and please my husband at the same time. This was not working out so well for the children and me. Satan was still strong in our home, and he did not want us to be with the Lord or learn His wisdom.

I went to bed one evening feeling very sad. Phil had been gone for two weeks of training and wouldn't be back until the next day, so I had plenty of time to look at my life and reflect on what I had been learning at church. I lay thinking about how I needed to change my ways. It seemed like hours passed before I finally fell asleep.

The next morning I got my children up for school and onto the bus. I went back into the house and started doing laundry and cleaning up the kitchen. When the laundry was done, I folded it, brought it upstairs to the bedrooms, and put the children's clothing away. Next I headed for my room.

As I opened the door, a funny feeling came over me. I looked at the wall right in front of me and saw a shadow of Jesus' face. It looked beautiful, and I was in awe. Then I felt a strong presence of evil. Almost in slow motion, the shadow of Jesus transformed into the face of Satan. I became very scared and ran out of the room.

I rationalized the situation as I stood in the hallway by the bedroom door. "Come on, Michelle!" I said out loud. "This is just a shadow on the wall made by the curtain and the sunlight flowing in. The curtain must have moved to change the shape. Just go in and open the curtain, and it will go away."

I walked back into the room and felt the evil presence again, but I was determined to prove it was only a shadow. I moved the curtain, but the shadow was still there. I opened the curtain wide and stepped back in disbelief: still the shadow was there, and now I also heard laughing. It was so evil that my whole body had goosebumps. I stood there for a few seconds, unable to move.

When I got control of my thoughts and body again, I ran. Satan was in there, and I was terrified. I ran down the stairs and out the front door. I stood in my yard for a few minutes, but I knew that I needed to go back into the house and pray. The only ones who could remove such evil from my home were God and His Son Jesus.

I opened the door slowly and walked back inside. I went right to the living room, knelt down, and began to pray. I was on my knees for almost twenty minutes, asking the Lord to remove this evil presence from our home. I had a hard time believing that God would do as I asked, but I knew that He had the power to cast it out.

I got off my knees and went back upstairs. I slowly opened the bedroom door. I peeked in at the wall; the shadow was still there. I slammed the door shut and ran back down. I got on my knees again and asked the Lord why Satan was still in my bedroom.

The Lord revealed to me that I had little faith and trust in Him. "And whatever things you ask in prayer, believing, you will receive" (Matt. 21:22).

I prayed for a third time, this time with new understanding: I needed to trust in God and believe that He would take care of me, and He would protect me in my time of need. I remembered Isaiah 41:10-13 and I claimed it:

> Fear not, for I am with you; be not dismayed, for I am your God. I will strengthen you, yes, I will help you, I will uphold you with My righteous right hand. Behold, all those who were incensed against you shall be ashamed and disgraced; they shall be as nothing, and those who strive with you shall perish. You shall seek them and not find them—those who contended with you. Those who war against you shall be as nothing, as a nonexistent thing. For I, the Lord your God, will hold your right hand, saying to you, "Fear not, I will help you."

Once again I walked up the steps, saying the whole way, "I believe in you God, I believe in you." This time, as I slowly opened the door, I felt a peace that surpassed all the evil that had been in the room earlier: I felt the presence of God. I fell to my knees by the bed and said a prayer of thanksgiving, praising His name and asking for forgiveness of my unbelief.

I never told anyone about what happened. I thought everyone would think that I was crazy or telling a tall tale. At that time I did not fully understand about the great controversy and the war between Jesus and Satan that is raging all around us. I only knew that I needed to stay connected with God, and that He was the only One Who could save me from Satan and his demons.

The children and I drove to church every Saturday until one day my muffler broke. Phil said we didn't have the money to fix it. I was not happy; we were down to one car, and it was his. He worked every other Saturday, which meant that the children and I would not be able to attend church. He let me use the car a few times, but then one Sabbath there were seminars, and the children and I stayed to listen.

We got home around four in the afternoon, and Phil was waiting in the living room when we walked in. I could see that there was going to be a confrontation, so I told the children to go upstairs and get changed out of their church clothes.

The yelling began. "Where have you been?" he said. "Church don't take that long. I had a buddy of mine want to go out for a while, and no car to get there." He was very angry, and I knew it was not over the car; I hadn't called to tell him I was going to stay late.

"We were at the church." I responded, but I didn't get to finish before he cut me off.

"Church ended a long time ago. So are you going to tell me the truth now?" He was yelling in my face.

I looked him dead in the eye; I was now very angry. "If you would shut up and let me finish, you would have known that we had a guest speaker today because they had seminars all week. He spoke for the services and then again after potluck this afternoon.

"Furthermore," I continued, "you have a motorcycle you could have driven to see your friend on and to work. We are married. I should be able to use the car when I need to, since we still have two forms of transportation. Or you could just help me get my car fixed so I can drive it."

That was all it took for the yelling to turn into screaming; then into a physical confrontation. I ended up in the bedroom in tears, tired of the constant fights.

Phil took off to his friend's house on his motorcycle, and from there they went to the bar. He didn't come home until three in the morning. I felt him climb into bed, but I pretended to be sleeping. I wanted nothing to do with this man. He was becoming a thorn in my side.

During several of our fights, I told him that I wanted a divorce, and he told me that he had only married me because of his sister. That cut to the bottom of my heart. He had married me because he felt he had to? Only because he wanted to honor Candy; not because he loved me?

We continued on this path for several years. Some days were good, and others were bad. I didn't attend church as much as before because he wouldn't let me use the car; I didn't know the people at church well enough and was afraid to ask them for a ride. The children and I still said our prayers together and read Bible stories before bedtime, but that was all we could do without ending up in a confrontation with my husband.

CHAPTER 32

Pregnant!

As the first year of our marriage ended, Phil came up for a transfer to another post. He was excited; he hated living at Fort Drum. All he had talked about for the last six months had been seeing if he could get stationed back in Germany. He put in for a transfer there, and it went through. He was going to be stationed in Hanau.

He took us all to get pictures taken for our passports. We were excited; the children and I had never been out of the country before except to Canada (and we didn't really count that as another country because we had gone there often while we lived in Kincheloe).

The Army packed all of our belongings in crates and shipped them out to Europe. I was very happy. I thought that this would be a new start and that our marriage would get better. I was determined to make it work. Both his family and mine were in agreement that we should have never gotten married and that it would not last, but I was going to prove them wrong. I was going to fight for this marriage.

Then Phil informed me that we would not be going to Europe with him. He had to go ahead of us to apply for military housing. Once he had secured that, we could fly over. In the meantime he made arrangements for us to live with his mother and stepfather in Upper Michigan.

I didn't find out until after we had been with his parents for a few months that we actually could have gone with him and stayed in the military motel. He just wanted to go over alone to see all his old German friends and party before we got there. I was very disappointed when I found that out; I felt unloved and unwanted. On top of that, Phil called one day and told me that we could not afford to bring all of our animals over to Germany.

Let me explain about our pets.

Our family had two cats and a dog. Phil had bought me the cat after he made me angry one day at the mall in Watertown. He had yelled at Ben for no reason, making a scene in one of the stores. His friend had told him that he was wrong and that he had better find a way to earn my forgiveness. Phil went down to the pet store and bought me a long-haired, black and white kitten, then asked if he was out of the doghouse yet. I forgave him.

> I thought this would be a new start. Then Phil informed me that we would not be going to Europe with him.

I wanted to hold the kitten, but he said he wanted to. He was more of a dog lover than a cat lover, so this gave me hope that he was changing ... until I figured out why he was doing it. Every time a young woman walked by, they stopped to pet the cute kitten sticking its head out of his jacket. Only after we got outside did he give it to me, then he made a comment about how kittens were a good chick magnet.

My heart was broken often in this way by Phil. I felt very ugly and worthless thanks to him. I thought it was because I did not do enough to please him, so in time I would start to think of ways to make him happy and get more attention. I would dress more provocatively and act promiscuously toward him. It stopped being about what I liked or wanted as I tried everything that I could to get him to focus his attention on me.

When you have a true relationship with God and have accepted Jesus Christ as your personal Savior, you will know in your heart that He made you beautiful just the way you are. God formed me in the womb, and He knows the beginning from the end: "Before I formed you in the womb I knew you ... " (Jer. 1:5a). "I am the Alpha and the Omega, the Beginning and the End, the First and the Last" (Rev. 22:13).

God knew everything about me before I was even born. He knew every hair on my head: "But the very hairs of your head are all numbered" (Matt. 10:30). If God cares so much for me that He paid close attention to every hair that He placed on my head, then I should have known that He cared about how I was being treated. When I was hurting, God was looking down on me in love. I just needed to let Him in so that He could wrap His loving arms around me and comfort me in my time of need.

> We should always take our burdens and sins to the foot of the cross. Only Jesus can wash us as white as snow. "Come now, and let us reason together," says the Lord, "Though your sins are like scarlet, they shall be as white as snow; though they are red like crimson, they shall be as wool." (Isa. 1:18)

The day we got the kitten, once we got home, the children kept asking if I had a name in mind and saying what they would like to call her. I told them that I wanted to name her. But I could not think of a name, so I decided to pray.

I knelt on the kitchen floor beside my kitten and asked the Lord to tell me what He wanted. For the first time ever in my prayer life I was silent and listened for His voice: "Be still, and know that I am God ... " (Ps. 46:10a).

I heard Him say, "Annabell."

I got off my knees, picked her up, looked at her cute, little face, and said, "You are my little Annabell, sent from God as a gift to me."

I looked up the name. It means, "favor, grace, or loveable." God was blessing me through this kitten that would be in my home for the next fourteen years. She was filled with a lot of love and shared it with the whole family. She was the greatest cat, and reminded me of my childhood calico, Mitt Mitts.

Later Phil decided to go back to the mall and get another. He got a brown and black tabby and named him Rocky. He then decided that he wanted a husky, found an ad in the paper for a husky mix, and bought her for $75. He brought her home and named her Sheba. Sheba had been very abused and was in need of some tender loving care. She had a litter of pups, and Phil kept one of the puppies. But he gave it to someone at work after a week; it was too much work for him to take care of it, and his stomach could not handle cleaning up its urine and droppings.

The funniest thing happened after Phil gave the puppy away: Sheba started nursing my kitten, Annabell, taking her on as her own. It was so cute. Annabell and Sheba grew to love one another in a way I cannot explain.

Now you know about the pet portion of our family.

So there I was, waiting for Phil to bring us to Germany, living with his parents, uncomfortable at first and then really cranky (I hadn't been feeling like myself lately, and I didn't understand why), and he was now telling me we could not bring all of our animals.

Well, God had blessed us with these animals. It was up to us to take care of them.

Phil's mom had become really attached to Rocky, so he gave his cat to her. Sheba went to stay with Uncle Dean and Grandma Alice in Trenary. At least Annabell would get to experience a plane ride to Germany.

But not yet: Phil had put in for housing, but we still had not heard anything back. He said the waiting list was six to eight months long. I was not happy to hear this. Meanwhile I had no transportation, because our car had been shipped overseas, and I was longing to attend church. But I knew that God was in control.

I looked up the closest Seventh-day Adventist Church and called. It was in Sault St. Marie, but the nice church members found a ride for the children and me with a wonderful, elderly woman who lived about seven miles down the road from us, on the Indian reservation. Her name was Bea. That was not her real name, but it is what everyone called her. Bea was the sweetest woman; very kind and God-fearing. She was very loving and caring, and always looked out for my children. She invited us over for lunch and talked with us.

During this same time, that sensation of not feeling like myself started to turn into pain in my left ovary. It got so bad sometimes that it almost brought me to my knees.

With all the excitement, I hadn't realized that my monthly cycle had not come for two months. I called the doctor on the reservation and set up an appointment. She was very nice. She did some tests and came back into the room a half an hour later with a smile. "Michelle, you are going to have a baby!"

I looked at her in shock and repeated, "I'm pregnant?"

"Yes, pregnant!" However, she was concerned about the ovarian pain, and told me that I was in danger of miscarrying. She said that the first trimester would be hard for me; this time would tell whether or not my body would reject the baby.

I went back home with a heavy heart. I knew my mother and father-in-law would be excited to have a grandchild, but I had to give them the good and the bad news.

I told them the first part, and as I thought, my mother-in-law was very excited. She had accepted my first two children as her own, but this would be her true, biological, first-born grandchild. It overwhelmed her heart with joy. But then I had to tell her the bad news. She had a worried look on her face but said, "Everything will work out."

I told her that I would call Phil in the morning and give him the news (because of the drastic time difference between the US and Europe, I knew that Phil was in bed). When I did, he was very excited. Then I gave him the bad news, saying, "Only time will tell if my body will keep or reject this little person growing inside of me." He said things would work out. We spoke for a few more minutes, then hung up.

I went down to the basement family room, knelt, and prayed, "Lord, if you keep this child safe within me and let me have this baby, I will raise the child up for you. Please, Lord, save my baby."

Every morning I went to the basement to pray, and every night I offered up the same prayer at my bedside. Each night, I added that not only did I want this child to follow Him and be raised up in His ways, I wanted Ben and Nautasha to also be mighty witnesses for the Lord.

As I entered my fourth month of pregnancy, I was still in pain, but it was not as bad. The doctor suggested that I not take anything for the pain. She didn't want to hurt the baby or have me miscarry. After two more weeks, when I went back to see her, my pain was gone.

The doctor connected me to a heart monitor, and the most wonderful sound came out: a heartbeat. I don't know who was smiling more; me or her. The baby was well, and I was most of the way out of danger. Still, she wanted to monitor me until she felt that the baby was safe.

Then it dawned on me. How was I going to fly while pregnant? I would not be able to go to Germany if I was too far along. I asked the doctor about this, and she told me that I could fly up to six months into the pregnancy; they would not let me after that. My heart sank.

I prayed on the way home that God would help us to get moved up on the housing list more quickly, and that He would make a way for us to get to Germany before it was too late. Only He could help our family now. I needed to trust in His ways even if I didn't like it.

CHAPTER 33

The Flight to Germany

At five months pregnant, I still had not heard a word from my husband about housing. The church was praying for me and the baby. I was very blessed to have such a wonderful church family. They lifted my children and me up in prayer every Sabbath, even though they wanted us to stay. They knew God's will was better than that of men.

Finally one day in the middle of the week, I received a phone call from Phil. He was so excited. "You will never guess what," he said.

"What? Just tell me," I said.

"We got moved to the top of the housing list. I just looked at three apartments and found the best fit for us. We have military housing, Michelle! You and the kids are going to be scheduled for flights out here soon.

"Once I have the information," he continued, "I will call you and make sure that everything is all set. We have to pay for Annabell to come. It's $75 to fly her over; the military won't cover her cost."

I was so excited that I was jumping up and down. I asked him a ton of questions about what the apartment looked like and how many bedrooms it had, until he told me that he had to go but would call me again soon with more details. When I hung up the phone, I screamed, "*Yes!*"

My father-in-law had just gotten home, and he asked me what all the commotion was about. I told him the good news. He was happy but also very sad; he loved Ben and Nautasha and played with them every day. They sat on his lap, and he also cooked for them. My father-in-law was a commercial fisherman, so he would bring home fresh fish all the time, then fry or bake it up for the children for supper. They loved grandpa's fish, and it made him feel good to make them happy.

We had to take Annabell to the veterinarian for additional shots that she needed to enter Germany. They told me not to feed her or give her water for twenty-four hours before the flight. The vet said that she would be fine and would eat once we arrived, but that the fast would help prevent her from using the bathroom in her kennel or getting an upset stomach.

I bought a small carrier for Annabell and some little things that my kids and I could eat while in the airports. Airport food was expensive, and we didn't have the money to buy every meal.

The flight from Jefferson Airport in New York to Frankfurt, Germany, would be seven to eight hours. This did not include our three flights to *reach* Jefferson—first through Detroit, then Chicago—or all of our layovers. In total, we would spend fourteen to sixteen hours that day either in a plane or an airport. This was going to be hard on me; being pregnant, having two small children who needed to hang onto me, pulling our luggage, and carrying Annabell in her kennel.

Ben was a big help to me. Up until Chicago our trip was pretty uneventful, but once there he pulled his little carry-on behind him and watched his sister Nautasha very closely while we went through O'Hare Airport. He kept telling her, "Hang on to Mommy's shirt and don't let go, okay?" She would nod and smile at him. I think it made him feel like a big boy to be able to help his sister in such a big place, which was amazing and scary to them at the same time.

We landed on one side of the airport and had forty-five minutes to make it all the way to the other side to catch our next flight. I was happy we only had our carry-on bags and Annabell at this point.

I grabbed Nautasha's carry-on bag, threw mine over my shoulder, grabbed the kennel, and looked to Ben to make sure he was with me. I told

Nautasha to hang onto the suitcase handle with me as we raced as fast as a four-year-old could go. Then Ben said, "Mommy, look: moving floors."

I looked up and said a quick thank you to the Lord. I led the children onto the moving walkways and told them to keep on running. They giggled as they realized that they were moving faster than the other people. I was worried that we would not make our flight, but at that moment I had to smile at my children. The walkways were something I would have just taken for granted had it been just me racing through the airport.

We made it to our flight with two minutes to spare before they closed the doors. Once on the plane, I said a prayer of thanksgiving and moved to buckle in the children.

Ben told me that he could get it himself. I just smiled and watched as he looked at the gentleman next to him to see how it worked. After he buckled up, he looked at me with the biggest smile. I think he felt like he was a young man that day instead of my little nine-year-old boy. It was a sight to see as he sat straight and tall in his seat. My heart melted. He had helped me the way a young man would have, and that made him feel very important.

> *Nine bags, two children, and a kitten.... All this for one pregnant woman to take from one side of the airport to the other.*

When we landed at Jefferson Airport, we had to claim all our luggage, then bring it to the overseas baggage area to be processed all over again to make sure that we had nothing which could not be taken out of the country.

We each had two suitcases to check and one carry-on. That totaled up to nine bags, two children, and a kitten in a kennel (who rode at my feet). All this for one pregnant woman to take from one side of the airport to the other and check in for our flight to Germany. The only way I made it through all of this was by the grace and mercy of my Lord and Savior, Jesus Christ.

Hours later as we got ready to land in Frankfurt, the children were super-excited to look out the window of the plane. The lights were amazing in the surrounding towns and cities. The children giggled and fought over who got to look. I just smiled at them and told them to share. I had to admit, I was excited, too. I had never been overseas before, and it was amazing to see the differences.

When we got off the plane, we had to go through customs. The children and I were nervous. Everyone was speaking German, and we hadn't learned the language yet. How were we going to communicate? A man in uniform came up to us and spoke, directing us forward. I looked at him in desperation and said, "Do you speak English?"

He looked at me with a smile and said, "Yes! I am sorry, ma'am. If you would follow me, I will take you to the right counter. There will be someone there who can help you." I smiled and gratefully followed him.

As we approached the counter, the men and women looked stern and very unkind. It was a scary and uncomfortable situation for the children and me. The man asked for our passports and then the questions began: "Where did you come from? Where are you going? Do you have any illegal drugs or substances? Why are you here? Do you have papers and shot records for this animal?"

The questions were brief and to the point, and I was expected to answer promptly. I said a small prayer: "Dear Lord, please help us to get through customs."

As the man behind the counter looked over our passports, military ID cards, and Annabell's papers, I overheard the man behind me talking to someone. "That man had been stuck at the counter for over an hour," he said. "Don't go in that line, or you will be there awhile. They are talking of searching all his luggage."

My heart sank. I didn't want them to search our bags or take us to a security room. This was scary enough for the children and me. I didn't want them to be more frightened than they already were. I knew I needed to claim the prayer I had just offered and stand on God's promises.

My attention returned to the man at the counter as he looked up, handed me our papers, and told us to proceed through the gate behind him into the next room. We could pick up our luggage there. He dismissed us, saying, "Next!"

I picked up our things and walked away with the children. My heart was beating fast. I was getting nervous: I didn't see Phil anywhere, and not everyone understood English. "God," I prayed, "please help us find our way."

I instructed Nautasha to hold onto the suitcase again and made sure Ben was on my other side. We went through the gate to another security checkpoint. We had to place all of our bags on the belt, including Annabell, and they went through the x-ray machine.

My children found the picture of our cat to be most interesting. "Is that Annabell, Momma?" Nautasha asked as she looked at the screen.

I smiled down at her and told her, "It is indeed our little Annabell. She is being x-rayed. That is what God made her bones to look like."

"Will the machine hurt her, Momma?"

I smiled again and told her that Annabell would be just fine. She did not seem convinced, so after we went through the metal detector, I told Nautasha she could get Annabell off of the belt and make sure that she was okay. She ran to the belt, then exclaimed in a loud voice, "Annabell is okay, Momma! Can't you hear her meowing?" The security guards smiled at her, and Ben, being the big brother that he was, decided to help get the bags and kennel.

We now headed for the luggage claim area. We waited for about fifteen minutes before the belt started to move. Everyone ran up and crowded us. I grabbed my children and pulled them back to wait for the crowd to disperse, using my feet to move Annabell's kennel. After ten minutes, it was calm enough to walk back up. I watched as the luggage went around, and when I saw some of our bags, I told Ben, "Hold your sister's hand and keep her next to you. Don't leave my side. Do you understand, son?" He looked at me with a stern face and nodded. He was his sister's protector. My heart was filled with joy at the role my son was taking.

I grabbed Nautasha's two suitcases. Then Ben's came through. But where were mine? I waited, then I saw one coming through the flaps. It was the small one that held some of our valuables. The suitcase with all of my clothes was missing.

I asked a guard if he spoke English.

"Yes, ma'am," he said, "I do."

I explained my situation. He told me where I needed to go to put in a baggage claim, then pointed to a large, rolling cart in the corner and told me to put my luggage on it. I was grateful, because I had been trying to figure out how to juggle bags, children, and kitten.

We entered the next room through the security doors. Many people were embracing their loved ones. We looked around but still did not see Phil anywhere. I was starting to get worried. The children were a little scared, and I kept reassuring them that everything would be fine.

A half an hour went by, and still there was no Phil. The children were tired of sitting. They started to run around the airport waiting area. When I yelled to them, they came over. I explained that this was not the place to play; we needed to be good and wait for Dad.

They sat down with sad faces. My worry was turning into anger. *How could he forget us like this?* I thought. *He knew when we were coming in. Maybe we should have stayed in the States.* I was brought out of my thoughts by my daughter's hand on mine and her little voice.

"Mommy," she said, "are you okay? Are you scared?"

I touched her little face and smiled. "Daddy will be here soon, and then we will go to our new place," I reassured her.

She started asking me a million questions about our new apartment. I answered her the best that I could. I didn't know what it looked like either, since Phil had only given me brief details. But it was enough to quench her curiosity.

After about an hour of waiting, Phil came walking up. "Sorry I am late," he said. "I overslept and raced down here as fast as I could. Is this all the bags? Are you all ready?"

"No. I am missing a bag, and I don't know how to get to the baggage claims department," I said with a sharp tone. He knew I was not happy.

Nautasha ran to hug his leg, and said, "I missed you, Daddy." He patted her back and said he missed her too. Ben just stood there.

"How's it going, Ben?" Phil said. "Did you help your mother?" Ben just nodded yes.

They played video games from time to time, but Phil and Ben did not have a very good relationship. With Phil, Ben kept to himself.

Phil walked away to speak in German to the security guard, then he came back and grabbed the luggage cart. "Let's go talk to the claims office. They will find your luggage."

I looked at him in awe. "Phil, are you seriously not going to hug your wife? Did you miss me?"

He just smiled, walked over, and hugged me, wrapping his arms and one leg around me while laughing and cracking jokes.

The Flight to Germany

Again, he had hurt my feelings. Why couldn't he just love me sincerely? Why did everything have to be a joke? I walked along with the children, carrying Annabell, while Phil pushed the cart. He told us all about why he was late. I just listened.

We went to the parking lot and filled up his friend's truck with our luggage (our car had not arrived in Germany yet). As we drove out, my eyes were wide with amazement. The sidewalks and streets were made of cobblestones, and the buildings were different than those in the United States. It was like entering an old movie.

Finally, we arrived at our new apartment. It had a patio deck off of the living room on the second floor. The kitchen was small, and the oven was half the size of my stove in Fort Drum. The bedrooms were small as well, and the bathroom had just enough room to turn around between the shower, sink, and toilet. We had no beds or furniture, because ours were still en route from the U.S.

Phil had obtained some beds from the Army, and he told us that furniture and dishes would arrive the following day. I asked him how he had gotten all of this, and he said, "The military has a place where we can rent all the household goods we need until ours come in."

The next day I was amazed as they came in with sofas, a table, and chairs. They even brought us some kitchen utensils, pots, and pans. We were very blessed. Then, just as we were getting ready to leave, we heard a knock at the door. It was a man holding my lost suitcase. I was shocked; I hadn't known they would deliver it to our door. This was a blessing for me, since I only had one set of clothes packed in my carry-on bag. After the man left, Phil took us shopping for food and to register Ben in school.

The food there was different than ours, so he took us to the on-base commissary which had a lot of food from the U.S. It made it easier for me to cook, until I learned about German food and culture. Later we realized how much we loved their food (we also realized how fattening most of the stuff we loved was).

Germany was different, but it was wonderful to learn the language and to shop in the *marktplatz* (marketplace). A *marktplatz* is a square space in the center of a German town. A fountain is usually in the middle. All around it are shops where you can find all sorts of foods, trinkets, and much more. The children and I loved to go there. The kids also fell in love with spaghetti ice cream; it was one of their favorite treats.

Learning to get around Germany on a bus when you didn't speak the language very well was hard. However, many people helped me out, with lots of love and understanding. I knew that they were going out of their way to translate to the bus driver where I was going, and that God was watching over me. This gave me a sense of peace. I praised God for the mercy that He gave me through His people.

CHAPTER 34

Arrival of Household Goods, and Moving Again!

―――◦◦―――

After two weeks of waiting for our things they finally arrived. Phil came running in, grabbed me by the hand, and dragged me to the door. "Our vehicles and household goods are here. They let me off work early so we could go sign them out and get the house items delivered." He was relieved. He had been catching a ride to work with a friend, and sometimes they worked different shifts, so it had been getting very stressful for him.

I grabbed Nautasha and got her shoes on. Excited, we ran to his coworker's car. When we arrived, Phil and I went in, looked things over to make sure it was all accounted for, and signed a bunch of forms. The lady there checked to see when their next delivery date was and told us she could have our household goods brought to our home by the following week.

Phil asked about our car, and she sent him over to another office. There he signed a few more papers while a man told him what dock it was in. The man said that Phil's motorcycle had not arrived yet but that it should be coming soon. Then he gave him the keys to the car.

I faintly remembered Phil talking about finding a way to bring his motorcycle with us, because he had found out we could only ship one vehicle and would have to pay out of pocket for the second. I asked him now how he had managed to get it there. He said that the military had accepted it as household goods.

It had been shipped in a separate crate, and my husband asked if they knew an approximate date that it would arrive. The man said he was not sure, and explained how some shipments went other places first. They had no control over when things came to them. Regardless, my husband was a very happy man that day.

We thanked Phil's coworker who had lent us the car, put Nautasha in our own, and headed for home. We laughed and talked all the way there. This was the sort of time I longed to have with my husband; one where we were happy and could talk and laugh. He told me all about places he had been to in Germany the last time he was stationed here, and how he wanted to take me to see them. I sat and listened as I watched him remember those places.

> This was the sort of time I longed to have with my husband; one where we were happy and could talk and laugh.

It was a good day for us. I was beginning to have hope in our marriage, and I prayed that God would bless my husband and help him to be a good husband.

Once our household goods arrived, I was pretty busy. I was a little over six months pregnant and feeling the effects of not being able to move the way I used to, but I managed to get our house set up so that it was livable. Then I called the military rental place so that they could retrieve the furniture and kitchenware which we had rented. They were very nice and came out the next day to pick it all up.

I am glad I did not unpack all of our boxes, because Phil came home later in the week and told me he was looking at a four-bedroom apartment. At six months pregnant, they approved you to move into a bigger apartment to suit the needs of the family (not before, in case of a miscarriage and because housing was limited, due to all the soldiers stationed there with their families). We had already been very fortunate to get housing so

Arrival of Household Goods, and Moving Again!

quickly, and now a four-bedroom opened up just as we received our household goods. I knew God was watching over our family.

The apartment was on the other side of base. It was not in as nice a neighborhood as the first one we were in, but I praised God anyway. It was twice the size, and the oven was a little bigger. I unpacked our stuff and put it all away that week. I was happy to be settled into a home again.

We met the neighbors above and below us, and they were really nice. I became really good friends with the woman upstairs, who was a German woman named Petra. Her husband John was in the U.S. Army and was stationed here for his second tour. He had met and married Petra here and wanted to sign up to stay longer, since Petra's family lived there and their children were just toddlers.

Petra and I talked often. She introduced us to some German friends of hers. One of them had all teenage daughters. We asked if her sixteen-year-old, Susie, would like to babysit for us.

I was having a hard time with my pregnancy and needed help caring for Nautasha when things got overwhelming. Her mother agreed, so Susie came and stayed with us during her breaks from school. She was great with the children, and did a good job of keeping them occupied. She also helped me clean and cook. She even started to teach me German. I enjoyed her company very much.

While there were nice parts of living there, at the same time I had not been to church since we arrived in Germany. One day I asked Phil if there was a Seventh-day Adventist Church in the area, but he told me that he had never heard of one over here. He also did not direct me to someone so that I could find out. It was like he didn't want me to go to church, or else he was just not interested in helping me find the kind I wanted.

Phil came home early from work one afternoon excited about something. I came out of the kitchen and asked him why he was already back.

"They called me today from the shipping office," he said. "My motorcycle is here, and I need you to drive me over there to pick it up."

I put away what I was working on and got Nautasha ready to go. We had to bring a gas can along, because in order to ship the bike he had had to drain all the fluids out. We drove down to the shipping yard, and he signed out his bike.

Phil got it running right there. He was like a kid in a candy store. He sat on his motorcycle and revved it up, while saying, "Oh, yeah! Listen to the engine roar: *'arrrrrrrr, arrrrrrrrr."*

I just laughed at him. Then I got nervous; I had barely passed my German driver's test to get my enhanced license so I could drive over here, and I didn't know the roads very well at all. I expressed this to Phil, but he told me just to follow him home and I would do fine.

I did, and it worked out great. This was my first driving experience in a different country, and I was excited.

CHAPTER 35

Baby in Distress, and an Unfaithful Husband

———⊸◦⊶———

As with my first pregnancy, I was getting bigger and eating more. Phil would call me fat and other names. He told me that I walked like a duck, and that soon I wouldn't be able to see my feet. He said so many mean things about my weight that I fell into a state of depression.

I knew I was not going to lose weight, and to comfort myself I would eat. I liked to get German banana juice from the store. It was rich, creamy, and very fattening if eaten in large amounts. I drank two quarts a day.

The bigger I got, the more Phil teased me. Then he started flirting with our babysitter Susie right in front of me, and taking her on motorcycle rides. I became so stressed that it began to affect the baby's health. I went to see my doctor, and he was concerned.

As he did every time I had an appointment, Doctor Weber gave me an ultrasound right there in his office. Because he would do this, I had not only gotten to find out the sex of the baby, but also to watch him grow. Yes: I was having a baby boy!

This time he said that I was showing signs of premature labor, which was not good, since at seven months the baby was not fully-developed. The emotional stress I was under was causing much distress for the baby, too.

Doctor Weber knew that the baby and I were in danger. He informed me that he was going to admit me into Hanau Stadtkrankenhaus (the local hospital).

I was taken to the labor and delivery floor. They placed my bed on a slant, with my head lower than my feet. This was supposed to help stop the labor. A doctor then came in and gave me shots to stop my contractions. He said it was dangerous to deliver the baby this early because its lungs were not developed. He also gave me steroid shots to help the baby's lungs to develop faster, just in case I went into premature labor again.

I was kept in the hospital for two weeks. During that time I went into labor several times. They monitored the baby and me every few hours, day and night. They wanted my contractions to stop before they would release me to go home.

While I was there, Phil came to see me and brought the children, but he never stayed very long. I was glad to see them. I missed my children very much, and I longed to go home.

During the second week, I was given permission to shower as long as I had someone with me. The staff was busy, so I called and asked Phil when he was coming. I told him that I needed his help. He came later in the day, and it was a blessing to be able to shower.

> *As I washed, he said that he had something to tell me. "Oh?" I said, bracing myself.*

As I washed, he said that he had something to tell me. "Oh?" I said, bracing myself for the fight that I envisioned him and Ben having had.

"I just wanted you to know that Susie and I slept together last week. I don't know how it happened. It just did."

I stood under the shower in shock as many emotions came over me and my mind processed what he had said. I could not stop the tears from running down my face. I felt thankful that the running water hid the hurt which I was feeling. I didn't know what to say.

Phil was still talking. He said that he was sorry and never meant to hurt me. I could only comprehend parts of it. I still could not believe what I had just heard. "I just wanted you to hear it from me," he said.

These were the words that made the most sense to me. I understood right away what was happening: he didn't want *Susie* to tell me what had happened. He was trying to cover his tracks by getting to me first, so that I would believe him and not her. My tears turned into anger. After I got out of the shower, I asked him to leave. I told him I needed time to think.

He did not expect this response from me. He kept apologizing for what had happened and telling me it was the first time he had ever cheated on me.

I could hide the tears no longer. I asked him again to leave. He tried to hug and comfort me, but I rejected his love and sternly repeated my request. He walked out of the room looking very unsettled, but not sorry for the hurt he had caused.

I lay in the hospital that night with a heavy and broken heart. No matter what I did to get his attention, Phil was always going to look at other women. And now he was not just looking but touching. My depression was even deeper than before. I longed for a way out of this world.

When I arrived home, Petra was there to greet me with her big smile. This made my homecoming very special. She sat with me while Phil brought in my stuff. She noticed that I was not saying much to him and asked what was wrong. I said that I would tell her later. Understanding, she nodded.

The Doctor had given me orders to take it easy, or I would be on bed rest for the remainder of my pregnancy, so Phil asked for the next few days off so he could keep an eye on me and help with whatever I needed done. We no longer had a babysitter to help, since I had asked Phil to fire Susie.

However, he didn't do much during my recovery. He sat and played on the computer while I watched Nautasha, cooked, and cleaned up.

Phil *watched* me like a hawk, and he was overly nice to me. He offered to help clean up a few times and helped with little things here and there, but it was very minimal. He studied me more than anything. But he could not figure out what I was thinking or feeling.

I kept silent, answering only when spoken to and giving him one-word answers. When we went to bed at night, there was plenty of room between us on the king-size bed. Our children could have slept between us, and I would have never felt them. I was hurt and angry, and I didn't even want Phil to touch me. He made me feel dirty inside. My heart could not bear the pain of what he had done.

I knew it was making him nervous, so I finally asked him, "Why are you home from work? You're not doing much of anything. If I need help, Petra will come down and help me."

He looked at me with wide eyes, and it dawned on me: he thought I was going to leave him.

"Phil," I said, "just to ease your fears, I am not going anywhere. I can't fly home. I am too far along in my pregnancy. They won't allow me to fly until after I have the baby."

He asked how I knew that. I told him what the doctor had told me in Brimley, when I lived with his mom and dad before coming to Germany.

Phil didn't say much to me after that. He turned back to his game, and the next day he went back to work. He did call and check on me throughout the day. He almost never did this. He was still worried that I was going to leave him and that he would not see his baby.

I would have loved to go home right then and there, but I knew I could not. Instead, I went to my knees in prayer and kept asking God to give me the strength to endure my trials. But I was feeling no relief, so I just stopped.

I told Petra and Breanne what had happened. Breanne, my friend from Fort Drum, currently lived an hour and a half away from us in Landstuhl (nine months before Phil got stationed in Germany, Breanne's husband Richard had put in for an overseas assignment). Petra was upset. She felt like she could have done something to stop Phil and Susie from committing adultery.

While I was in the hospital, Petra said, she had had roaches in her apartment really bad, and the Army had come to spray. They told her that she would have to find another place to stay, because otherwise the fumes would make her and her children sick. Since her husband John was in the field for two weeks doing training exercises, she had asked Phil if she and her children could stay at our apartment for a few days. Phil had said yes, and that he could use help. So Petra had come down with her children and helped keep up the house. She watched my two children as well as her own.

Petra looked at me. "He gave up your bedroom, and the children and I slept in your bed," she said. "Susie asked to stay the night because I was there. She was supposed to sleep in the room with Nautasha or else with me and my children. She was in the bedroom with us for a while, but said she couldn't sleep and walked out of the room. I thought she went to your daughter's room and fell asleep with her. I knew Phil was sleeping on the sofa that night, but I never dreamed she would go out there with him."

Petra was very upset. "I would have said or done something had I known what was happening. I am so sorry, Michelle. I feel so responsible. Had I not stayed, she wouldn't have asked to stay."

She went from being upset with Phil to being very angry at him. I hugged her and told her it was not her fault. Petra was a good friend, but I didn't want her to get into the middle of my failing marriage. She already had enough problems with John.

Breanne told me to leave Phil and come to her house. She said she would let me stay with her, Richard, and their three boys until after my baby was born. Then the Army would help me fly home with the children and our household goods. Phil would lose military housing and would have to move back into the barracks with the single soldiers.

I thought over this idea for a long time. It sounded good to me. However, I think Richard must have called and talked to my husband.

One day he came home from work livid, telling me he would come and get me if I moved in with Breanne and Richard. We ended up in a big argument that day. He tried to make me feel that it was all my fault, like he did all the other times, but this time it did not work.

I brought to his attention why we were going through this rough time in our marriage, and that is when he said the most hurtful thing to me:

"If you weren't so fat, maybe I would not have wanted it from someone else."

I looked at him in shock. "I am pregnant with your child. It took two of us to get me this way. Save your excuses for someone else, and man up to what you did wrong."

He looked away, mad. He knew this argument was not going to twist around onto me. He had already admitted what he did wrong.

I went into Ben's room and the tears started to fall again. I started the vacuum up and pushed it across the carpet. Phil came in behind me, turned off the vacuum, and turned me to face him. With his hands on my shoulders, he said, "Can you ever forgive me?"

I looked him in the eyes. Through tears I replied, "I don't know."

I wanted to turn Phil in, because Susie was only sixteen. However, in Germany, that was not a crime. What I didn't realize was that, because we were U.S. citizens and on a U.S. military base, all of our laws applied to Phil. He could have gone to a military prison for what he had done.

But as things stood, we were stuck in this house together in a foreign country. Peace eventually had to be made.

Susie came and talked to me one day while Phil was at work. She had called a few times, but Phil kept telling me not to believe a word she said. She just wanted to break our marriage up, he told me. But it was hard not to listen to her.

She sat on the end of my bed and told me the whole story of what had happened. She cried the whole time, and when she was done, she asked me if I could ever forgive her. I knew that she was very sincere.

When I told her Phil's side of the story, her eyes got wide with disbelief. She looked me straight in the eye and said, "He is a liar! I tell you the truth."

Her broken English got worse when she was upset. Many times she spoke half-English, half-German. I had to tell her to slow down and speak English.

She told me again that she was sorry, that he was not a good man, and that she wanted nothing to do with Phil ever again. She still wanted to be friends with me, but she refused to come over unless she knew Phil was not home.

After talking with her, I knew that my husband had been lying to me again. I knew that he was good at manipulation, but I didn't always catch it, in part because all I wanted was for someone to love me.

I decided there was nothing I could do to get Phil to be honest with me. He always wanted it to be someone else's fault. But I wanted peace back in my house. I wanted our marriage to work. I didn't want to give up, even though I was not happy. The only way I could see to restore things was for me to surrender to his lies and tell him I believed him. So I stuck to Phil's story so that he would accept me again.

Now *I* was lying to bring peace, and breaking the ninth commandment: "You shall not bear false witness against your neighbor" (Exod. 20:16). I wish I would have looked to the Lord for my happiness and guidance, but I was so depressed and felt so unloved that I could no longer hear the calling of my dear Savior's voice.

CHAPTER 36

Birthday Request

It was getting close to Nautasha's fifth birthday. I decided to have cake and ice cream and cook her favorite meal, macaroni and cheese. It was a special day for my little girl. I asked her several days before her party what she wanted, and her response brought tears to my eyes.

"Mommy, the only present I want for my birthday is for my baby brother to be born. Can you have the baby for me, Mommy, on my birthday?"

I smiled at my sweet little girl and told her, "It is not in my hands but God's when the baby will come, but it is so sweet of you to want your baby brother for your present."

She said, "Then I will just pray and ask God to give us the baby on my birthday." All I could do was laugh and hug her. It was the sincerest request I had ever heard from my daughter. At that moment, she was filled with such a selfless love; a love which I knew could only come from our Father in Heaven.

Ben tried to tell her that she would have to share her birthday and would get less gifts, but Nautasha didn't care. She was determined. She just kept telling everyone that she only wanted her baby brother for her birthday.

Her day came, but still there was no baby. Nautasha was sad, but she enjoyed her party with friends and family. I asked her that night as I tucked her into bed, "Did you enjoy your birthday party?"

She smiled big. "*Yes*," she said while nodding her head up and down. Then she put her hand on my belly, as she often did to see if she could feel her brother kicking (when he kicked, she would smile and then ask me if it hurt, and I would reassure her that he didn't hurt me one bit). She said, "Mommy, I really wish God would have given me our baby for my birthday."

I told her, "God sometimes says no to our prayer requests, because He knows the future and what is best for us. We just need to trust in all His ways and know that He is leading us to do what is right in His sight. Later, He usually lets us see why He said no, and then it becomes so clear to us that His way was best.

"We can't see the future," I continued, "so sometimes we do not understand. Remember what it says in the Bible in Proverbs: 'Trust in the Lord with all your heart, and lean not on your own understanding; in all your ways acknowledge Him, and He shall direct your paths.' So if we trust in God and all His ways, we will be blessed, and He will help us to understand why later.

"I love you, baby girl." I said. "I am glad you had a good birthday and that you wanted your baby brother for your present. That was a sweet birthday wish, and it showed momma just how much you will love your little brother, because you didn't ask for more toys. I am so proud of you."

I kissed her goodnight and tucked her into bed. As I walked to the door to turn out the light, I looked over at my sweet girl, all tucked in and with a sweet smile on her face. My heart melted.

As I turned out the light, she said, "Good night, Mommy. I love you."

"I love you too, Nautasha. I love you too."

I walked away from her bedroom in awe. This was a moment in time when I felt truly loved and was able to see what loving another person felt like.

God had just shown me true love through my little girl: it was sweet, pure, honest, and sincere. I tried to comprehend it. I was seeking love, but I really didn't know how to love the way God does:

As the Father loved Me, I also have loved you; abide in My love. If you keep My commandments, you will abide in My love, just as I have kept My Father's commandments and abide in His love. These things I have spoken to you, that My joy may remain in you, and that your joy may be full. This is My commandment, that you love one another as I have loved you. (John 15:9-12)

CHAPTER 37

The Birth of Tristin

I was feeling very worn out and was not sleeping well. The baby had been due on March 23rd, and it was now the 26th. If I lay on my back, the baby would push on my bladder, causing me much discomfort and many bathroom trips. When I lay on my sides, my hips would go numb or else start to hurt from the weight of the baby. Lying on my stomach was like being on a beach ball all night long. I was in need of a good night's rest, but until this baby decided to enter the world, I knew that I would not receive those precious hours of restful sleep.

That night when Phil and I went to bed, I was feeling discomfort in my stomach and back. By 11:00 p.m. I had dull pains in my lower stomach. I woke Phil up.

"Phil! Phil!" I said softly as I shook him. "I think I am in labor! You need to get up and take me to the *krankenhaus*."

He awoke and looked at me. "Are you sure?"

"*Yes*, I am sure! Let's go!"

I pulled the covers off, climbed out of bed, and got dressed. Phil jumped up and pulled on his pants. I had never seen him move that fast before, not even when he was late for work. I was happy because soon I would have my body back.

As Phil brought me into the emergency room, he spoke to the receptionist in German and told her that I was in labor. She made a phone call and two young men dressed in white came and pushed me in a wheelchair to the elevator.

They took me to the delivery floor, and Phil stayed with me for a few hours. Then the doctor informed us that it was going to be a while and had the nurse sign me into a hospital room (where I would also stay after the baby was born). This was to keep the delivery rooms open for the women who were ready to give birth.

Phil brought my belonging up to the room. They already had me in a hospital gown. After the nurse got me all set up, she gave me a shot to stop the contractions for a few hours so that I could sleep. Phil then said he would be back tomorrow and walked out the door.

My heart sank again. What if the baby came tonight? He wouldn't be here to see his son being born. The nurse had told him he could stay and sleep in the bed next to me, so why didn't he want to be with me? I felt very alone.

The nurse I had in the morning was so sweet and very loving. She would walk into my room every day that she worked and say, "*Guten morgen! Wie geht's mein schatzi?*" I knew that "*guten morgen*" meant "good morning," but I didn't know what "*wie geht's*" meant, so I just smiled and laughed.

She said, "'*Wie geht's*' means, 'how are you?' You should respond by saying, '*Gut und dir?*' which means, 'Good, and you?' And '*mein schatzi*' means, 'my sweetheart,' which we say a lot at home to the children. So the translation is, "Good morning! How are you, my sweetheart?"

Once she had explained what she meant, I knew she was going to make my stay here a good one. She had fun teaching me German, and I had fun learning from her.

I asked her if there was anything I could do to hurry this delivery up. She suggested that I walk the halls and the stairways, if I was up to it; but I needed to let someone know how far I was going and whether I was on the stairs or in the hall, just in case I went into labor and could not get back to them.

The nurses at the desk timed how long it took me to walk a flight of stairs and the hallway. If I was not back in time, they would come looking for me. I found this out when I ran into some people from the military base in the stairway and gave them directions. The young lady and I got to talking for about ten minutes, and a nurse came to see if I was okay.

I told her that I was sorry and I didn't mean to scare her. She smiled and asked how I was feeling. I said that the pains were getting worse, but not enough to deliver the baby.

The nurse smiled again and said, "Just keep walking." Then she went back to the nurse's station.

By that afternoon Phil still had not come back to the hospital. When I returned to my room, the phone rang. I answered it with hesitation.

"Hello?" I said.

"Hi, honey! Did you have the baby yet?"

My husband was calling to see if I had had the baby? I wanted to tell him that he should be there, and then he would know if I had had the baby or not. But I just said, "No, not yet."

> My husband was calling to see if I had had the baby? I wanted to tell him that he should be there.

"Are you getting close?"

"My pains are a little stronger, but not bad yet."

"Well, call me when your pains get worse, and I will come back. Got to go take care of the kids and find a sitter so that when you call, I can come. Talk to you soon. Bye." He hung up the phone.

I was sad, angry, and hurt. I felt like he would never love me, no matter what I did, including giving him a son. As for a babysitter, Petra had said she would watch the children. The more I thought about the situation, the more frustrated with Phil I became.

My pains grew stronger, but I decided not to call him. If he wanted to be here, he would come. I was ready to have this baby on my own if I needed to.

These thoughts flooded my mind as I went on another walk. Then, as I rounded a corner to do another flight of stairs, I ran into my husband.

"I found a sitter and got here as fast as I could," he said. "When you didn't call, I figured you must be in labor, so I raced down here. Are you having stronger contractions yet?"

"A little stronger. The nurse told me to just keep walking."

He walked upstairs with me and down the hall. We said hello to the nurse as we passed by, then turned around and walked back the other way. By the third round, I told Phil, "Let's walk another flight of steps and see if we can speed this up."

Phil started cracking jokes about how the baby was stubborn like me. Just as he finished talking, a long, sharp pain went through my stomach, and I almost fell over. Phil grabbed me and helped me start back up the steps. I didn't make it very far before I had another contraction and had to stop.

It was taking me a long time to get up the stairs, and I hadn't told the nurse that I had decided to do two flights instead of one. Just as we reached the top of the landing, the door opened and the nurse walked in.

"She is having stronger pains now," Phil exclaimed. "I had a hard time getting her up the steps." The nurse had Phil hold on to me while she ran and grabbed a wheelchair. Once she came back, she and Phil helped me into it and brought me to the elevator. She raced me down to the delivery room.

A midwife came in and hooked me up to the baby monitor. She checked the heartbeat of the baby and did an ultrasound. She then asked if I wanted to sit in the jacuzzi for a while to help soothe the pains.

I had not experienced this with my other two children. I said, "I will try anything that helps." My husband and the midwife helped me take off my hospital gown and get into the jacuzzi. The pains were still strong, but the water did help to lessen the pain.

I was only in the water for about ten minutes when I felt the head of my baby pushing down. "Phil," I said, "you better go get the midwife. The baby is coming out."

When I looked up, he was gone, but within a minute or two he was back with the midwife (in Germany, the doctors don't deliver your baby unless there are complications; you only have a midwife to accompany you during your birthing time). She came running over to the jacuzzi and had me move closer to her so that she could check how many centimeters I was dilated.

She said something to Phil in German, and he instructed me to get out of the jacuzzi. By this time, I was in so much pain that I could hardly stand. Phil helped me get out and put my gown on, while the midwife left to prepare the delivery room for me.

I looked up at my husband and saw the worried look on his face. I realized at that moment that he did care about me; just not always in the way that I would have liked him to.

The midwife came running back into the room. She helped Phil walk me across the hall. I was not far from the delivery room, but because my contractions were so intense, I had to stop every twenty seconds. Had my husband not been holding me up, I would have fallen to the floor.

The midwife looked worried and instructed Phil to get me on a table that was shaped like a snow angel, with the middle of the legs cut out. It was nothing like the birthing tables in the United States. As I lay down, the pain grew even stronger than before.

Phil looked at me and said the meanest thing: "You sound like our dog Sheba when she howls!" Then he laughed.

I was not amused by his comment and gave him a nasty look. He kept laughing. I truly believe this was his way of coping. I felt that he was very uncomfortable and nervous and just didn't know how to react to something that he did not know how to fix.

But then, as my pain and contractions continued to increase, Phil became worried. I was seeing a caring side in him that I had never observed before. He asked the midwife if there was something she could give me for the pain.

I didn't want any medication; I just wanted the baby out. Still, the midwife gave me a shot in the butt cheek. Phil asked, "How long till it will take effect?"

The midwife said, "*Zehn minuten.*"

"*Ten minutes?*" Phil exclaimed.

About a minute after the shot, my baby boy was pushing his way out. The midwife coached me through the birth, with Phil translating when she didn't know how to say something in English. She kept telling me that I was doing fine and the baby was on his way.

Finally, it was over. I heard the midwife ask Phil if he wanted to cut the umbilical cord. She laid my boy on my stomach as Phil made the snip.

My baby never cried. He just lay on my belly, opening and closing his eyes, trying to adjust to the light. He finally kept them closed and wiggled from the chill of the room. The midwife cleaned him up, wrapped him in a blanket, handed him to me, and left the room.

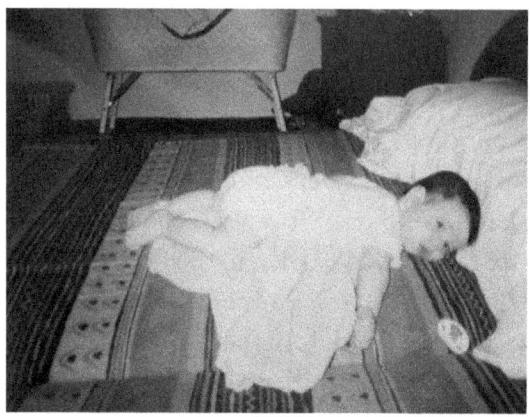
Tristin as a newborn.

I looked down at my beautiful baby boy with his full head of black hair. He was snuggled up to me and very content. I was amazed that he was not crying. He was different than my other two children had been when they were born.

I looked up and saw Phil staring at him in awe. "He is so tiny." Was that all he could say?

The midwife returned with the doctor. He checked me over, said something to the midwife in German, then left the room. She smiled at me and said I was doing great. Then she grabbed a camera, snapped a shot of the three of us together, and asked me what the baby's name was.

I looked down at him and then back at the midwife. "Tristin Joe."

She walked away with the picture but came back a few minutes later with a card in her hand. She handed Phil the card and said in broken English, "You have a healthy, seven pound, six ounce baby boy, measuring in at nineteen point seven inches long."

I looked at the card. It read:

Zur geburt ihres kindes!

Das baby wurde am 27.03.99

um 16:48

im Stadtkrankenhause Hanau geboren

Tristin war bei der geburt

3200g schwer

7.06 pound

und 50 cm lang

19.7 inch

The Birth of Tristin

Es gratulieren ihnen

Hebamme Marion

Arzt Dr. Rleiz

Translated, it read:

> The birth of their child! / The baby was born on 03-27-99 / at 4:48 pm
>
> Born in Hanau City Hospital
>
> Tristin was at birth / 3200g Difficult / 7.06 pound / and 50 cm long / 19.7 inch
>
> We congratulate you
>
> Midwife Marion / Doctor Dr. Rleiz

It sure is amazing that God let me see how wonderful the German culture is. When you have a baby there, they keep you in the hospital for a week to observe you both. They want to make sure you are healthy. They even go so far as ultrasounding the baby's stomach, as well as the mother's, and they do a lot of bloodwork on both people, checking for HIV and other diseases. The whole experience was wonderful. If I could have had all my children there, I would have.

The part that I really found interesting was that, when I decided to leave my baby in the nursery at night, the nurses did not feed him between 10:00 p.m. and 6:00 a.m. I found this disturbing until I asked them why they did this. I found out that this was how they trained babies to sleep through the night.

After I got home, I really appreciated being able to go to bed and sleep through the night. However I still had to listen closely because Tristin never cried.

I was very thankful that I was a light sleeper, because Phil never heard Tristin when he woke up. When he was hungry or needed a diaper change, he would only make a little "uh" noise.

Tristin did not cry until he was three months old. Even then, it was only a very short "wah." He didn't cry hard until he was six months old.

He truly was a blessing from God, and he still is.

CHAPTER 38

Depression Sets In

A**fter I had been home from the hospital for a few weeks, Phil went back to his old ways. He played video games or sat on the computer until it was time for bed. On weekends he went to bars with his friends and did not come home till between 3:00 and 6:00 a.m. (in Germany, the bars don't close until early in the morning, and even if they stop serving at 2:00 or 3:00, the dance clubs stay open until 5:00 or 6:00 a.m.).

Phil left me at home with the children. Every time I asked him, "How come you never ask me to go out with you?" his response was the same:

"I never said you couldn't. Find a sitter and come."

He hurt my feelings deeply when he responded to me this way. All I wanted was for Phil to want me to be a part of his life; to ask me to spend time with him and go places together. But the times I did find a babysitter and went out with him to a bar, I could feel the Lord tugging at my heart, telling me that this was not a place for me to be.

I wish I would have been more in tune with God through prayer and the study of His Word while I was going through these trials. I know I would have made different choices and stood strong in Him. However, because my heart was set on trying to please my husband instead of God, I chose to walk down a very dangerous path.

My favorite author says:

> Brethren and sisters, it is by beholding that we become changed. By dwelling upon the love of God and our Savior, by contemplating the perfection of the divine character and claiming the righteousness of Christ as ours by faith, we are to be transformed into the same image. (White, *Counsels for the Church*, p. 80)

After reading this I realized that what we behold, we become. If we are not beholding Christ but instead the things of this world, then we become like the world and not our Savior. "But we all, with unveiled face, beholding as in a mirror the glory of the Lord, are being transformed into the same image from glory to glory, just as by the Spirit of the Lord" (2 Cor. 3:18).

When I went to bars with my husband, he treated me like a tagalong, leaving me sitting at the bar or table alone while he danced very inappropriately with other women. After a few times, I stopped going. My heart could not take the pain of his adulterous actions.

At home my mind would whirl with thoughts of what he was doing, because I knew he was not being faithful to me. All Phil wanted was to have fun with as many women as he could. Meanwhile, my depression grew stronger as the days passed.

Each day Phil would take the car and go to work, Ben would go to school, and Nautasha, Tristin and I would walk to the store a mile and a half away to pick up groceries; or else we would just enjoy a day out walking through the shops. Nautasha enjoyed the sights of Hanau and all the differences between it and the United States. She loved watching new things and walked long distances with a smile. Tristin slept in his stroller, soothed by the gentle rocking movement.

My children were at peace and very happy on those walks, but my thoughts were a different story. I was so depressed that I would think terrible thoughts. When I saw a semi coming, I imagined how easy it

> *My children were at peace and very happy on those walks, but my thoughts were a different story.*

would be to push the stroller over to Nautasha and step out in front of the truck. Then my pain would be gone and my children would be safe.

I no longer wanted to live in the pain and misery of feeling rejected by my husband, but I kept these thoughts to myself for a long time. I fought against them and began to pray again. As I prayed, I was moved by the thought that I needed to get help or else, one time, I *would* step out into the road or drive into oncoming traffic to end my life.

I told my husband that I was depressed and needed to see someone. He looked at me funny and laughed. He didn't think I was serious until I stated that I didn't want to live any more. His smile turned into a frown, and he told me to call my family doctor and see what I could find out about getting in to see the right person.

I scheduled an appointment with the doctor, and when I went to see him, he was very concerned. He set an appointment for me to see a psychologist in Landstuhl, Germany, a few days later.

It was about a two-hour drive there, so Phil and I needed to get up early. Traffic was always heavy in the morning, but it always flowed pretty well once you got past the cities and towns.

There is something interesting about German autobahns (we call them freeways in the United States). There really is not a speed limit unless you are going through a city or town or passing by an exit. That means that a four to six-hour drive in the United States takes two to three hours there. We would drive at speeds between 115 and 117 miles an hour (the governor on our car kicked in at 118), yet people would pass us like we were sitting still. When an accident occurs there, it is always fatal. However, to our surprise, Germany's highway accident and death toll was lower than that in the U.S.

On the way to Landstuhl to see the psychologist, Phil talked to me about what was going on in his life, and we laughed about a few things. I loved times like these, but it was more like a friendship than anything else. We seemed to be really good at being best friends, but incompatible as husband and wife.

When we arrived at the clinic, Phil laughed and cracked jokes about being at a nut house. I think this was his way of trying to make me smile, but all it did was make me feel worse. As I entered, I felt uncomfortable and wanted to leave; but the Lord moved me to stay and see what would come of this visit.

A gentleman called me back and asked Phil to stay in the waiting area. I do not recall his name, but I do remember that he had the rank of commander. He had a gentle, caring character, and was filled with compassion. He listened to me as I told him all the thoughts that went through my head when I walked, drove a car, sat in the bathtub, or looked out the window of a tall building. They all revolved around taking my life.

However, I never told him *why* I was feeling this way. I didn't want anyone to know that my husband was not a good man. I was protecting him even though he made me feel unwanted and unloved. What I did tell the commander is that I really wanted to live; and I just wanted all these bad thoughts to go away.

He listened with a gentle expression on his face. He told me that he wanted me to attend depression classes and work on techniques to help me to overcome my thoughts. He wanted me to start focusing on happy things that I loved, like my children. Then he suggested that I find a job and some purpose in my life.

I was grateful for the commander. He gave gentle, compassionate care to a woman in desperate need whom he didn't even know. He made me feel like my life mattered to those around me, especially my children.

His kind acts then remind me today of God and of how we are all special to Him. I know in my heart that God sent me to see that man. He was watching over me even when I felt like I was falling away from Him.

I attended the classes, where I was shown how to breathe deeply, relax my body, and think happy thoughts. I used these techniques often, and they helped me greatly over the next two years.

I also took the commander's advice and applied for a job as an associate at the military PX/BX Exchange (this is like a Kmart for retired and active soldiers and their families). I worked with German crystal and other collectibles like Precious Moments. When someone liked something, I unlocked the case for them to look at it. If they wanted to purchase it, I went to the warehouse cage, unlocked the secure area, and found the product they wished to buy. Then I accompanied them to the cashier.

Most of the items where I worked were very expensive, and the store did not want people walking out with merchandise without paying. You would think this would not be a problem, since these were men and women with families who were serving our country, but sadly it was and is a very big problem in our world. Just because it was a military base did not make people exempt from stealing. Still, despite their faults, I enjoyed my job, and I looked forward to working with the men and women of the military.

CHAPTER 39

Flood, Loss, New Job, and Church at Last

---•◦•---

We wound up moving back over to the other side of base. It was the same building we had been in before, except this time they would put us on the top floor, where there were six bedrooms. It was the only housing they had available that met our family's needs. The reason we would have to move was a sad one.

One day Phil and I took the children to see Breanne and her family in Landstuhl. Because it was a few hours' drive, we decided to spend the day there. We had a wonderful visit, then headed for home. On the way the children wondered how our dog was doing after being left at home alone all day.

Six months earlier, we had decided to get a puppy for the children. The children named him Gus Gus. He was a mixed breed; we believe he had Lab and Cocker Spaniel in him. Gus Gus was very smart. He could lock and open doors, and often broke out of his kennel.

Before we had gone to visit Breanne, we put him in the bathroom. That door swung in, and he had not figured out how to open it yet. First Nautasha and Ben used the bathroom, washing up their hands and faces with a washcloth, which they left in the sink, then we placed Gus Gus in the room and told him to be good. He loved to be with us, so he started to bark and whine. Phil said he would be okay, and we all left.

While we were gone, Gus Gus turned on the hot water in the sink. The spigots looked like door handles, just shorter. They were long, not round, so they were easy for him to pull with his paw.

The washcloth plugged up the sink, the water flowed onto the floor, and the bathroom became very hot (our hot water supply came from something almost like an on-demand heater). In the meantime, the water leaked down into our neighbor's apartment. They knew we were out of town, so they called housing, who sent someone over.

When we got home, the military police were just arriving. Phil ran up and opened the apartment. There was water everywhere. He ran to the bathroom door but could not open it. He and the officer picked the lock, but the door still would not open far enough. Our dog was lying in the way. They managed to push him out of the way far enough to get into the bathroom and turn off the water.

The officer figured that Gus Gus had tried to jump onto the toilet to get out through the window, then fell backwards and broke his neck. He wrote a report of what happened and asked what we would like to have done with our dog. One of the options was to let the vet cremate Gus Gus and spread his ashes in what they called the doggie graveyard. This was what we chose.

As they wrapped Gus Gus up in a blanket, I stood with tears flowing down my face. I didn't want the children to remember their dog looking this way, so our neighbors downstairs took them for a while. I thought this was sweet, considering that we had just flooded their apartment.

As the officer was getting ready to leave, Phil said the most horrible thing: "I bet you never had a case where a dog committed suicide. This will be a new one for you." Then he laughed.

I was irate. I started yelling at Phil, telling him that Gus Gus was a part of our family and that his words were mean and cruel. I expressed how happy I was that the children were downstairs and could not hear what he had just said. He just blew me off and laughed.

While we cleaned up the house, I did not want to talk to him at all. He realized this and kept apologizing for his comment.

The water damage was so great that the downstairs neighbors and our family both had to move to new places. And so we ended up back on the other side of the base.

The children loved it there. The hallway was long, so we got them a plastic bowling set. They played until one time the downstairs neighbor complained that it sounded like a herd of elephants running across the floor. The children were very upset that they could not bowl anymore, so we got them a dwarf bunny rabbit to play with instead. This also helped keep the peace with the neighbors.

With Nautasha in kindergarten and Ben walking her to school, I only had Tristin to worry about. I found a full-time babysitter and applied for a transfer to the stockroom for the PX/BX. I ended up getting the job and began to work thirty-four to thirty-six hours a week, sometimes forty … but never a steady forty (otherwise the store would have had to put me down as a full-time employee and give me benefits).

I believe the Lord put me in that position. I met a lot of new people while stocking; and I loved my job and did it well. Management saw this, and I was given work in other areas of the store when they were shorthanded.

One morning while I was stocking, I ran into a gentleman and his wife. I asked if they needed help finding something. We got to talking, and the conversation somehow turned to the topic of God and church.

They asked if I attended and what my beliefs were. I told them that I was a Seventh-day Adventist and that I was not currently attending any church, because I didn't know of one in the area. The gentleman smiled really big at me and told me they were also Seventh-day Adventists, and that he had some great news for me. I looked at him curiously.

"Do you know the Catholic church on Pioneer, just on the other side of base?" he asked.

I nodded. I knew where it was very well, because it was only a few blocks away from the apartment where poor Gus Gus had recently died.

"Well, every Sabbath we have services there, and we would love to have you and your family come and join us."

I stood there in disbelief. The whole time, I had been only a few blocks away from the church and hadn't even known about it? Then my confusion turned to excitement. "I would love to come and worship," I said.

They smiled and gave me a hug, then told me the times for Sabbath School and church services. My heart sang with joy after they left.

How in the world could I have lived so close without someone telling me there were Seventh-day Adventists who had services at the military chapel? I started to think that Phil had known all along and just didn't want me to go to church. I asked him about it after I got home, and he said, "I am not into the whole church thing. I had no idea that there was a service at the Catholic Church for Adventists on Saturday. For all I knew, it was a Catholic service. You know that they meet on Saturdays, too."

The answer he gave never sat well with me, but I blew it off. I was happy that the children and I could attend church again. Every Saturday we got up and went to the chapel.

Phil still worked every other Saturday, and sometimes more often if they were shorthanded. Because Germany has a winter season, Phil stored his motorcycle and used the car to get back and forth to work. However, this time it was no big deal when he took the car, because a tunnel went under the highway to the other side of the base: we could walk to church when we had to.

When the people I had met at the store found out that we were walking, they gave me their phone number and told me to call whenever we needed a ride. They had two small children of their own, so the gentleman would drop off his wife and kids at church, then come and pick up my children and me. God was working everything out for us. It was a great blessing.

CHAPTER 40

Another Vision

Phil was not that thrilled that we were back to attending church, and this started confrontations. The arguing got worse as the weeks and months passed, and he became more physically and verbally abusive. The couple who picked me up for church became concerned for me. I didn't tell them much about my life at home, but they somehow knew that something was wrong.

One Sabbath when I went to church, I had many bruises on my arms. The gentleman pulled me aside and asked me twice if my husband was abusing me. I assured him several times that the marks were from working in the warehouse and stockroom.

I don't think he believed me, but I was telling him the truth. Phil was smart: when we fought, he knew pressure points and how to hold me without leaving a mark on me. It is scary now, thinking back, how he could have really hurt me and no one would have known. I truly believe that the Lord was protecting me through all those trials which I was enduring. And still I did not give up on Phil being saved.

I talked to Chaplain Darroux and told him I would like to dedicate Tristin to the Lord. He was excited and encouraged me to dedicate all three of my children. Nautasha never had been, and Ben was older now and would understand more about what it meant. We worked out a Sabbath day for the dedication, then I went home and told Phil that I would love to have him there.

The morning arrived, and he got up and got ready to go to church. My heart swelled with great joy, and I praised God. I wanted my husband to accept Jesus into his heart, so I prayed that God would touch Phil's heart that day, and that he would start going to church with us on Sabbaths. This was a huge prayer, but I knew that God could answer it.

On April 15th of the year 2000, Chaplain Darroux dedicated all three of my children to the Lord in the Pioneer Military Catholic Chapel in Hanau, Germany, with my husband at my side and the presence of the Lord all around us. It was a day I will never forget.

Phil started coming to church with us from time to time. After a short while, though, he stopped altogether and started hanging out more with his friends at bars and motorcycle rallies. The people he spent time around were all about the pleasures of the world and having as much fun as they could.

My heart was breaking all over again. I had thought that things would change once he was going to church with us, but Satan pulled at my husband's heart, and Phil's desires had nothing to do with the Lord or His salvation. This escalated into yet more confrontations, and our children were really being affected.

Ben was becoming uncontrollable, acting out at school and at home. Nautasha was not too far behind him. She crawled under her desk one day at school and cut one side of her hair off (my little girl was a little princess; she had had the most beautiful long hair). And Ben would fight after school while his sister held his backpack.

I was becoming very stressed out. I didn't know what to do. I had no family here to talk to while things got worse. I could call someone, but with a time difference of eight to nine hours, it was hard to catch my family at home. If they were there, it was late and they were usually in bed.

I went to bed one night feeling lonely and far away from home. My husband was sitting in the bed reading. I didn't feel like arguing with him over turning off the lamp, so I closed my eyes and tried to go to sleep. That is when the Lord brought me a vision.

I was walking down a hallway in the stockroom at my workplace when I looked up and saw a bright circle of light. In it were angels, and the city of God was in the middle. God himself was standing in the center of the circle, calling me to come home.

I was in awe. I wanted to walk to the Lord, but I could not move because I was too scared. I knew I was a sinner and did not want to approach Him in my state of sin. Then I felt the presence of Jesus behind me.

He put His hand gently on my upper back and said in my ear, "God is calling for you to come home."

I looked back to the circle, and God had both his arms outstretched, waiting for me to come to Him.

"Go, Michelle! Walk with the Lord," Jesus kept urging me.

I saw that the path to the Lord was a narrow one, but as long as I kept my eyes on God it looked like it would be easy. I longed to go to God; I wanted to step forward.

Jesus urged me a third time to walk to the Father.

I hesitated, then as I looked up, darkness started to cover the circle of light. The presence of Jesus was no longer with me. The blackness came in from all sides of the circle until it had engulfed it. Now all I could feel was evil, stronger and stronger all around me, as I stood helplessly, watching the light of Heaven be taken away from me.

I took a deep breath and sat straight up in bed. My husband stared at me with wide eyes, his book still in his hands. I jumped out of the bed, ran into the living room, and sat in a chair. Phil was right behind me.

"What happened in there? You sucked in air like you were not breathing."

I looked up at him, wondering how to explain what I had just seen. I felt that there was no other way but to simply tell him what had happened the best that I could.

> I took a deep breath and sat straight up in bed. My husband stared at me with wide eyes, his book still in his hands.

When I was done, he looked at me with disbelief and went back to the bedroom to read. His brushing me off like I was a nutcase did not help me. I needed to understand what was happening and why I had had this dream vision.

Looking back now, I can connect the visions from my teen years and my mid-twenties. But at the time, I did not put them together. I had blocked out the time I spent in the hospital as a teen, and I did not receive a memory of it until the time when I wrote my testimony.

In the moment I got up, grabbed my phone, and called Chaplain Darroux. I told him the whole dream. He explained to me that the Lord had given me a vision. I asked him what I needed to do.

"Seek the Lord in prayer, and ask Him to reveal the dream to you. Seek Him with all your heart. Only God can reveal the answers to your questions."

After talking to him, I bowed my head in prayer and asked the Lord to reveal to me what this vision meant. He showed me that I was living a life of sin, even though I was attending church. I was not standing strong in His promises or commandments.

CHAPTER 41

The Fire

---⊃⊙⊂---

When the end of the week was upon us and the Sabbath was near, Phil would decide it was family time. We took the children to bars to eat, went shopping or to the movies, or attended motorcycle rallies for whole weekends. The rallies were very inappropriate for children (and anyone who was a follower of Christ), and I knew that doing these things was wrong. However, I saw that he was trying to do things together as a family, and that was a big step for him.

I had been praying for just that, so I thought that God must understand and was answering my prayers. However, I was deceived; I was still trying to please my husband and God at the same time.

I did not put my full trust in God to make a way of escape. I did not watch Him work in our marriage and lives, because I was too busy trying to win over my husband. I eventually realized that I could not serve God and try and win my husband's heart. I would have to "choose this day" whom I would serve. So I decided to take a stand and stay strong in the Lord.

When I did this, my marriage went downhill fast. It spun completely out of control, and the children acted out even more than before. I hadn't thought that it was possible for things to get worse. My heart was heavy with all that was happening.

One afternoon the military police came to the door to ask where our son Ben was. An officer explained that our son and his friend, while experimenting with smoking, had started a fire on the pallets behind the apartment complex next to us.

Because someone had previously spilled oil or gas on the pallets, they had lit up very quickly. If a neighbor had not seen the fire, the whole apartment complex would have gone up in flames in minutes. The neighbor had called the emergency hotline and explained the situation very quickly, then he ran into the building and banged on every door to get people to evacuate.

By the time the fire department came, the backside of the building had in fact caught fire. But luckily, the firefighters managed to get it under control and saved the apartments. Still, there was a lot of smoke damage, both to the outside and the inside of the building.

> I stood and faced the officer with a look of disbelief. My son wouldn't do such a thing ... would he?

I stood and faced the officer with a look of disbelief. *My son wouldn't do such a thing ... would he?* My thoughts raced, and I became very worried about Ben. I remembered that he had come home and gone right to his room. I hadn't thought much of it, because everything in our family was a big, emotional mess. I called Ben out, and the police officer talked to him.

Phil was very angry and blew up at Ben after the police left. His face was red and the tone of his voice was threatening. "What were you thinking?" he said, "Do you realize this is going to affect my job? Pull your head out of your backside, and do what is right. If I get in trouble for your mess-up, and we have to leave Germany, you will feel the consequences."

I sent Ben to his room so I could talk to my husband. That conversation didn't go very well. He wanted to beat the life out of Ben. He kept telling me, "I had to fight to get stationed back in Germany, and I will be darned if that kid is going to ruin it for me!"

I asked him if he cared about this family and our children at all. That made him even angrier, and the argument was on. Very nasty words were said by both of us that day.

I told him, "I want a divorce. I can't live like this anymore. You are rude and inconsiderate to all of us. All you care about is going out with your friends and sitting on the computer. We are not a family to you; this is just a place to live. All we are doing here is helping you to live in an apartment and not in the barracks. I just want to go home."

This sent him over the edge, and he lashed out at me with very hurtful words that I cannot repeat. He called me some very ungodly names and then attacked the Lord with cruel and hateful speech.

I was not shocked at his choice of vocabulary. He used words like this all the time (and then yelled at the children when they used them). I used to tell him, "You can't say those kinds of words and expect the children not to say them later. If it is not okay for the children to speak them, then they should not be okay for you to use in front of them." He would state, "They need to do as I say, not as I do!"

I was in a battle that was never-ending.

CHAPTER 42

Flight Back to the United States

---◦◦◦---

When Phil got home from work the next day, he was very mad. He said, "Well, you got your wish. I had to make a choice in front of my commander today, and I am sending you and the kids back to the States. I am going to stay and finish my tour here in Germany.

"I will call my mom and dad in a little while to see if they will pick you up from the airport and let you stay with them. I will ship the car and all of the household goods back, too. I found a Camaro that I like and will be getting that for when I can no longer ride my motorcycle." Phil then walked into the other room and stayed on the computer until he went to bed.

> *How could this be happening? What had happened to my dream?*

He had stated all this like he was satisfied with what he had chosen to do. He was so self-involved that he could not see how he was hurting his own family.

We really didn't mean that much to him. My heart was breaking all over again. How could this be happening? What had happened to my dream of a big, white house, with a big yard, and a beautiful, white picket fence? The problem was that it was only a dream; one which many of us have. In reality, I was never going to have that in this marriage.

As the days went by, Phil and I got all of the paperwork and arrangements figured out for the trip back home. Tristin was a little over a year old now. I already knew how hard it was to fly with children, luggage, and our cat. I realized that I could not take all three kids as well as the cat this time; it would be way too much.

Phil started to soften toward me in this area, and we worked things out so that I could get everyone home safely. Phil was going to keep the cat for a while, and once he had the money, he would fly her home. All I would have to do would be to pick her up from the airport.

As Phil softened, my heart did as well. I told him that I was sorry for the harsh words I had stated. But it was too late, now; he had already chosen to send us home.

I found out that he had had other choices with his commander, but he was just tired of fighting with me, and the children were getting on his nerves. The only thing he regretted about his decision was not being with Tristin to watch him grow up.

I realized all of this, but I just didn't want to stop loving him. I kept wanting him to change and love me. I continued to struggle with this emotionally. I had a hard time leaving it up to God and trusting Him to get me through this.

The day of departure, we arrived at the airport and checked in our luggage. Phil hugged Nautasha and Ben goodbye and told them to be good. He then took and hugged Tristin. With tears in his eyes, he said goodbye to his son. Lastly, he half-heartedly hugged me, gave me a quick kiss goodbye, and walked away. He didn't stay at the airport with us because he was not allowed to go into the secured area we were entering to catch our flight.

As I sat in the waiting area and waited for our flight to board, tears rolled down my cheeks again. I felt the pain of separation; it was like someone had cut half of my heart out.

I was holding Tristin at the time, and he looked at me with sad eyes. Nautasha said, "Don't cry, Mommy. We will be okay. I will miss Daddy, too, but I promise to try and be a good girl for you." She then wiped the tears off of my cheeks with her little hand.

Ben sat there with a sad expression on his face. I knew that he felt bad because of what he had done; but he could not fix this any more than I could. My heart broke for this young man. I knew he was suffering emotionally, but I would not find out how badly until later in his life.

The flight attendant called over the loudspeaker, "All passengers going to New York, please have your boarding passes ready and approach the gate."

I pulled ours out, grabbed the children, and said a quick prayer with them before we boarded. I told Ben that I needed him to be a big boy again, this time to help his sister with her suitcase. Ben grabbed his carry-on by the handle and held Nautasha with his other hand, while she grabbed the handle of her own bag. As they smiled at one another, I knew that they loved each other even if they fought from time to time. Nautasha grabbed my shirt with her free hand and held on tightly to me as we walked to the gate.

The flight back to the United States was a long one. When we arrived at Jefferson Airport in New York, I had to reclaim all of our baggage, haul it to the other side of the airport, and check it all back in, then catch our flight to Detroit Metro, which would leave in an hour and a half. This time we had twelve suitcases, including the carry-ons, to haul across the airport. On top of that, I now had Tristin and his car seat. I had thought it was hard the first time, but this was close to impossible. I knew for certain that God was helping me get through it, as we managed to get everything checked in and onto our next flight with ten minutes to spare.

We had a long layover in Detroit. I was grateful that this part of the trip was over, but the children were getting hungry and cranky. They argued about everything either one of them said. I finally got tired of it. I had to yell at them both to sit down and wait for our next flight, which was headed to Pellston Airport.

I decided to buy them a snack to hold them over till we got on the plane. That seemed to help for a while, but once we boarded, Ben and Nautasha started yelling at each other again and calling one other names. Ben did not have a very good attitude, and I was not willing to deal with it at that moment. I had to intervene again, telling them that they were both going to be grounded if they didn't stop. Tristin, however, was a very good boy for most of the trip. He only got cranky and cried when he got overly tired and needed to sleep.

I had never been happier to see my smiling father-in-law's face than I was when we arrived at the airport in Pellston. Oh, how I had missed him and Phil's mother! They were good to us, even when I had a selfish attitude. I hugged them both. The children were excited, too; they came running and hugged their grandma and grandpa.

It was an hour and a half drive back to their house. This gave us time to tell them all about Germany and the things that we had done there. I was happy to be home on American soil.

CHAPTER 43
The Power Struggle

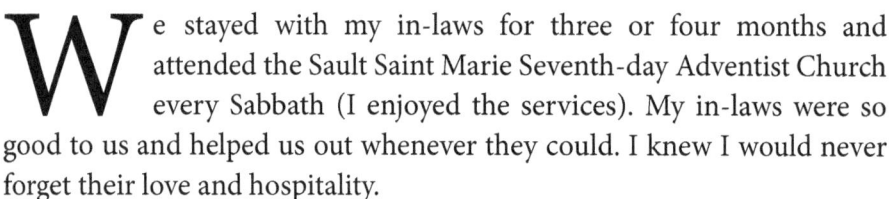

We stayed with my in-laws for three or four months and attended the Sault Saint Marie Seventh-day Adventist Church every Sabbath (I enjoyed the services). My in-laws were so good to us and helped us out whenever they could. I knew I would never forget their love and hospitality.

Still, living in their house for that long was hard on all of us. We loved them very much, but I knew it was time to move on, so I decided to move closer to my own family.

I found a job in Gladstone working at an adult assisted living home and moved to Escanaba, where I rented an apartment on the corner of North Tenth Street and First Avenue. It was a nice, little three-bedroom, and we enjoyed living there.

Our belongings arrived in the States, and they were brought right to our new apartment. The car had already come while I was staying with Phil's parents, so my brother-in-law took me to Illinois to pick it up (prior to our car arriving, I had been using my father-in-law's truck and my mother-in-law's car to get around).

I couldn't wait to attend church and see Carol and Joe. I hadn't seen them in many years, and my eagerness to hug them both was overwhelming. My first day back was such a blessing. I enjoyed the services and met some new people. Ben stayed close to Carol and Joe for most of the time that we were there. I could tell that he missed them, and they missed "their boy" (every time I saw Carol, she would ask me, "How is my Ben?"). It was so comforting to see the love she had for my son, and to know he would always see Jesus through her and Joe.

I enrolled Ben in the Seventh-day Adventist school and bought him school supplies and a new backpack. I wanted him to have a Christian education. Because the school started at first grade, I decided to home-school Nautasha, since she had been held back and needed to repeat kindergarten.

I became fast friends with a woman name Tonya, whom I had known since Ben was a baby. I had first met her at the Riverside Seventh-day Adventist Church in Rapid River. I didn't talk much to her then, but she remembered Ben and I well. She, too, was home-schooling her daughter, so when I started working fulltime at the adult foster care home, Tonya offered to watch Tristin and Nautasha and helped home-school Nautasha. This was a blessing to me.

Tonya guided me in my walk with Jesus and helped me to see that there was so much more to knowing and loving the Lord than what I had already learned. She brought me deep into the Scriptures and was like a mentor during this new journey in my life.

Her friendship was God-given and just what I needed at that time, because Ben was struggling with things that I had no understanding of. He was getting into trouble at school; they even suspended him once. I had to go before the board at church and present my case, explaining how much I wanted Ben to stay in their school. They reluctantly granted my request.

Then I realized that he hadn't started acting out until Phil had flown home for a two-week visit over the Christmas holiday. I was always trying to mend their relationship, but to no avail. Ben hated Phil and had stated it on several occasions.

While Phil was home, there had been a power struggle between the two. You see, Ben had become the man of the house while Phil was gone; he helped me out with many things. But when Phil came, that all changed, as he would yell at Ben for doing things that I let him do.

It got so bad one night that Phil made Ben go to his room. Once there, Ben locked his door, opened the window, and popped out the screen. Then he grabbed his winter coat, jumped out, and ran away.

After half an hour, Phil went to Ben's door to let him out. When he realized that it was locked, he became angry and threatened to break down the door if Ben didn't open it; but there was no response to his threats.

"I'll fix him," Phil stated, as he went to get tools. When he came back, he yelled, "When I get this door open, you're getting your backside whooped good. Do you hear me? This is not a game, and you will pay for your actions."

Once Phil got the door unlocked, he swung it open so hard that it hit Ben's dresser on the other side. Then he stormed into the room. "Come out from hiding now. If I have to find you, you're going to get whooped worse."

I tried to calm Phil down, but he wasn't listening. I finally had to yell at him, "If you would have listened to me earlier, none of this would have happened. You can't treat Ben like that. He needs you to be there for him."

He was so angry that he started yelling at me. "You know what your problem is? You baby him way too much. He just needs his backside tanned."

The first few days that Phil was home had been wonderful. We had been like the family I prayed for, but it hadn't lasted long. It was getting to the point where I could not wait for him to get back on the plane to Germany.

I looked over at the window and saw that it was cracked, then I saw that the screen had slid down by the end of his bed. I ran and opened the window while Phil kept yelling and making threats that Ben had better come out of hiding.

I saw my son's footprints on the ground outside. By this time Phil saw what I was doing and came over to the window. He called Ben a bad name, then said, "He ran away. Great! Now we have to call the police. Just great! This is not how I want to spend my vacation time at home. Why does he have to ruin things?"

I was worried about my son out in the city on a cold night, but all Phil could think about was how Ben had ruined his night. I turned around and told him, "I can't wait for you to leave. I would take you to the airport tonight if I knew they would fly you back to Germany."

I left him standing there and walked over to the phone to call the police station. They came to my apartment and got a picture of Ben and a description of what he was wearing.

Phil closed and locked the window after the officer left. He said, "He is not coming back in the house through his window. He wants to be a man? Then let him walk through the front door."

The police returned about forty-five minutes later with Ben. The officer stated that he had had a talk with my son on the drive home. Then he questioned Phil about what Ben had told him regarding Phil's abusive actions toward my son.

Phil told the officer that Ben liked to tell lies to get him into trouble. I could tell that the officer did not believe him. However, there were no outward signs of abuse on my son, so the officer had no grounds to remove my children from the home. He finished taking Phil's statement, then said goodbye.

As he was walking out the door, the officer rubbed Ben's head and said, "Goodbye, buddy. Be good. You know what you need to do."

I sent Ben to get ready for bed and told him I would be in to talk to him in a little while. I told Phil that I would handle this and that he needed to stay out of it. Phil got angry again. He went into the living room and turned on the television.

I talked with Ben, then prayed with him and tucked him into bed. Phil left the next week, and things went back to normal.

I knew my son was hurting, but I was still trying to save a marriage by myself instead of letting God lead my actions and thoughts. I was in love with Phil, but he often broke my heart. I missed him a lot while he was gone, but once he came home, I couldn't wait for him to leave. It was like I could not live without him, yet he made my and the children's lives miserable.

All I really wanted was to be loved, but I was looking for it in the wrong places. To be loved the way I wanted, I first needed to know God's love. Then I would understand true and unconditional love:

> *All I really wanted was to be loved, but I was looking for it in the wrong places.*

> Love suffers long and is kind; love does not envy; love does not parade itself, is not puffed up; does not behave rudely, does not seek its own, is not provoked, thinks no evil; does not rejoice in iniquity,

but rejoices in the truth; bears all things, believes all things, hopes all things, endures all things. Love never fails. (1 Cor. 13:4-8a)

God loves us so much that He gave His Son to be a sacrifice so that we could live in Heaven with Him one day. I cannot help but marvel at such a selfless act of love for a world that is so deeply embedded in sin.

CHAPTER 44

Charley

I enjoyed living in Escanaba and working with the elderly, but my heart still longed to be near to my family.

My family laughed and had a lot of fun together. In particular, the holidays had always been my favorite time to be with them. Our family was so big that it was like having a party rather than a holiday meal.

My grandmother would host the dinners at her house. She always put three long tables from the kitchen in the living room so that there would be room for all of us to sit. My mother and all of my aunts helped my grandmother cook the best meals. Then they made the most delicious desserts to follow. They put a lot of hard work into our family meals, and we all loved them.

When we were done eating, my uncles and cousins would go outside to play, while my grandmother, mother, and aunts would clean up the kitchen. Once they were done, they all would come and join us outside. I remember one year when my uncles had a few old car hoods; we used them to sled down the hill in the yard. That was a day I will hold dear in my heart.

Those were the days I now longed for, but even though I lived closer, I didn't get out to see them much. And meanwhile our holiday gatherings had started to fade away, as my aunts and uncles moved away with their families and my grandmother got older.

My thoughts shifted to my mother. I was really missing her. Even though we had had a rough time when I was growing up and a hard time living together as adults, I still loved her dearly.

Uncle Dale, who lived in Trenary, said that the children and I could move in with him if I wanted to come back home. He had just gone through a bad divorce and was living alone in a four-bedroom house. He said that I would have to pay half of the rent.

I agreed and applied for a job at the Trenary Home Bakery. My mother's friend still owned the bakery, but the son and his wife were now running it.

I had gone to school with the son and was excited to see him. My friend hired me, and I told him I could start at the end of the month. I needed to put in my two-week notice at my job in Gladstone; by then Ben would also be done with school, so it would be easier to move.

The lady I worked for in the assisted living home hated to see me leave. I was really good with the people there; she told me I would be hard to replace. Even after I moved to Trenary, she asked me to work part-time in the evenings until she could get someone to fill my role. She had a hard time finding someone who cared about the disabled adults; a person who would love them and had a kind heart.

I had never realized how much people watch what you do when you are around them (or working with them). Her kind words made me feel good. Still, I knew that all the love I gave came from God, and that all the glory for who I was as a person should go to Him, not me.

I loved being with all of the tenants at that adult foster care home, but there was one time while I worked there that I will always hold dear in my heart. I want to share this special part of my life with you.

When my work shift was over, I would go to the end of the hall and pull up a chair to visit with my friend Charley. He was in his late seventies and had a cancerous tumor growing all around his heart. The tumor was so big that it stood out three inches from his chest. But what Charley looked like never bothered me. He became my friend, and I grew to love him as if he were a member of my own family.

He loved the Lord, and we prayed together quite often. He also loved to read, but his eyes were so bad that he could not enjoy books any more.

One day, Charley was telling me how he longed to read again. That is when I offered to stay a half hour after every one of my shifts to read to him.

The Lord prompted me to read to him *The Marked Bible*, by Charles Taylor. As I started, Charley's eyes lit up. He lay on his bed in the small room with the light of the sun shining on his body through the window.

I began with one of the poems in the beginning of the book. It spoke of God's truth and Jesus' abiding faithfulness, since He always walks with us. Charley's eyes filled with tears as he lay there looking up at me. I read on, and he listened intently.

Whenever I finished a chapter, he asked me if I was going to read to him again the next day. I would smile and tell him, "Of course." If it was my day off, I would ask my friend Tonya to watch my children, and I would drive over to my workplace just to read to Charley.

It was while I read *The Marked Bible* to him that he expressed his love for God and how he longed to have a relationship with Him.

I never realized how much of a difference I had made in Charley's life until later. After I left, he was sad and asked for me a lot. Ten days after I left, his health went downhill and he had to be put into the hospital. A week later my friend went to sleep to await the coming of our Lord.

I truly believe that God prepared Charley to go home. I could only pray that God had moved his heart, and that one day I would walk in Heaven with my friend.

"And whoever compels you to go one mile, go with him two" (Matt. 5:41). Even though I did not have to be at work during those visits, walking that extra mile could be what made the difference in Charley's salvation.

CHAPTER 45
Trenary: Home Again

---◦---

I told my husband that I was moving to Trenary to live near my family until he was stationed back in the United States. I also told him that I had found a job there which would be able to pay for the children and my living expenses (the military paid him extra because his family was stateside, but Phil was not good with money; he often spent impulsively, which made it hard to pay off the bills and loans that we had incurred).

I packed up all my belongings, and Uncle Kent and Uncle Dale helped me move. We stored most of my things on the porch at Uncle Dale's. Some smaller items were kept at my grandmother's and Uncle Kent's houses. My cat Annabell needed a place to stay (Phil had flown her back while I was still in Escanaba) because Uncle Dale's landlord did not allow pets; Uncle Dean took her. He was still living with my grandmother at the time, so Annabell stayed in his room and slept with him.

Now he had our dog Sheba as well as my cat. I would go over to their house just so that the children and I could see them. Annabell would meow and purr around our legs and feet. She really did miss us; she had been a wonderful friend and companion. Sheba would howl until we pet her. Ben and Nautasha took her for walks. On those visits it was nice to be back in the country for a little while.

I worked at the bakery Monday through Friday and had the weekends off. I had to be to work every morning at 5:00 a.m. and sometimes earlier, depending on what orders for bread and toast we had going out that week. The nice part about going in so early was that I got off between 12:00 and 2:00 p.m.; I could spend the rest of the day with my children.

While I was at work, Uncle Dean (you'll remember that he was Dale's twin) would come over and watch the children. It was the funniest thing when Tristin would come out of the bedroom, half asleep, and say, "Good morning, Uncle Dale."

Uncle Dean would laugh and say, "I am Dean, buddy."

Usually Uncle Dale would already be at work, but one morning he had the day off. That day when Tristin said to him, "Good morning, Uncle Dean," he then saw the real Uncle Dean walking in the door. Tristin became confused, looking back and forth from one to the other, while Uncle Dale laughed. To this day they still tell Tristin this story, even though now he can now tell them apart.

CHAPTER 46

Marriage Troubles

I started attending the Adventist Church in Rapid River regularly shortly after I moved to Trenary. This was the same church where I'd met Tonya. I loved it there, and I was intrigued by Pastor Wise's seminars on Daniel and Revelation.

I became very interested in learning and following the Word of God. I talked with the pastor and told him that I wanted to be rebaptized because I had fallen away. He talked with me about this commitment and offered to do Bible studies with me again. I agreed and looked forward to them every week. Pastor Wise helped me to understand the Word of God and to draw nearer to the Lord. I was excited as I learned more about the promises of God and how much He truly loved me.

I came to miss my husband. I longed to have him there with us. He was missing out on so much with the children as they grew; especially Tristin, who was still little and learning new things every day. I began to call Phil daily and talk to him for ten to twenty minutes at a time, telling him all about the children and the Bible studies I was doing with Pastor Wise. Because Uncle Dale did not have a home phone, and all I had was a cell phone, I got a few prepaid cards and used the pay phone across the street from my uncle's house, just outside the gas station.

I would walk over, rain or shine, and call Phil. However, after a few weeks, he was not as excited to hear from me as I was to hear his voice. Some days he would talk to me; on others he would get mad at me for calling him.

He would tell me, "You are interrupting my time with my friends. I am just heading out the door to go out." Or else he'd say he was the middle of watching a movie with people and couldn't talk.

I would get angry and hurt. He was thousands of miles away and yet was still treating me as if I was in his way all the time. How come he didn't miss me the way that I missed him? I was his wife; his love for me should have been great, even overwhelming, while we were separated by so many miles. I began once more to feel depressed, worthless, and very unloved.

Still, I was going to call him even if he didn't want to talk to me. The least that I could do was to show Phil how much I loved him.

I got home from work one day and was excited to speak with him. Tristin had grown so much, and I just couldn't wait to share with him the things that Tristin was doing. I ran over to the pay phone.

When Phil answered, he told me that he couldn't talk. I told him that I had something exciting to share with him.

"Can't it wait till another time?" he said. "I am busy." Then I heard a child in the background, and a woman talking to the child.

I asked who was in his room with him. He named a girl and her baby, and said that they had been spending time together and he had been helping her out. I asked him who else was there.

Phil got angry and said, "Does it matter if she is the only one here?" This started an argument on the phone, and he hung up on me.

I was grateful that Uncle Dean had decided to take the children to see their great grandma Alice that day. I walked back across the street, sat in the living room, and cried. I knew in my heart that Phil was cheating on me again. The pain I felt was so intense that I didn't want to live anymore; not like this.

I got on my knees and prayed for the Lord's guidance and for peace to come into my heart in this time of such darkness and sorrow. I felt a calm come over me. I got up and went to get my children.

On the way there, though, I let Satan in. I decided that I was not going to get depressed anymore; I was going to get even. I would stop calling Phil, and if he called me, I would not talk to him. I was going to treat him like he had been treating me.

After a week, Phil started to call my grandmother's house to see what was going. I told her I had no desire to talk to him. She asked what was going on, so I broke down and had a talk with her. She advised me that this was not a good relationship; that I needed to consider what I should do and then do so wisely.

After having no success calling my grandmother, Phil got the number for my workplace and started calling me there. My supervisor was not pleased: I would not take Phil's calls, and he was tying up the business line.

I had to address it, so one day I answered and told him to stop calling me at work.

"What is wrong?" he asked. "I haven't heard from you in over a week."

I wanted to reach through the phone and shake him into reality. "This is not the time to talk about this. I am at work. I will call you afterward, if you have 'time' to talk to me."

Phil heard the tone of my voice. He asked what time I would be calling and said he would make himself available.

I hung up feeling very angry at him. I didn't want anything to do with him. Once more I wanted to get a divorce.

When I called him later that day and told him how he made me feel, all his apologies spilled out. He exclaimed that his tour was almost up in Germany and that he was going to make it all up to me. I got off the phone feeling happy. I felt like he was making steps to change. I was content once again and prayed for us to be a family again.

Phil called me at work a few times the following week to let me know that he was going to be stationed in Fort Polk, Louisiana. He was excited because Sam, a friend of his whom we had met at the biker rallies in Germany, was stationed there. Sam and Phil had spent much time together, and it was Sam who had talked him into requesting orders to be stationed at Fort Polk.

When he told me the news that he was moving back to the United States and we were going to be a family again, I told him I had some good news as well. "I have asked Pastor Wise to rebaptize me. We are setting up a date, and I would love to have it done while you are here."

All he could say was, "Oh! What brought this on?"

He didn't understand the meaning of baptism or why I wanted to do it again. I knew that if I tried to explain, he would change the subject. All I could do for now was pray that he would come to my baptism and that God would touch his heart.

When Phil finally made it home from Germany, he was anxious to move on to Louisiana as soon as possible. I told him that we could not leave until after Sabbath because that was the day when I was being rebaptized. I repeated that I would love for him to be there to support me in my decision.

Pastor Wise had planned for it to occur in the evening, starting at the church and then moving down to the river. I was excited to give my heart to the Lord again and to have all my sins washed away. I felt Him calling me to walk in the ways of righteousness. I wanted to learn more from His Scriptures about how to be a disciple for Jesus.

That Sabbath morning, the children and I went to church and worshiped with our brothers and sisters in Christ. When we got home, my husband wanted to go to Escanaba to shop and go out to eat.

I told him that God did not want us to work on the Sabbath or make others work. We got into a huge argument over this. He got angry, put his foot down, and told me, "We are going." I reluctantly got into the car.

When we got to town, I sat in the car while Phil went into the store. I made the children stay with me even though he wanted us all to go in. When he came out, he was upset with me and tried to smooth the whole argument over. "I don't understand why you can't shop," he said. "I think it is wrong for us not to be able to have family time. I don't think God would take that away from us.

"Well," he continued, "it is over and done with. At least let me take you all out to lunch so that we can celebrate your baptism."

I looked over at him. "Phil, it is the Sabbath. We can't make someone cook for us."

This led to another argument, but in the end I went to Pizza Hut with him. The children were excited and could not wait to get their food. However, I was worried, because I knew that they would think it was okay to shop and eat out on the Sabbath.

I sat in the restaurant wanting to leave the whole time. I felt the Lord impressing upon my heart that this was wrong.

The waitress came over and took our order. Phil ordered a pepperoni pizza. I looked at him after the waitress walked away and asked, "Isn't there pork in the pepperoni? My grandmother said it is all beef, but I thought there was pork in it."

He said, "I don't know. I think it is all beef."

I had stopped eating pork after reading in Leviticus:

> Now the Lord spoke to Moses and Aaron, saying to them, "Speak to the children of Israel, saying, 'these are the animals which you may eat among all the animals that are on the earth: among the animals, whatever divides the hoof, having cloven hooves and chewing the cud—that you may eat. Nevertheless these you shall not eat among those that chew the cud or those that have cloven hooves: … the swine, though it divides the hoof, having cloven hooves, yet does not chew the cud, is unclean to you." (Lev. 11:1-4a, 7)

I kept looking at the door, and my heart was not at ease when the waitress brought out our pizza. I just felt unsettled about the pepperoni. My husband saw my anxiety and reassured me that there was no pork. I finally gave in and ate. I was overjoyed when we left and headed for home.

An hour later while preparing for my baptism, my stomach started to hurt. I prayed that God would take it away. I got in the car with my family and we headed for church. When we got there, I had to run to the bathroom.

My stomach hurt so badly that I could not leave the bathroom. My baptism was getting ready to start. Finally I prayed. "Lord, please forgive me for any wrong I have done. Help me to feel better. If anyone can take this pain away, it is You. If anyone can heal me, it is You. In Jesus' name I pray this, amen."

A few minutes later, I was in my robe in the sanctuary. My stomach did not feel the greatest, but it was better.

I realized that it must have been the pepperoni I ate. I found out later that pepperoni does have pork in it. I had not eaten pork in a long time, so it had had an effect on my body that was not very pleasant.

The pastor said a prayer, then called me up to the platform. We went over the twenty-seven Fundamental Beliefs and "My Commitment in Baptism" questions. Then it was time for me to give a short testimony.

Aunt Lu was in the pew smiling up at me. How I loved this woman with all my heart. I knew that she was the reason why I had given my heart to the Lord, and this was my opportunity to share that with her. By the time I got done thanking her for never giving up on me and for how she made me feel loved by God (and her) when everyone else judged me and gave up, we were both in tears.

> *Aunt Lu was in the pew smiling up at me. How I loved this woman with all my heart.*

I knew that day meant a lot to the both of us. Aunt Lu's health was failing, and she just didn't have the strength she used to. Cancer had taken over her colon. I had seen firsthand her loss of energy and how the illness was consuming her. She was fighting a battle that soon would bring her to a restful sleep to await the coming of our Lord and Savior Jesus Christ.

Not long before then, I had wanted to do something nice for Phil, so I had asked Aunt Lu if she would help me make a quilt for him. She had agreed, so I went to her house for a few days to work on the quilt.

I wanted to do a solid piece with wolves and owls on it. It was going to be a reversible quilt. This made it easy, and it only took a few days to make. On the first day, we cut the batting, put it into place, and pinned it together. Then we went to her sun porch, put the quilt in her homemade frame, and tightened it down to prevent it from moving.

As we strung the yarn through the quilt to secure the batting to the material, I noticed that Aunt Lu had only put a few in place. She looked over to me with a big smile and said, "I need to rest for a while. I will sit and watch how you do it."

I smiled back at her, but in my heart, I was worried for my dear Aunt Lu. I didn't want her to leave me.

That was the last time that we would spend together working and sharing the love of Jesus through prayer and conversation about the Bible. At my baptism, I knew that her health was not good, but I never imagined that it would be the final time I would see her.

After I gave my testimony, I looked over at my family and then at my husband. I was surprised to see tears in his eyes. It gave me great hope that God was working on his heart. Pastor Wise redirected my attention when he told everyone that we were going down by the river.

I followed him down the trail to where I would recommit my life to the Lord. Even Aunt Lu made the walk down the narrow path to the edge of the river to watch me. She was up front with my mother, hugging her. It made my heart overflow with a joy I cannot describe.

Pastor Wise and I walked into the water. He first said a few words of encouragement to the people on shore: "If you wish to give your hearts to the Lord and are interested in having a personal relationship with your Father in Heaven, and if you want to make a commitment in baptism, please see me afterward." Then he put his hand up in the air and said, "I baptize you in the name of the Father, the Son, and the Holy Spirit."

He plunged me beneath the waters of forgiveness. As he raised me up and hugged me, he said a prayer. As we started back onto the shore, I heard a song and tears filled my eyes:

Shall we gather at the river,

Where bright angel feet have trod;

With its crystal tide forever

Flowing by the throne of God?

Yes, we'll gather at the river,

The beautiful, the beautiful river;

Gather with the saints at the river

That flows by the throne of God.

(Lowry, "Shall We Gather at the River?")

It was a day of great rejoicing on the shore near our little church. I prayed that it would touch the heart of my husband so that he would long to have a deeper relationship with his Father in Heaven.

CHAPTER 47

Fort Polk: Sam's House

―――⋙◉⋘―――

We were packed up and heading out to Fort Polk. The goal was for Phil to be there on time to sign in for duty. Phil called Sam and asked about places to live, and Sam opened up his home to us. He had a three-bedroom house and said we were welcome there until housing became available on post. Phil was happy.

Since we had no place of our own to stay, I was curious why Phil wanted us to go with him before he was approved for housing. I only found out later that he had talked to my grandmother, and that she had told him I was not happy with him and wanted a divorce. She had also told him that she supported me if I wanted to file.

He was not in control of my decisions when we were apart, and that made him nervous. He knew that if I was with him, he could persuade me to do what he wanted. It was such a toxic relationship, but I was blind to all of it. All I wanted was for my husband to love me with all his heart and only have eyes for me.

The ride from Michigan to Louisiana was a long and hot one, as it was the beginning of August and very hot and humid. I drove the car with no air-conditioning, while Phil drove the U-Haul truck, which did have AC.

I told him several times as we approached the warmer states that it was too hot to drive without air-conditioning, especially because I had Nautasha and Annabell with me. My poor cat was laying on the floor of the car, panting uncontrollably.

He was getting irritated because I kept mentioning the heat and saying that driving with the windows down offered very little relief. He offered to take the cat in the U-Haul truck with him, thinking that this would stop me from complaining. I wished he could see how miserable we were feeling or experience it for himself.

Finally, when we hit Arkansas, I refused to go any further until he fixed the air-conditioner. He called a dealership and explained the problem. They got us in right away. Back on the road with cool air, I was a happy wife and mother.

After arriving in Leesville, Louisiana, the children and I could not wait to relax and get a good night's sleep. We walked into Sam's house, and he was happy to see that we had made it safely. He took us through the house and showed where we would be sleeping. Tasha was going to bunk in the hallway on a cot, while Tristin would sleep with Phil and I in the bedroom across the hall from Sam. But when Sam opened the door to the other bedroom, where he told us our son Ben would be sleeping, my heart stopped.

> "This is my shrine, where I worship the gods," Sam said, "but your son can stay in here."

"This is my shrine, where I worship the gods," Sam said, "but your son can stay in here as long as he doesn't touch any of my spiritual belongings."

I asked, "What religion are you?"

"I am Wiccan," he said. "I believe in nature and the gods that created it." He then bragged about the spells which he cast on people when they made him mad.

I asked if Ben could sleep in the living room; then Sam wouldn't have to worry about his things.

Sam said that this was not a good idea because he often stayed up late and got up early for work; the boy wouldn't get much sleep. He was very adamant that Ben sleep in the bedroom and that he trusted Ben not to touch his things.

I stood looking into that room after they walked away. What was I going to do? How was my son going to sleep here at night with all this evil surrounding him? I could hear Phil and Sam talking in the living room with the children. I was moved to pray right there. "Dear Father God in Heaven," I said, "please keep my son safe from the evil that will surround him in this room. Send your legions of angels to protect him and fill this room with your Holy Spirit, that no evil may come near my son. In Jesus' name, I pray this. Amen!"

Every day I walked into that room and prayed over it. Every night, as I tucked my son into bed, I prayed over it again. Sometimes, in the middle of the night, I walked into the room while Ben was sleeping and prayed over my child a third time.

I had to protect my child, and the only way I knew how to do this was by giving Ben to God and asking Him to protect him. I did not have power over the spirits and the fallen angel, but I knew that Jesus did, through the Father:

> Then the seventy returned with joy, saying "Lord, even the demons are subject to us in Your name." And He said to them, "I saw Satan fall like lighting from heaven. Behold, I give you the authority to trample on serpents and scorpions, and over all the power of the enemy, and nothing shall by any means hurt you. Nevertheless do not rejoice in this, that the spirits are subject to you, but rather rejoice because your names are written in heaven." (Luke 10:17-20)

One evening Phil and I were out late, taking care of some business to help us get ready for when housing became available. Sam watched the kids that evening. I was not really comfortable with that at all, but Phil had insisted that they would be fine. By the time we got back, the children were sleeping and Sam was in the living room. I told Phil and Sam that I wanted to check on them.

Phil said, "They are fine. Come and relax in the living room with Sam and me. We can watch a movie." Phil pulled me by the arm and sat me next to him on the sofa.

I was not happy. I just wanted to pray over my son, but Phil and Sam kept engaging me in conversation. After a while they preoccupied my thoughts with Army life and what we were going to do for fun that weekend.

I dozed off on the sofa, and Phil woke me up to go to bed. Half-asleep, I stumbled to the bedroom, climbed into bed, and fell back asleep.

I woke up the next morning feeling refreshed. Tristin and I walked out into the living room. Phil and Sam had left for work, and the children were watching television.

"How come you didn't wake me up?" I asked them.

"We just got up a little bit ago, Mommy," was Nautasha's response.

Ben didn't look rested. His poor little eyes were bloodshot. I asked him if he was okay.

He stumbled over his words. "I-I-I-I saw something last night." With tears in his eyes, he described the most evil demon, who had threatened to do him bodily harm. Ben told me he had prayed but it just would not go away: even as he prayed, the demon threatened to kill him. He had spent most of the night in fear.

Ben was eleven years old and believed that he was old enough to take care of himself, but he had found out the night before just how real the fallen angels from Heaven were. I wish today that he could have known then just how powerful prayer is when you believe what you are praying for; but not even my own faith was quite that strong yet, so the truth did not reflect into my children's lives the way that it should have.

That morning, I got on my knees, hugged my son, and prayed with him: "Please, dear Father, protect my son and our family. Help us to trust in You. And please, Lord; help us to get into military housing soon. In Jesus' name, amen!"

This made Ben feel better. I knew he was tired, so I let him take a nap on the sofa for most of the day.

The Army had told Phil that the waiting list for military housing was three to six months. We had already been at Sam's place for almost one month, and now I was not sure how much longer I was willing to live here and let my son be placed in this kind of danger. I began to earnestly pray for God to get us another place to stay. I knew that He was the only one who could speed up the housing process.

Phil came home from work early that same day. "Michelle! Michelle!"

I came out of the kitchen, surprised to see my husband home two hours early. "What is it, Phil?"

"The housing office called today. We have twenty minutes to get to base and look at an apartment. Let's go!"

I slapped together the sandwiches I was making, handed one to each child, and told them to follow Daddy to the car. We raced to the base and arrived at the apartment just before the man who would show it to us arrived.

We didn't really care for the setup of the apartment or the neighborhood. I sighed. I had hoped it was the apartment that God wanted us to have. Phil told the man that it just wasn't going to work for our family.

Then the man said, "Wait a minute! I think I have something over on Sayers Court. Let me make a phone call and see if that one is ready to be shown today or not."

He got on his cell phone and walked over by his car. As I watched him talking, I began to pray, "Please, God, give us an apartment today; one that will be in a good neighborhood. Please, Lord, take us away from the evil that has engulfed Sam's house. Lord, we need your protection. In Jesus' name I pray this, amen!"

The gentleman came back over and looked at us with a smile. "You folks are in luck. If you will follow me over to Sayers Court, I will show you the apartment there. It should not have been available until tomorrow, but the cleaning crew just finished cleaning it up."

I looked up and said, "Thank you, Lord."

You see, if we did not take the apartment that was offered to us on that day, we would have been put back at the bottom of the waiting list. The only way to avoid this was if the Army had more than one to look at. Then they let you choose which you would like to live in.

When we arrived at the other location, we saw a nice neighborhood with several duplexes. We looked through the one that was open, and it was perfect for our family. It had four bedrooms, two bathrooms, a big living room, a kitchen/dining area, a walk-in closet in the hall, and a laundry room across from the closet. To top it off, the neighborhood was safe and friendly.

We told the gentleman, "We will take this one."

He smiled and said, "Wonderful! If you folks will follow me back to my office, I will get the keys and all the papers for you to sign. You can move in today if you like."

I looked at the man in awe. *God is so good!* I thought. I didn't think it could get any better than this.

At the office the gentleman said, "You folks are really lucky. There were ten families ahead of you. It was the funniest thing: they all seemed to find housing off-base and wanted to be removed from the list. If they hadn't, you folks would have been waiting at least another two or three months."

I sat in the chair in that man's office fighting back tears. I knew only God could have performed an act as big as this one. He had opened the door for my family to move out of Sam's house.

CHAPTER 48

New Apartment

Phil and I were excited to move into the new apartment, but he had to work the next day. I tried to talk him into just moving the beds, along with some kitchenware so that we could eat. But he said, "No, tomorrow is Friday, and I can get out of work early. We will have the whole weekend to move in."

In my mind, I was screaming, *No!* But arguing with Phil would get me nowhere. I looked at Ben and saw his smile change to a sad expression.

That night when we got ready to go to bed, Ben asked in desperation, "Can I sleep on the floor next to my sister?"

"No," Phil said with a stern tone. "You can sleep on the cot in the room you were given. I don't want to be tripping over you on my way out to work in the morning."

Ben bowed his head and walked away. My heart broke for him. I tried to tell Phil that he was having nightmares in that room (I knew that if I told him demons were tormenting our son, he would laugh and call me crazy). Phil said it wasn't going to hurt him to stay in the room for one more night.

That night I tucked Ben in and said a powerful prayer for the Lord to protect him. Then, leaning down to whisper in my son's ear so that no one else could hear, I said, "Trust in God, and he will protect you. I will be praying for you." I kissed him goodnight and went to bed. I did not sleep well; my thoughts kept going back to my son. I continued to pray for him throughout most of that night.

The next morning Phil woke me up and told me there was something I needed to see. He was laughing as he walked out of the room. I got up and followed him into the hallway. He pointed to the bottom of Nautasha's cot: there was Ben, sleeping underneath it, curled up in a blanket.

After Phil and Sam left for work, I woke Ben up and told him he could sleep on the sofa or climb into bed with me. He took his blanket and went to the couch. I smiled, looked up, and said a prayer of thanksgiving to the Lord. God had protected my son.

We managed to get all of our stuff out of storage and into the apartment in one day. Phil and I set up the children's beds and our kitchen table, then moved our furniture into the living room. There were still boxes everywhere; it was going to take a few days to get everything organized. I didn't mind, though. I was happy to unpack our belongings and put them away.

As everything got put in its place, I also knew I had to get the children enrolled in school. I spent a good amount of one day doing this and buying their supplies. The children were excited to be at a new school and looked forward to meeting new friends.

After I got this taken care of, I found a phone book in our new mailbox, opened it up to the yellow pages, and looked for Seventh-day Adventist churches in the area. The closest one I could find was in DeRidder.

I asked my husband where that was at supper that evening. He asked me why I wanted to know. When I told him I was looking for a Seventh-day Adventist Church to go to, his reaction blew me away:

"Why don't we jump in the car and go for a ride?"

Phil found the church at the edge of DeRidder and pulled into the driveway. "This is it!" he said. "This is the church you were looking for." I remained shocked as he even walked me through how to get home, making sure I was paying attention so that I could find my way back to the church. This was a nice gesture from him, but it was to be short-lived.

As I resumed attending church and grew more spiritual, I was convicted that we should not be watching television on the Sabbath unless it brought glory to God. Instead, I starting taking the children on nature walks. I also told Phil that we would not go shopping on the Sabbath. I was going to stand up for God and do what He was convicting me of through His Word. I wanted to follow Him and keep His Word in my heart, and I knew that to do this I had to apply what I had learned.

I also wanted to please my husband, but not by displeasing God. I knew it was going to be a struggle and that there would be some arguments, but I knew in my heart that God wanted me to live this way.

One afternoon I received a phone call from Phil informing me that I needed to stay home that day. The moving company had contacted him and said that his belongings were in from Germany. Since he had lived in a barracks room for the last year, I knew that he would not have much. The biggest thing would be his motorcycle.

However, to my surprise, when the men opened their moving truck, there were a lot of boxes, a sofa, and some other furniture. I could not believe how much stuff he had had in the barracks.

As the movers started unloading, I had them put all the boxes in the living room. I was not sure what I was going to do with the sofa yet, so they set it down outside while I rearranged the furniture to make space. Once I was ready I went out and told them they could bring in the sofa.

I was getting ready to direct them where to put it when one of the men's hand slipped and the couch fell on its side on the ground. He apologized, and I told him that it was okay; accidents happened. Then, as the young man picked the sofa back up, its cushions fell off and a bunch of adult magazines spilled out.

> *as the young man picked the sofa back up, its cushions fell off and a bunch of adult magazines spilled out.*

The men made nasty comments. I picked up the magazines and told them I would surely take care of this filth. I tore them up and threw them in the trash can for pick up the next morning.

While I unpacked Phil's boxes, I also found some adult videos. I broke them and threw them away, too.

I waited until the trash was picked up to confront Phil about what I had found. This led to a big argument, so I was glad that the children were outside on the playground. I told him I wanted a divorce and went to our bedroom.

Things were not getting any better. If anything, they were getting worse. Phil played on his computer every day from when he got home from work until the time he went to bed. Very rarely would he come in and watch television or play with the children. If he heard us laughing, he would come out to see what we were doing or just make a comment from the computer, asking what was so funny. He left his games only long enough to eat dinner.

On Sabbaths it was different. Phil would sit on his computer till we got home from church, or he would come home from work and change clothes, but either way he'd be ready to spend family time shopping, going to the movies, or eating out. Each time I would refuse to go with him and or let him take the children.

This caused great confrontations between the two of us. "You are brainwashing our kids into this religion," he would say. Most of the time, he voiced his opinion in front of them to try and place doubt in their minds about God and the church. This was a struggle that would not end any time soon.

CHAPTER 49

New Jobs

Time passed, and I decided to get a job again to help out with our finances. I started working on the base at Klein Hospital as a custodian in the emergency room, the intensive care unit, and labor and delivery. I was on call to care for these departments as well as the custodial room and the hospital laundry.

I liked my job, and it paid well. Whenever I was given work, I did my very best. Because I went the extra mile for my employers, they called me all the time to fill in for other employees. I ended up working anywhere between sixty and seventy-five hours a week. However, this wore on my body and my home life.

The children needed an adult in the house who would watch them and help them with their homework. Phil was not to be disturbed when he was on his computer, and if the children were having a disagreement, he remained very abusive when correcting them.

I called my grandmother's house one day to see how everyone was doing in Trenary. Uncle Dean answered the phone. We talked for quite a while. I learned that he had broken his foot and was having trouble finding work.

I asked him, "Would you like to come and live with Phil and me and help with the children? You can look for a job here at Fort Polk. We would love to have you."

He paused, then told me he would have to think about it.

After I got off the phone, I talked to Phil about Uncle Dean staying with us. He thought it would be a great idea. The next day we called back, and Phil also encouraged my uncle that he would be welcome.

Two weeks later Uncle Dean called and asked if we still wanted him to come. We were thrilled and set up a weekend to drive to Michigan and pick him up. Because he didn't have a lot of personal items, we decided to take the van Phil's stepmother had given to us as a gift.

Uncle Dean would have to share a room with one of the boys, or else we would have to put the boys together. We agreed that my uncle should have his own room, while Tristin and Ben could bunk together.

Tristin was really excited about this arrangement, because he loved his big brother and wanted to be with him all the time. Ben, on the other hand, was not too thrilled. He wanted his space, and he didn't want his little brother getting into his toys. There were some challenges to having the two of them sharing a bedroom, but we had seen this coming since there were ten years between them.

One day a while later, Uncle Dean surprised Phil and me when we came home from work. He had moved in with Tristin and given Ben his own room back. He wanted the boys to be happy, so he had sacrificed his space in order to bless one of our children. It was a sweet gesture.

Uncle Dean continued to look for jobs on- and off-base. I was also looking for new work. One day he found a listing in the newspaper: an ENT doctor in Leesville was looking for a file clerk. He thought I would be interested since I was taking an online medical decoding class. I applied and got hired. Around the same time, my uncle was called for an interview at the PX Exchange on post. A few days later he was hired.

After a year at the doctor's office, I began having problems with the nurse (who happened to be the doctor's wife). I am not sure what I ever did to offend her, but she made life hard on me. She would single me out and tell me I could not do certain things, while the other workers would not be reprimanded for doing the same things. I could no longer take the abuse.

My uncle told me that there was a position open at the PX in the stockroom and warehouse. I went online and applied, and the next week I received a call from the manager, who wanted me to come in for an interview. I told her my hours at the doctor's office, and she worked around my days off. The day that I went in, after answering some intense questions about how I would perform my job, I was hired on the spot.

I put in my two-week notice at the doctor's office. His wife told me I did not have to wait to quit: she stated that I could be done tomorrow if I wished. She was not sad at all when I handed her my letter of resignation, but her husband did not share in her happiness. He was sad that I was leaving, but wished me happiness at my new job. He told me that if I ever needed a referral, he would gladly give me one.

He was a really nice guy and an outstanding doctor. He cared deeply for his patients and made sure he did all he could to care for them. He even gave free office calls to some who had little money. He taught me a lot about medicine and had me sit in and assist him on several in-office surgeries, even though I was only a file clerk. I will always be grateful for his kindness.

Working at the PX Exchange was a blessing. I loved the people I worked with, and I enjoyed doing physical labor at my job. I was happy at work and with the children, but not when I was with Phil. He seemed not to care about anything but his computer.

For example, the children kept coming home from school and telling me all the things other kids were saying on the playground. I was shocked, but Phil just blew it off, saying, "Kids will be kids." I did not share his opinion on this matter, so I brought it to the attention of the principal. However, nothing was done, even though they had corporal punishment for the children there.

I expressed to the school that, when my own children were in trouble, I would like for them to call me, and I would punish them. When they decided to punish my son with the paddle, and did not contact me until afterward, that was the last straw: I pulled my children out of public school and home-schooled them. Phil gave me a hard time about this as well, but I stood strong even though he refused to help.

It was hard to home-school and also work, but Uncle Dean helped me out. I worked from 4:00 a.m. to 11:00 a.m. or 12:30 p.m., depending on how busy we got. Meanwhile Uncle Dean worked the evening shift; so he helped the children with homework in the mornings, and I would school them in the afternoons. This worked out well.

CHAPTER 50

I Can't Take Any More!

It was getting to the point where I couldn't take much more of my marriage. I was living with a man who couldn't care less about his wife or her thoughts. I knew that he could not love me the way that I needed him to love me. I started to pray for the Lord to intervene.

One day not too long after the 9/11 attacks, Phil came home from work and told me he was being deployed to Iraq. My heart sank. I wanted him out of the house, but not in danger. I prayed and gave this to the Lord. He brought Scripture to my mind to comfort me: "And you will hear of wars and rumors of wars. See that you are not troubled; for all these things must come to pass, but the end is not yet" (Matt. 24:6).

After I prayed, I knew that God would protect Phil. I helped him get all his military gear together. I even took care of him when the gas chamber made him sick.

This was a training exercise used to help the soldiers understand that they needed to fully rely on their gas masks. While in the chamber, the soldiers were instructed one by one to take off their masks. After removing it, they had to recite their last name and Social Security number with just one breath of air.

Very few soldiers finished saying their Social Security number before they ran out of air and bolted for the chamber door. Phil was one of them; but he did not make it out in time and breathed in some of the gas. He was sick for a few days, then he was back to his old self.

The time drew near for his company to leave for Iraq. My heart sank once more. I didn't like living with him (or being with him) anymore, but my heart longed for him to have a relationship with God. I was not sure why God was letting this happen. There was a good reason; I knew there must be ... but I could not see past what God had placed before me.

The children and I drove Phil to where his company was boarding a bus headed for Virginia. We said our goodbyes, and the children hugged and kissed him. Once he was seated on the bus, Tristin looked for him and, once he found his dad, just kept waving. Phil had tears in his eyes as he opened the window to say one last goodbye to the children. My heart was heavy; we all knew the danger of going to a war zone.

Once his bus arrived in Virginia, they would be loaded onto planes and transported to Kuwait. After two weeks to a month, they would be assigned to their posts in Iraq. This would be the dangerous part of the trip.

They were not flown directly into Iraq because of air raids and fear of the planes being shot down. Instead, they had to go in by trucks and tanks. Still, as they drove, they had to watch for air attacks, ground attacks, land mines, and IEDs.

An IED, or improvised explosive device, is a homemade bomb constructed and deployed in ways other than in conventional military action. The Iraq military made a fair amount of sharp metal IEDs. When they exploded, pieces of shrapnel would shoot through the air at high speeds, acting like bullets. Anyone hit would either die or become severely injured. Such was a successful IED.

When my husband arrived in Kuwait, he was able to contact me and let me know he made it there safely. I was relieved and said praises to the Lord for hearing my prayers.

Phil ended up being stationed in Kuwait for about a month before they moved him to Iraq. I knew that we would not be able to talk as much once he was there, so until then, four or five times a week, we talked on the internet. He also tried to call home once a week. Now that he was overseas,

I started to lose the bitterness in my heart for him. I prayed daily for his safety and for him to have a relationship with God.

However, as the weeks passed, he started emailing me about all the women and the adulterous actions that were happening there. He thought that it was funny, but I was not amused by his comments. When he started to compare me to the women there and to tell me how beautiful they were, I decided I had had enough of his mental abuse and withdrew from talking to him online.

I became bitter. Satan was coming in through the cracks in my armor and driving my thinking. I was still attending church, and I was the primary Sabbath School teacher, but I was not getting the food which I needed from God to fill the holes in my heart.

My husband started calling home more often because he rarely saw me online anymore. One time I told him, "I am sick of the way you treat me. I will never be good enough for you. I want a divorce." Despite the prior times I had mentioned this, that conversation still shocked him. He really did not see himself as having done anything wrong that would merit me asking for a divorce.

I started filing. My attorney told me, "By law, I am not permitted to serve him with divorce papers until he is back in the United States." I understood, but I was not happy. My heart started to harden even more.

> "By law, I am not permitted to serve him with divorce papers until he is back in the United States."

During that time I was unfaithful to God and to my husband. Today I am very thankful that Jesus washes our sins away when we are sincere in our prayers and seek to follow God with our whole hearts.

I was promoted at work to stockroom supervisor. I continued to do my job well and always worked hard. I stayed late if they let me; I hated leaving a project unfinished and strived to accomplish all that I could in one day, even if it seemed impossible. Most of the time the manager had to tell me to go home. Because of my hard work and dedication, I received many awards.

Other employees got angry at me and began to call me a brown noser. Their jealousy shined through very brightly. Regardless of their jealous behavior, I helped them when they needed it and was always nice to them.

One of the other female employees asked me, "Why are you so nice to me? I can't stand you and I treat you like dirt. You might as well say I hate you. Yet you treat me like I am your friend."

I replied, "God would have me treat you no less than I would treat anyone else, no matter how much you hate me. I am not accountable to you, but I am accountable to God."

She walked away confused, but after that day she treated me with a little more kindness. I remembered Matthew 5:44: "But I say to you, love your enemies, bless those who curse you, do good to those who hate you, and pray for those who spitefully use you and persecute you."

That experience made me think of how I was acting toward my husband. He treated me with so much ugliness that I became ugly back to him. Because I longed for a wonderful, loving marriage, I spent my time thinking about how bad Phil was instead of how much more I needed to be praying for him.

If I had been praying earnestly for my husband and letting go of self, God would have helped me through that trying time in my life. However, because I made my own choices instead of laying them at the feet of Jesus, I prevented my Savior from helping me.

God gives us free will. I needed to learn to surrender mine to Him so that I could have a character more like that of my heavenly Father.

CHAPTER 51
Moving Back to Michigan

Almost a year had passed when I got a call one day from my husband. "We are coming home soon," Phil told me. "My company is in Kuwait again. I will call you again soon to let you know the exact date we will be arriving and where we will be meeting our families."

His voice sounded sad. I realized that I had broken his heart by filing for a divorce. For a moment, I felt like I should cancel it and stay with him. Then my heart hardened again as I thought of all the mean and unfaithful things my husband had done to me. I decided I would push forward with the divorce.

The day Phil was to return, Ben and Nautasha did not want to come to pick up their dad, so only Tristin and I arrived at the gym on Fort Polk. We got there later than I wanted to, and the whole gym was full. Tristin and I found a place to stand on the side of the floor, then waited for the soldiers to enter.

It was a sight to see. They marched in with an air of patriotism and a sense of the freedom that they brought by serving our country. It brought tears to my eyes as I watched more than a hundred soldiers go by.

They formed ranks and the commanding officer stood in front of them. Watching the orderly way they obeyed every command, I thought of how we should obey God's every command. Guilt raced through me again, and the thought of staying once more passed through my mind. God was trying to reach me, but I kept hardening my heart.

When the ceremony was over and all the medals were handed out to the soldiers, they were dismissed to find their families. The room turned into a great, big mass of people. It was like looking for a needle in a haystack.

I brought Tristin outside and decided it would be better to wait there. Phil came out and found us. I gave him a hug and welcomed him back. He didn't want to let go, and when I pushed him away the sadness that was displayed on his face was almost more than I could bear. When he took Tristin in his arms, he had tears forming.

He looked at me with his tear-stained, blue eyes, and I could see clearly the pain that lay within his heart. I felt very badly about the way I was hurting him. I knew how he felt because of how often he had made *me* feel so unloved and unworthy of his compassion. I would never wish that feeling on anyone else, because I knew how that pain could tear up your life.

Time passed and I continued to have second thoughts about leaving. However, everyone I talked to about this decision told me to proceed.

I should have confided in someone in the church. By the time I thought about going to the pastor, Phil had already approached him and told his side of the story. Phil was doing all he could to save our marriage, and I was doing all I could to get away from it.

The pastor called me into his office and asked me about what was happening. Then he told me a little of how my husband was feeling. I immediately became defensive and could not wait to leave. I felt conviction falling upon me, but I resisted God's call. He let me go on making my mistakes but never gave up on me.

I called my cousin Josie, and she came to help me move back to Michigan. I moved in with her and her children in Center Line. This would be a new world for me.

I was now going to live on the outskirts of Detroit. I was not a city girl and didn't know a lot about city life, except that there was a lot of crime and you needed to be careful where you went and at what time. This would be very different from the country life I had grown to love, with the peace of God and nature surrounding you at every turn.

Once at Josie's, my family helped me to get my belongings into a van trailer to take and store them at the company where my cousins worked. My cousins in the area were so nice to me; I was grateful to have family. We then spent the rest of the week getting my personal things in order.

There was so much to do. The days flew by, and getting organized took longer than I thought. I realized I had not had time to look for a church.

I enjoyed visiting with my family, but most of them were not religious. My aunt, her youngest daughter Mary, and Mary's family were the only ones that went to church (Mary home-schooled her two boys, and they were very well-mannered). Therefore, when Sabbath came, the children and I decided to have church at Josie's house, since she and her family were leaving for the day and would not be back until later that night or the next morning.

I made the children breakfast and tried my best to have services at the house with them. We prayed and read from one of the children's devotional books. A little later I went to the kitchen to find them something to eat for lunch, but I discovered that we were running low on food.

I found some macaroni and cheese that we had brought with us. I started to boil the water and put the noodles in, but then I realized that we didn't have any milk to mix the cheese into. I looked over to Ben and said, "Honey, I know it is Sabbath, but I need you to run down to the end of the block to the corner store and purchase some milk for me so I can finish the meal. Only get what is needed for the meal."

"I am not going to the store for you," he said.

Ben had been very rebellious lately. Still, I looked at him in disbelief. I firmly stated that he was going, but he told me that he was not going to break the Sabbath.

I knew that he just didn't want to go to the store. Ben didn't really like going to church, and he was using the Sabbath as a ploy to be disrespectful. However, I didn't feel like arguing with my twelve-year-old son.

So I looked to my seven-year-old, Nautasha, and asked her if she would run to the store. It was only half a block away, and I didn't think it would be out of the ordinary if I sent her. She gladly took the little bit of money I handed her and left.

After fifteen minutes of waiting, I became worried. I told Ben to go and see where his sister was. Again, he refused me. I didn't have time to argue with him, so I told him, "You are being very disobedient and disrespectful. The least you can do is watch your brother while I go look for you sister."

I walked out the door and down the block to the store, figuring that Nautasha was just looking at candy and wondering whether she could get away with buying some. I was upset with Ben, and my daughter was about to get a spanking for taking so long.

I got to the store and asked the clerk if he had seen a little girl come in to buy milk. He nodded his head and told me that she had left about ten minutes earlier.

> My heart stopped. My daughter was missing.

My heart stopped. My daughter was missing. I ran out of the store and looked around in all directions, but I could not see her anywhere. I ran home to the boys. I had to call the police.

When I ran into the house, Tristin asked where his sister was. Ben looked ashamed and worried. He just looked down when I scolded him. "This would have never happened had you just gone to the store like you were asked," I said to him. Then I calmed down and started to pray, "Dear Father God in Heaven, please protect my little girl and help me to find her. Please bring her home to me safely. In Jesus' name, amen."

I searched for the phone. When I finally found it, I started dialing 911. Then I heard the door open and looked up.

There, standing in the doorway, was Nautasha. I ran to her and asked what happened, then told her how worried I had been.

Nautasha explained that when she had walked out of the store, she could not remember which way led back to Cousin Josie's house. She had started walking down the street, but after two or three blocks, when she didn't recognize anything, she started to pray. A lady was sitting on her front step watching her children play in their front yard. Nautasha had walked up to her and told her that she was lost, then asked if the woman could help her find her way back to Cousin Josie's house.

Nautasha described the house and front yard to the lady, who was very nice and offered to drive her around to look for it. Nautasha finally spotted my truck and told the lady. The woman dropped her off and told her to be careful, because this was not a good neighborhood to be getting lost in. I was very happy my daughter was safe.

A week later there was a dead body lying in front of that same store. The police said it was drug- and gang-related, and they didn't think they would find out who was responsible for the murder.

I knew right then that God had protected my daughter the day she was lost. I said a prayer of thanksgiving unto the Lord, and I also prayed for the family who had just lost their daughter to a gang incident.

CHAPTER 52
Trailer in the Country

I found a Seventh-day Adventist Church close by in Warren and started attending. I had not given up on God, and I was glad He would never give up on me. I was not all the way grounded in the Lord's Word, but I was still seeking His guidance. This is what gave me hope in life.

Living in the city, I started feeling the effects of evil all around me. I just wanted to get out; I didn't like the darkness that I sensed daily. My cousin Josie knew I did not like it there and told me that she had friends who had a house on the outskirts of Grayling.

I was overjoyed at the news and the fact that they would let me rent their trailer. The man and woman also told me that they used to have horses, and they would be fine with us bringing ours. The trailer was not available to move into yet, so I had to wait for them to call me back.

When that phone call came, I was jumping up and down and could not wait to tell the children we would be moving in a week. They were excited. I told them it had a big yard, and that we could bring our horse from Louisiana and set up a pen for him.

About the horse: while living in Louisiana, Phil had introduced me to Lieutenant Farmers, who owned lots of horses. She told me that I could spend time with them any time. I missed being around Bridget, so I went out there as often as I could.

I became attached to an Arabian Appaloosa mix. They called him Sam, but later I found out his papered name was, "That's My Horse." Sam and I formed a bond; he followed me all over. He was a great horse, and I loved to spend time with him. I started to pray for God to bless me with Sam, because I knew I could not afford to buy him.

One day I decided to bring my son Ben out to see the horses. I asked if he wanted to ride Sam. Ben was excited, so I helped him onto the horse. My son rode bareback as I led him around the field. Ben became very comfortable, so I tied the lead rope to the other side of the halter and put the rope over the horse's neck like reins.

Ben was doing very well, but all of a sudden Sam spooked: he had stepped on a red ant hill. My son fell to the ground and went right underneath the horse. My heart stopped as I stood there, knowing I would have no time to react.

Then the most amazing thing happened: after Ben fell off, Sam lifted his back leg up and turned his head to look at him. Then he walked over to Ben, sniffed him, and gave him a little nudge, as if to say, "Are you all right?" I stood there in shock.

I stepped out in faith and asked Lieutenant Farmers how much she wanted for the horse.

"One thousand is what I am asking for this gelding. He comes from a good line and has been shown in English and Western. He would be the perfect horse for you and the kids."

I looked down. I knew I could not afford a thousand dollar horse. "I don't have that kind of money. I sure wish I did," I said as I stroked Sam's velvety nose.

"I'll tell you what," Lieutenant Farmers said. "If you can pay me $150 a month, I will sell him to you, but the horse has to stay here until he is paid for. Now, this won't include your boarding fee: I'll charge you $75 a month for boarding since you are buying him."

$225 a month? YES! I told her that I knew we could afford that, but that I needed to talk to Phil. He later agreed to let me buy Sam.

I was excited to teach my children about horses. I showed all three of them how to ride bareback before I put them in a saddle. They would beg to go and see them. Nautasha used to ask the most, especially after we finished paying off Sam and moved him at another horse farm closer to the military base. It cost seventy-five more a month to board Sam at the new farm, but it was worth it, because we could go take care of him daily if need be while living on the base.

This was where Sam was still being boarded at the time of our move to Michigan. I had been sending money for the monthly boarding fee to ensure that he could stay there until I could go and get him.

Our move into the trailer went smoothly since we had lots of help getting all our things into place. The trailer had propane heat and a wood stove. I set up my bed in the stove room because there were only two bedrooms. The boys shared the big bedroom, and Nautasha had the little one close to the living room. I knew I would not be able to afford propane, so the children and I went out into the woods with a handsaw to cut wood for the winter, which was fast approaching.

We began to attend the Seventh-day Adventist Church in Grayling. I fell in love with Pastor Dave and his wife Diane immediately. They loved to give a helping hand and words of encouragement to anyone in need.

Pastor Dave found out that I needed wood for winter, and one day he stopped by just to loan me his little fourteen-inch chainsaw. He knew I had worked in the woods when I was younger, and he figured I could handle working his chainsaw. He walked me through how to use it and shared all the safety tips. The next day the children and I went out and cut a lot of wood. Using the chainsaw was a lot faster than doing it by hand.

Both of our dogs loved to run in the woods while we worked. We had brought them (and Annabell) with us when we returned to Michigan. Earlier, when we had gone to Louisiana, we had taken Sheba with us; while there I had rescued a baby pit bull from having to experience a dog-fighting ring. She had been abused at only four weeks old, but the vet took wonderful care of her and cleaned up the cut on her nose. Even though it took us over a month to get the fleas off of her, her health seemed to improve greatly. We named her Schatzi. We knew this little puppy was a treasure, a little sweetheart; her name fit her.

Trailer in the Country

I felt protected by our dogs while we cut our firewood. They would come and check on the children and me, and then run back into the woods to sniff around.

After a while we all got tired and wanted to be done. It was hard work cutting and hauling with only one child who could come close to working like an adult. Nautasha and Tristin helped out a lot, but they were so little that they could not haul as much to the truck as Ben and I. But with God's help, we managed to get the wood we needed.

As winter approached we seemed to have a lot of problems in the trailer, but I always went to church with a smile. The church family was amazing, and I was not afraid to ask for help when something broke. Also, since the church was on the same road as the Seventh-day Adventist camp Au Sable, we were fortunate enough to meet all the staff who ran it.

One day I told the people at church that our pipes had frozen; we could not flush the toilet or take showers. Because the wood stove was located in an addition that the owners had built onto the trailer, and because the stove did not have a blower, the heat did not reach the back bedroom or the bathroom that was down the hallway.

I hardly ever had to sleep with covers because the stove room got so very warm; I wish I could have said the same for the bathroom. I had gone down the hall that morning and found that the water we had left on to trickle in the tub had frozen like an icicle.

The camp staff offered to come out to see what they could do. They managed to get our water unfrozen and working again. I was very grateful.

Many other things broke down: the stove, the dryer, and the toilet; and the pipes froze often. I never complained. I was always happy to be in the country.

One day at church, Scott and Tammi, the camp managers, walked up to me. "Michelle," one said, "you have had so many bad things happen to you since you moved into that trailer, yet every time we see you, you are smiling. You are an inspiration."

I was shocked; I had never looked at myself that way. To hear it from them made me feel good and very blessed by God.

> "you have had so many bad things happen to you since you moved into that trailer, yet every time we see you, you are smiling.

Winter kept getting colder. It dropped below zero a lot. There came a time when the pipes were so frozen that we could not thaw them out. Then Scott and Tammi let me wash our clothes at their house, and we showered in the camp's bath houses.

Times were getting rough for the children and me in other ways. I was working as a waitress, because that was the only job available for me at the time, and in order to make it we had to go on state assistance.

During this time Phil did not give up on our marriage. He told me he was attending the Seventh-day Adventist Church in DeRidder, Louisiana, and doing Bible studies with the pastor.

When I learned this, I was in shock. Several times before I had left, Phil had tried to get me to stay. He would tell me things like, "I read my whole Bible while I was in Iraq, and I want to be a Christian." Then he would say, "I will start going to church on Sunday if you and the children go with me." He had also started to give me ultimatums about Sabbath-keeping and Sunday-keeping so that I would quit attending the Seventh-day Adventist Church. I knew then that he was only trying to win me back and not really trying to have a relationship with God, and it would make me mad.

So what he said during that phone call blew me away: "I wish you could be here for my baptism." He sounded sad and very sincere about giving his heart over to the Lord. In fact, a week later, he was baptized in the DeRidder church.

Phil called me up another evening and told me that he was being sent to Korea for a year. He wanted me to put the divorce on hold and move back to Louisiana to take care of the house and the bills.

I said I didn't understand why he wanted me to come back if Uncle Dean was still living with him.

He told me that once the divorce was final, he would have to give up housing, and if he was in Korea, he would have no way of moving his stuff unless Uncle Dean did it for him. Phil knew that Uncle Dean didn't know a lot about the military paperwork that housing would need, when it came to moving and getting things put into storage.

I told Phil that I needed to pray about it before I said yes.

I had just finished reading the book *His Robe or Mine*. The Lord had been working on my heart through it. I prayed earnestly that night and asked the Lord what to do. Christmas was fast approaching, and Phil wanted an answer before he came home to visit his family for the holidays. He could get a truck to move us if he had advance notice (I didn't know it at the time, but his stepmother Debbie had said she would pay for the moving truck if he could get me to come back to Louisiana).

The Lord answered my prayer, telling me to return. I was reluctant, but I did as the Lord asked. I called my attorney and put the divorce on hold.

He was shocked. He stated, "Your divorce papers were just about to be hand-delivered to the judge's desk. Your divorce would have been finalized this week."

I acknowledged his concerns and told him I was very grateful for all that he had done for me, then I hung up the phone. Next I called Phil and told him what I had done and that I would move back. He was very happy and started making many promises that later he would not be able to keep.

I would need a job once I got back to Louisiana, so I called the PX Exchange and talked to my old boss, Mrs. Hugh. She agreed to hire me back on the spot, telling me to fill out the required online application. I did this and let her know once I had submitted it. The next day we did a phone interview. I am not sure why it was called an interview, because we just talked about all that had happened in our lives since I had left.

The stockroom/warehouse manager and I had become fast friends. She considered me to be like a daughter and had taken me under her wing. Most people took her the wrong way, but I loved Mrs. Hugh. She was a six-foot-tall black woman who stated her opinions very boldly. Underneath that boldness lay a love for her personal Savior, Jesus Christ.

I admired her hard work and the dedication that she put into her job. She was a true mentor to me regarding how to go the extra mile for God. I will never forget her kindness or love for me.

While yet in Grayling, I didn't have much for the children for Christmas. Still, I knew that God was with us, and that was all that mattered. Two days before Christmas, during the evening hours, I heard a knock at the door.

Ben and Nautasha ran to open it. All the staff and church members from Camp Au Sable were there. They started singing Christmas carols to us, at which point Tristin ran right up behind his siblings. My heart overflowed with the love of God at that moment, and I could hardly hold back my tears. The children watched with big smiles on their faces; Nautasha in particular, who loved music and singing. I will never forget her beautiful smile as she watched the group sing carols of praise unto the Lord.

When they were finished, they started handing boxes to me. These were filled with presents for the whole family. After the second box, I thought they were done, but two more came through the door. Rocky, the camp cook, said, "There is a box for each one of you filled with presents. May God bless you all this holiday season."

Our Christmas tree was now full of gifts from the staff and church family of Camp Au Sable. My love for these people was so very great.

I wish today that I had time to tell every story of how each one of them touched my heart. They were all wonderful people. I will always hold the camp and its staff dear to my heart. I know we will all enjoy Heaven together.

Phil made it home the day before Christmas Eve. We spent that night at the trailer with the children, opening the gifts we had been given. On Christmas Day we went to Phil's parents' house.

Then we started packing up. My church family came to help us load the truck. We moved out of the trailer that day and headed back to Louisiana.

CHAPTER 53

Hurricane Rita

---◦◦◦---

The children and I settled into the old house and resumed our home-schooling. It was nice to be back in Fort Polk, but different. I really did not have a love for my husband back yet. I felt that he sensed this and was trying his best to treat me special.

A few weeks later, he left for Korea. I managed all his bills and took care of the house and children. Uncle Dean helped me out.

The children loved him, and he spoiled them rotten as if he were their grandpa. When I smiled and let him know this, he always responded with a smile, "I know I am a pushover when it comes to the kids, but I love them; and you only live once."

Phil called me every day. He really was trying to change his life around. I could hear this in his voice and reactions on the phone. My heart once more started to long for that loving marriage I had been dreaming of. We began to talk about plans for the future and what he wanted to do after he put in his twenty years with the Army. Things were starting to look up, and I praised God for bringing us back together.

Then, after two months of living in Korea, Phil started to backslide. He told me that he was going to bars with friends, and he spoke often about the women who spent time at those bars. They were not women of God but of harlotry. Phil seemed to be intrigued by them. A sadness fell over me again. I feared for our marriage and Phil's salvation.

I knew that if I let it go on, things would go back to the way they had been before. So one evening when he called, I addressed this situation. After I talked to him, he apologized and seemed to get his priorities back into order. I thanked God for answering my prayers. I prayed every day, throughout the day, for my husband. I longed for him to stay strong in his relationship with God.

When Hurricane Rita hit on September 24th, 2005, Fort Polk was only hit by a tropical storm (the hurricane had died down by the time it reached us). Still, many trees, electrical lines, telephone poles, and much more were down all over the roads. We lost our electricity for a week and were restricted to our houses until further notice.

During this time, my family had no way of contacting us, and it was hard to call out, even locally. Most of the cell phone towers were down, as well as the land lines. The few that were not damaged by the hurricane were always busy, as many people called their families to assure them that they were safe. We would have very little phone service until all the phone lines could be fixed and the cell phone towers replaced.

Meanwhile Phil worried about us. He still had about six more months to serve before he could come home, and he tried several times to contact us with no success. He finally called his company, and they assured him that his family was fine.

Once the restriction was lifted and we could leave our homes, Uncle Dean and I contacted our church to see what we could do to help. They shared their plans to supply clothing, bedding, and personal supplies such as toiletries to the victims of Hurricane Rita. As we were very involved in our church, we decided we wanted to help the Adventist Development and Relief Agency (ADRA) with this.

The Methodist camp just down the road from our church opened its doors to people from New Orleans who had fled from their homes and left everything behind. Those people had lost all they had, and some had no family or place to go. Uncle Dean, the children, and I visited and saw firsthand their tears and loss. Our hearts went out to them.

There was one African-American family which I will never forget. They were very close to each other, from the grandmother on down to the grandchildren. Jackie, the grandmother, was the stronghold of the family.

When we brought bedding and clothing to them, we asked if they had any other needs. Jackie asked if we could bring a few toys for the children to play with. My children decided they were going to go through their toys and give some to these children in need.

My heart was filled with joy as I watched my children tell Jackie's grandkids about some of the toys that they would bring. I knew that God was smiling down on them for wanting to give their favorite toys to these kids who had been victims of a bad storm.

I asked Jackie if we could pray for them, and she called everyone into the cabin. I was shocked as they kept coming in. She had many daughters and a son, and the daughters had families of their own. The room filled fast with husbands, wives, and children. At Grandmother Jackie's word, everyone bowed their heads and closed their eyes. When the grandchildren started to giggle and fidget, she only had to look at them and they would stop. I was impressed by this family.

As I prayed over them and asked for God's protection and guidance to fall on them, I heard small sobs here and there. I finished my prayer and everyone said, "Amen."

I looked at Mrs. Jackie and watched as tears rolled down her face. I thought I had brought back memories of the hurricane and their journey here as I prayed, but then she shocked me. She got up, hugged me, and said, "I know you are a woman of God, and I know this happened for a purpose. I know God is with us and has a place for us to dwell. My Lord holds me in His hands, and I am blessed to be here in this cabin with my family.

She continued, "I am blessed to have life and breath coming from my body to watch the Lord perform a miracle for my family. May God bless you, Michelle, and your family for your kindness. You truly are an angel from the Lord sent to help my family." She hugged me so tightly and with such love that I could not help but let the tears fall. She was a Godly woman who loved the Lord with all her heart and soul.

Mrs. Jackie asked me to sit and visit with her while the children went out to play. I listened to her story of how God brought them out of the storm and to this camp. Her faith was strong, and she never gave up on God getting them to safety.

She told me of all the things that she had had to leave behind, and how they almost didn't make it out of New Orleans. She had managed to grab the wedding picture of her and her deceased husband before walking out the door.

She also spoke of the many families that had gotten stuck on the freeway overpasses. Some were throwing other people into the water below to save provisions for the rest. Many children and adults died from that act of cruelty for others to survive. Truly, many people died from the storm, but others died because of greed or fear.

Some of the things that Mrs. Jackie told me I never saw hit the newspapers or on television. I began to realize that even when the news gives us a story, there is still way more to be told that is never revealed.

We stayed in contact with her family for a few years. Then, as life got busy, we lost contact. I look forward to seeing Mrs. Jackie in Heaven, never more to part. She showed me what true faith in the Lord was like. She trusted God to work everything out and was willing to wait upon Him for instruction and guidance as to where she should go and what she should do.

I never saw her take a step forward unless she first prayed earnestly, and she always had a positive word to speak, even when she had lost everything to a hurricane.

CHAPTER 54
Finding the Right House

———⊃⊙⊂———

I was finally able to contact my family after ten days. They were all relieved to find out that we were safe. My mother had pictured us on top of our house with the water raging around us. I had to explain to her that we were not down by the ocean. Once she realized that we only been hit by a tropical storm, she calmed down and praised the Lord for keeping us safe.

I didn't like the fact that we had had to wait out the storm; nor that we had lost power and food, couldn't call home, and couldn't leave our houses. So I asked Phil what he thought about us buying a house back home, close to the National Guard training camp in Grayling.

He was thrilled. He had been talking about that base with his friends and family, and that he would like to move from active duty into the National Guard one day. Now, as he only had seven years left to complete before he could retire, he would try and see if he could be stationed there for active duty instead.

I started looking up websites for realtors and found many houses, but they were just not the right ones. We even made a weekend trip up to

Grayling to look at three, but none of them fit us. We did find one which we liked, but the bank would not finance it; it was too old and didn't meet their requirements. I went home sad because we did not find a house yet very happy that we had been able to see our family.

I didn't give up. I finally found the perfect house in Vanderbilt, Michigan. It had four bedrooms, with a potential fifth, and an attached two-car garage. It was located on ten acres of land with a barn and a small corral for horses. The children, Uncle Dean, and I were all excited. I emailed the site to Phil, and we decided to buy the house.

Since he was still in Korea, I had power of attorney to sign for the house in his name. This was new for the realtor: she had never sold a house to someone who had not looked at it first.

We got all the paperwork started, and they gave us a closing date so that we could sign the papers and move in. Phil put in for leave to come home and move us back to Michigan. He was also going to keep the housing on post for as long as he could so that he had a place to stay.

I found a horse trailer for a good price. Sam was currently in a new boarding place, and the man who owned it had a Welsh pony he wanted to sell. We bought the little guy, whose name was Thunder, and loaded both horse and pony into the trailer.

Nautasha was excited to now have a pony to ride. It had been abused but it took right to her. The bond was amazing as they grew together.

I had most of the things that we needed packed and ready to go. We would leave the rest at the house in Fort Polk for Phil. I called and arranged for a U-Haul, which we picked up the day after my husband came home on leave.

We loaded all that we could into the twenty-four-foot truck and headed for Michigan. It took us two days to get there, what with having to stop and feed the horses.

They were ready for this trip to be over. I watched as they nervously stomped their feet. Sam hung his head almost to the floor throughout the whole trip until we would stop. When I opened the side door of the trailer, he would poke his head out of the door, breathe in the fresh air, and look for treats. Otherwise, Sam would not eat or drink while traveling.

We arrived at the house in Vanderbilt, and the realtor met us there. We went in and looked at the whole house in amazement. It was huge, at just less than 3,000 square feet. We went into the kitchen and signed all the papers. She handed us our keys and welcomed us to the neighborhood.

I was so excited that we had our own home; and a place that was so beautiful. When I looked around, I saw that God had placed something here that each individual of our family would like:

> *When I looked around, I saw that God had placed something here that each individual of our family would like.*

My uncle loved to watch and feed the birds, and there were a dozen bird houses along with three feeders. My husband hung his American flag on the flagpole in the front yard. Nautasha and I headed for the barn to see how we could set up the horses until we could fix the old fencing. And my boys loved the trails in the woods and the fact that we had a game room in the basement. Everyone was happy.

CHAPTER 55

Back to the War Zone, and Slowly Backsliding

---◦---

The two weeks of vacation time went fast for Phil, as we fixed up the barn and a few things in the house. He returned to Fort Polk, then flew back out to finish his time in Korea. In a few months, his tour would be up and he would be back in Louisiana.

While overseas he tried once again to get stationed at Camp Grayling Military National Guard Base, but every time he thought he had an opening, it closed and he was denied. It seemed the Lord was shutting every door of opportunity that arose for him to get stationed close to home.

The rest of the year passed by rather quickly. Before I knew it, Phil was once more on his way back to Fort Polk. We did not have the money to go and meet him this time, but once he was checked into his unit, he was permitted two more weeks of leave time. Phil spent them with us. We drove to Brimley and had a wonderful time with his family.

Again the two weeks flew by, and again it was time for him to go back to Fort Polk. We were getting along better, but I didn't like the separation. I longed for my husband to be home with us.

Within a few weeks, Phil was told that he was being sent to school for training in order to move up to E-6, or staff sergeant rank. He called and told me the good news. If he was promoted, that also meant he was getting a raise. This was a blessing for us financially, since with the horses we needed hay for the upcoming winter.

His training lasted for a couple of months. Phil passed the classes with high scores and was given a certificate of graduation. He was pleased with his accomplishment, and I was happy for him as well. He was beginning to feel good about himself, and things were falling into place even though we were apart.

Phil was able to come home for another week of vacation. We enjoyed going to Gaylord Seventh-day Adventist Church together and visiting with its members. Phil really got into Doug Bachelor's seminars and watched the Millennium series quite often.

I saw many changes in him, but I saw many struggles as well. During that week I noticed Phil start to fall back into his old ways; for example, his addiction to the computer grew.

Uncle Dean and I took care of the children most of the time; it seemed like they were in Phil's way. Tristin would try to get his dad to go outside and play catch, but Phil would always tell him, "Maybe later, buddy." Then he would never follow through. It was hard to watch sadness fall over the children's faces each time he told them that he was busy.

I was sad when he left to go back to Louisiana, and I prayed for his safe travels. He seemed distant, almost like he was uncomfortable with my prayers. I didn't quite understand why. I shrugged it off and gave him a hug and kiss goodbye.

Phil came home on another leave right around the holiday. We made plans to go to his parents' house to celebrate on Christmas Eve.

It was a wonderful night. My sister-in-law had a very beautiful, decorated Christmas tree. All of his family was there, and we had a wonderful dinner. My mother-in-law had made some wonderful homemade pies and lots of good food. That evening we heard stories of their Christmases as children, and we laughed at all the fun things they had done together as a family.

As the holiday went by, I noticed that Phil was spending a lot of time playing computer games which I did not approve of. I knew that they were not good for him nor for the children to watch him play.

Tristin wanted to spend whatever time he could with his dad, so I feared for my son's salvation. Phil and I got into many confrontations over this. I tried to keep the arguments away from the children, but it did not always work out that way. Then it was time for him to go back to base.

My heart longed for him to give his life back to Jesus. I wanted Phil to have a relationship with our Father in Heaven. I prayed and talked to my husband whenever I could about his salvation, but it started to make him angry. I knew that I needed to just pray for him and let the Lord convict his heart.

This was hard for me. I always tried to fix the problems in my family. Then I realized that instead of praying, watching God work, and trusting Him to lead me in what I should say or do to help, I was trying to fix people on my own.

Once Phil reported back for duty, he was informed that he was up for transfer to another base. He put in papers to go to Fort Drum. Since this was where we had started out as husband and wife, I already knew it was only a fourteen-hour drive as opposed to the twenty-eight-hours to Fort Polk. I was excited because this meant we could see each other more often.

Phil found out the next week that his transfer had gone through. He was given orders to report to the base in New York in two months time.

When Phil had been there for two months, he was informed that his unit was going to Iraq. I was devastated. I was worried about him, because this was taking a toll on his mental health. I also knew that he had not been attending church regularly and was falling away from God.

I mentioned this to him, and he blew it off. He said he was fine and that I had nothing to worry about. He joked about how we made more money anyway when he was overseas in a war zone.

But I knew deep down that something wasn't right. During his previous tour in Iraq, Phil had received an Article 15 (court-martial) for verbal sexual misconduct toward a female soldier. He had told me at the time that she was framing him and that he was being made an example of. I already knew that he had been court-martialed for the same thing in the past, and I felt troubled knowing that my husband was not being truthful with me. Nor was he seeking God as he needed to during these times of hardship.

Phil left on the long journey to Iraq. He ended up in Kuwait for three months before they found a duty station for him in Iraq. He seemed distant when I talked to him on the phone. Even on Yahoo Messenger, he didn't seem to want to stay online with me very long. He loved to play games with the children online and to make funny faces, but that only lasted so long as well. I also noticed that when he did talk to me, he treated me more like his best friend than his wife. This bothered me, and I was determined to fight even harder for our marriage. All I could do was pray that God would change his heart.

One day, out of the blue, Phil called the house. It was neither the normal day to call or the normal time. He said he wanted to talk to Tristin to make sure that he was okay.

I assured him that Tristin was fine.

He said, "I just witnessed a school bus full of Iraqi children get blown up. They were Tristin's age. They were sacrificed to kill American soldiers.

"Only a few soldiers were injured from the blast, but all the Iraqi children are dead. This made me think of Tristin. I started to picture him on that bus. I need to know if my son is okay!"

My heart broke for Phil. I knew that he needed to hear directly from his son that he was okay, so I called Tristin down to talk to his father.

He was excited that dad had called to talk to him, because Phil usually only talked to me on the phone (although, every once in a while, he would ask to talk to the children). Tristin answered the phone with quite the joyful attitude, and after about ten minutes, he handed the phone back to me.

I heard relief in my husband's voice. I told Phil that I would be praying for him. He said that he needed a lot of it and that I had no idea what was happening over there. He informed me that the news would never give me the whole story.

When Phil came home on leave from Iraq, he was really different. He got irritated very easily and had nightmares from time to time.

It reminded me of when he had come back from his first tour in Iraq. We had had a really bad storm one night. At about 2:00 a.m. it rolled in; lightning lit up the whole sky, then there was a big, booming sound of thunder. It was so loud that it shook the whole house.

Phil had jumped out of the bed and dropped to the floor, yelling, "GET DOWN! GET DOWN!"

> *Phil had jumped out of the bed and dropped to the floor, yelling, "GET DOWN! GET DOWN!"*

I rolled over to his side and looked down. "Phil, what are you doing?" I asked with a puzzled look on my face.

"GET DOWN! GET DOWN!" he yelled at me. "Where is my gun? I can't find my gun." He spread his arms all over the floor, looking for a weapon that he would never find.

He was having a flashback. Softly I said, "Phil, you are at home in Louisiana. You are safe. We are just having a thunderstorm. Please come back to bed."

It took me a few minutes to convince him that he was, indeed, home and in our bedroom. Eventually he climbed back up and went back to sleep.

The next morning, he never mentioned a thing about it. He only talked about it later, when we were telling stories about weird things that happened at night.

During this leave his temper flared rather quickly. Tristin tried to get his attention, but if Phil got upset, Tristin would get spanked. Then he would go up to his room to play with his cars or else go down to Ben's room and talk with his brother. The other children avoided him. They only talked to him when they knew he was in a good mood. On several occasions, Nautasha and Ben stated that they could not wait for him to leave.

I felt bad for the children, and I was concerned about Phil and his behavior. I talked with him several times and asked if there were things bothering him. When I told him that he was being too hard on the children and not spending enough time with them, he would yell at me, "What do you want me to do, Michelle? I am not perfect. They will just have to get over it."

These words cut deep. Once again I was having to fight to get my husband back. I saw him sliding away from his family and changing into a new person I did not like. I tried all that I knew to reach him, and I prayed every day for him.

When it came time for him to return to Iraq, the children and I were relieved. I loved Phil; he was just turning into someone whom I did not know. Even at the airport he acted distant. I hugged and kissed him goodbye and watched him go through the security gate to catch his flight.

I was still praying for our marriage and my husband's salvation. His walk with God was in serious trouble.

In the meantime, while he was away from us, the rest of us were growing in the Lord with every passing month. We got rid of a lot of our movies and started watching better ones. I disposed of all the secular music we owned, and instead the children and I listened to Christian radio stations and started to buy Christian CDs. I studied the Bible more and was asked to teach the adult Sabbath School class at our church once a month. I was the primary Sabbath School teacher as well. Being so active in the church gave me a sense of purpose and helped me to grow more and more in God's grace.

CHAPTER 56

Family Reunited, and Nautasha's Unhappiness

We managed to get a nice-sized pasture built for the horses. Meanwhile, Nautasha was getting a little too big to be riding the pony.

Just a mile down the road, the neighbor's daughter was going off to college and wanted to sell her horse, Meg. Meg was a sassy Arabian Paint mix with a white blaze. The daughter and I had ridden together often. Meg knew our Sam and our pony already, and they got along well (the girl later told me that this was why she wanted me to buy her horse).

I told her we would buy Meg, and she asked if I would take their Arabian Morgan, Thunder, as well. The latter had been abused and could no longer be ridden. I felt bad for the horse and didn't want to separate him from Meg. With two animals named Thunder, we ended up calling the Morgan "Big T" and the Welsh pony "Little T."

Nautasha was excited when I bought Meg, but I told her that she was mine for the time being. After watching her work with Meg for a while and making sure that her fear of the horse was gone, I allowed her to start riding the new horse. At first she only rode Meg for short periods around the yard, but once I saw that she was comfortable riding Meg on trails, I decided it was time for her to belong to my daughter.

That day, she could not believe that I had just given her a horse. She absolutely loved horses and longed to spend every waking moment with them.

Now that she had a larger horse to ride, Nautasha decided to pass the pony down to Tristin. Tristin didn't like to ride as much as his sister and I did, but on occasion he would join us for a trail ride.

I recall a time when we all went out in the late fall. We had ridden about a half an hour along the trail when we saw a herd of elk passing through the woods. The children and I stopped to watch those magnificent creatures which God had created. They were so beautiful. The male bull caught our scent and started to snort and stomp his hoof. At the same time, Nautasha's horse, Meg, did a dance; she was nervous around the elk.

Only after the herd had passed through the wooded area did the bull follow them. We also got back to our trail ride after saying a prayer to the Lord, thanking Him for allowing us to see such beauty so closely.

Time flew by. Before I knew it, Phil was due to come home. My heart did not long to see him. It had been a great five months of peace with the children in prayer, devotions, and nature. I did not want to give that up or let Phil ruin what God was doing in the hearts of our children.

I started to pray. I just longed for a marriage that was beautiful and filled with love; one where Jesus was at the center of the relationship.

Phil did not desire the same things I did. Although he had grown spiritually while we lived in Louisiana together, I knew that the war had changed him. He was turning back into the man whom I had first married, and I felt like I had to win his love all over again. Still, I was now more determined to make this marriage work than ever before.

I decided to go to Fort Drum and meet him as he arrived. We spent five wonderful days together, then he drove back home with me for a week of leave time at the farmhouse. But once he was home, he started acting funny.

He spent little time with Tristin and paid a lot of attention to Nautasha. When we woke up in the morning, he would ask if Nautasha was up yet. If she wasn't, he would go into her bedroom and wake her. I felt hurt by his actions; this was time we could have spent together as husband and wife, without the children.

Nautasha started to act strangely as well. She became moodier and didn't want to be around her stepdad. Phil often yelled at the children for little things, so I figured Nautasha was getting tired of his attitude toward her and Tristin. I began to pray for her to be more obedient.

I just thought Phil missed my daughter. She was growing up fast; and he had missed out on so much because he was gone so often. Therefore I suggested to him that we move out to New York with him; being apart would not help our marriage. He agreed that this was a good idea but said that he didn't want to live on-base again. We looked around in Watertown and found an apartment to rent.

I had to pack enough household goods to furnish the apartment. We decided not to take too much furniture with us. We ended up buying some from a soldier on post instead.

I was not really sure that I wanted to live in an apartment complex again, but it would turn out to be a great blessing when we discovered that the people on the second floor on the opposite side of the hall from us were Seventh-day Adventists. I ended up spending a lot of time praying with my neighbor, and she and I became fast friends; more like sisters. I cherished the times that we spent together. We came to love those neighbors dearly.

Nautasha put up a big fight when I told her we were moving to New York. She was very angry, and she begged me to let her stay with Uncle Dean to help take care of our farm.

Speaking of which, there was much to be done. I had to get my uncle set up to take care of things while we were gone for a year. We now had four horses, four White Pekin ducks, six Rawlings ducks, three turkeys, twelve chickens, thirteen rabbits, two dogs, five cats, three goats, three rats, a ferret, two cockatiels, a parakeet, two guinea pigs, a fifty-five-gallon fish tank loaded with fish, and a teddy bear hamster.

Nautasha had taught her turkey, Sparky, to mimic her. She would turn her head, and he would turn his. She would wink, and he would wink back at her. It was the craziest thing I ever saw (I always thought birds were not very smart, but God showed me differently). We all loved animals. My daughter in particular spent most of her time with them. Still, I did not give in to her request to stay.

Family Reunited, and Nautasha's Unhappiness

All the animals would be a lot for Uncle Dean to care of, and I was worried about Nautasha not having any animals to play with, so I asked the landlord at the new apartment if we could bring our cockatiels. I knew it wouldn't be much help to my uncle for us to take just two little birds, but I already knew that we would not be allowed to have our cats.

I prayed to God about the birds, and when the landlord said yes, I was overly excited and could not wait to tell my daughter. I thought it would cheer her up.

I was wrong; she didn't care. She was still against moving to New York.

The night before we were going to leave, I went to Nautasha's room to talk to her. She was not there. I knew where to find her, so I put on my coat and walked out to the barn. The moon was bright that night, and you could see pretty far. The stars were always beautiful out in the country, but this night they also seemed to be even brighter.

I walked up to the gate of the horse pasture and looked for my daughter. I saw her lying on Sam's back, looking up at the stars as the horse ate from a round bale of hay. Even though my daughter didn't say a word, I could feel her pain in the silence of the night.

"Tasha, honey!" I said. "It is time to come in. We have a long day ahead of us tomorrow, and you will need your sleep."

"I'll be in in a little while, Mom," she said in a sad tone.

I didn't push her to come. Somehow, I sensed that she needed to be out in the pasture with her best friends and God.

The next morning came quickly. We were all packed up and ready to go. I told Uncle Dean to find homes for the baby rabbits. One of Nautasha's friends came by and was happy to take her guinea pigs as pets.

We were trying to make life a little easier on Uncle Dean. Taking care of so many animals was a lot of work for one elderly man, and since Ben was now in Arizona with my brother Robin (I had sent him to live there, hoping this would help Ben with his ongoing rebelliousness), Uncle Dean would be on his own.

Nautasha was not happy that she had to give away her animals. The ride to New York was long, and she had a defiant attitude all the way there. Tristin, on the other hand, was happy, and he could not wait to see where we were going to live.

We got to our apartment that evening and unloaded only what we needed before going to bed. The next day we brought in everything else and started to get our apartment set up. The birds were a little nervous, but Nautasha and Tristin seemed to be able to settle them down.

Phil had to report back to duty, so the children and I decided to go shopping for food and a few other things that we needed. Once we were most of the way settled, I took them to the food court at Fort Drum and treated them to lunch. I was hoping that this would help with Nautasha's attitude, and it did, a little. She seemed to open up, and she loved looking around the PX Exchange.

I asked around about a Christian school for the children to go to, but I had no luck. There was not a Seventh-day Adventist School anywhere near us. I had to make a decision: I told the children that there was no school close by to go to, so I would be home-schooling them this year. They both seemed to be okay with this. I ordered their school books.

I knew money was going to be tight, so I went online and applied for a job as a stocker and warehouse worker at the PX Exchange. I worked from 5:00 a.m. to 11:00 a.m. three days a week. On the other two days I worked until 1:00 in the afternoon, unless they were shorthanded or it was a holiday, when I would work a forty-hour week.

I gave the children homework in the morning and schooled them from the afternoon into the evening. But sometimes I was so tired when I got home that I would let them do what they could on their own, while I took a nap on the sofa.

I would work, come home, school the children, then cook supper for the family. When I was done with supper, there was cleaning up and dishes. I also had laundry to do; plus Phil wanted to spend time together as a family in the evenings. This didn't include my personal devotional time in the morning before I left for work or the devotional and prayer time which I did with the children at night.

I got worn out. I told Phil that I could not stay up late anymore because it was too much on me. He was fine with it and encouraged me to get the sleep I needed.

Nautasha's attitude got worse. She would spit out hateful words at Phil while I was there. She never wanted to be around him; but Phil wanted to be around her all the time.

Once again it seemed to me that he wanted to spend more time with her than with me. I mentioned this to him, and he said, "Oh, you're just being jealous over nothing. It is all in your head."

I began to think that it *was* all in my head; that I was making it out to be more than it was.

CHAPTER 57

Back to the Farm

We lived in Watertown, New York, for eight months. During that time, my husband played more computer games and talked to women online; he was adapting back to his old ways.

After we came home from church, he would get on his computer. We argued over this often. "Phil," I once said, "it is the Sabbath; our special time with God. You are not setting a very good example for the children."

"Michelle," he replied, "if I wanted a lecture, I would go to work. I get enough of it there; I don't need it at home. I am not doing anything wrong. If the children wish to go on the computer on the Sabbath and watch television, I have no problem with it."

I walked away in frustration. I was worried, because Tristin wanted to follow in his dad's footsteps. I think that he felt this was the only way he could spend time with his dad, as Phil continued to pay more attention to Nautasha than to him.

The arguing and fighting continued. Because Phil was friends with them, I even tried having the elders of our church talk to him, but nothing seemed to work. I earnestly prayed for my husband to accept Jesus back into his heart, but it seemed to be in vain. Phil's heart was becoming hardened.

In May, the seventh month of our time in Watertown, Phil came home from work one afternoon and told me they were sending him back to Iraq for a third time.

"What?" I said. "How can they do that? You have only been home for a little less than a year." I was upset. I knew what this war had done to my husband's mental and emotional state.

(L to R) Nautasha, me, and Tristin.

"By the time I leave," he said, "it will be a year. They have every right to send me back over. I am not happy about this either, but it is what it is." He turned and walked into the bedroom to change, while I stood and wondered why God was letting this happen.

We told the children that evening. They asked us, "Are we going to stay here, or are we moving back home to the farm?"

I looked at their faces and knew that they wanted to go back to our house in Michigan and all of our animals. "We are moving back home to the farm," I answered.

The children leaped out of their seats, yelling and giggling. They could not wait. They would miss the friends they had made while in Watertown, but I knew that they didn't feel at home here.

I started making the arrangements. When the Lord provided money for us to get a moving truck, I knew He would bless us and help us through this time of need.

I called Uncle Dean and told him the news. He was happy that we were coming home, as he had been having a hard time keeping up with the house, yard, and animals. By the beginning of June, we were back at the farm.

Phil called the place in Watertown where he had rented a room the first time he came back from Iraq, to see if they had anything for him to move into for two weeks. They didn't have anything open yet but would call him as soon as a room was available.

Meanwhile, Nautasha's attitude toward Phil remained awful. I witnessed this in action when we held a surprise birthday party for him, since he would be leaving for Iraq on his actual birthday.

We invited the Gaylord Seventh-day Adventist Church and both of our families. It was a beautiful day outside, and we had games and a big potluck lunch. By evening a lot of people had left, but a few friends were still with us, so we decided to light a fire and have some roasted veggie dogs and make s'mores.

As I sat by the fire, Nautasha came storming out of the house. Phil walked out just behind her. I got up and walked over to ask him what was wrong.

"Our daughter is just having attitude problems. She's mad because she can't have her own way." He told me something about Nautasha wanting to spend the night at her friend Dani's house, and that he had told her no.

"Why?" I asked. "We have a few days before we have to leave. She and Dani are close, and they will miss each other."

When I said this, he got really defensive. "Michelle, I will be leaving for Iraq soon. It won't hurt her to be a family for another few weeks, without all her friends." Then he walked over to the firepit.

A few minutes later, Ben came up and said he wanted to talk to me (my son had recently moved back to Michigan and was living with my grandmother Alice). We went inside the house so I could grab a few more things for the hotdogs and s'mores.

> "Tasha said she hopes Phil dies in Iraq. She said he deserves to die."

"What is it, Ben?" I asked.

"Tasha said she hopes Phil dies in Iraq. She said he deserves to die."

I looked at my son in shock. "I will take care of this," I said. "Thanks for sharing. I am sure she is just mad at him and later her attitude with change." I patted his shoulder, and we went back outside together.

I took Phil aside and told him what Ben had said. He looked really hurt at first, then his face turned angry. He looked down at the fire and said that he would handle it later.

I wondered what was going on between the two of them. Nautasha was a teenager now, and I knew that she was going to have mood swings, but I never thought they would be this bad. She had called me into her room a few times, but when I asked what she needed to talk about, Phil always walked in, and Nautasha would tell me she had forgotten what she was going to say.

A week after we had moved all of our stuff back home, the gentleman from Watertown called us back and said that he would have a room for Phil in about three days. Phil explained to him that he needed something the next day, and that his family would be staying with him until he left for Iraq.

The gentleman called again later in the evening while Phil was packing our stuff in the car. When I answered the phone, he said, "Michelle, I just had a tenant call a few minutes ago. He will be all moved out by tomorrow morning. I won't have time to clean it before you get here, though."

I told him, "That is fine. I will clean it if you leave supplies in the room for me." He agreed to this, and I went out and gave Phil the good news.

The next morning, we all headed back once more to Watertown. Nautasha begged to stay with Uncle Dean for the two weeks that we would be gone. I told her that she would be home alone a lot if we let her stay, and I was not comfortable with that. She was very unhappy.

We arrived at the Watertown apartment where we would be staying, and it was a mess. I started cleaning it right away. In the bedroom, I saw bugs crawling around on the mattress. I grabbed the vacuum and sucked them up. Little did I know that this was going to cause problems later!

We slept in the room that night, and the next morning we called the office to let them know about the bugs. We figured out they were bedbugs. I didn't know much about them and neither did the landlord. They moved us into the upstairs apartment until they could investigate the situation. I looked up bedbugs for myself and found out how bad they were. I felt grateful that they had moved us, and that another room had been available so quickly.

The second unit was like a motel room. It had two queen size beds, a television set, a bathroom, a table with three chairs, a little refrigerator, and a microwave oven. It was not very big, but the cost was reasonable, and it would do. We had just gotten settled in when I got a phone call. It was my old friend Sheila from the local church.

"Michelle," she said, "I have a question for you. I know you are only here for a few weeks, but I was wondering if you could come and watch my grandchildren for me while I work? I have a daycare for them, but they do not have openings for both girls until two weeks from now."

"Let me talk it over with Phil, and I will give you a call back." We hung up.

Phil and I agreed that it would be better for me to watch the girls. That way, the children and I would have something to do besides sit in the apartment. When I called Sheila back, she was happy. We set up times for me to be there and discussed what the girls could and could not do.

I brought my children with me to help. We all went for walks and played games. It was a lot of fun, and those girls stole a place in my heart.

CHAPTER 58
Phil's Surgery

Phil had a lump on the side of his neck, and we were getting concerned. I thought it could be cancer. He went to the doctors, who did a biopsy. The results came back, and it was a fatty tissue tumor. They scheduled surgery for him to have it removed just days before he was to leave for Iraq.

I asked him, "Are they going to let you go overseas just after surgery?"

"The doctor said it is not a serious surgery," Phil said. "If I come through with no reactions, then I leave with the rest of my company."

I sighed. I had hoped he would not have to go again.

The day before his surgery, I realized that I could not be with him because Sheila had no one else who could watch her granddaughters that day. Phil and I talked about what we were going to do. He said his friend would drive him there and back. I also asked Nautasha to go with her dad to the hospital and keep an eye on him after the surgery. She told me that she didn't want to do it.

I was hurt. I didn't understand why she would not want to help her dad, even when he was going in for surgery. All she said was that she hated hospitals. I asked her to do it for me, and she finally agreed.

The day of the surgery went by slowly. I was waiting for Nautasha to text me that Phil was out and doing well. Tristin saw me watching the clock and encouraged me that dad was going to be fine. I wondered if he was saying it to help me or to convince himself.

Finally, that afternoon, I got a text from Nautasha. Phil had come out of surgery fine, was in recovery, and would be able to leave in a few hours. Relief flooded me. I could see that Tristin was relieved as well.

By 3:00 p.m., however, I had not heard from Nautasha or Phil, so I thought I had better call. Phil answered the phone, and we talked about his surgery and how he was feeling. He said he wanted to rest awhile, so I let him go after fifteen minutes.

CHAPTER 59
Home Again

―◦―

Those two weeks went by fast. Even in the new room, we had been getting bitten by bedbugs. It turned out they had survived in our vacuum cleaner and come along with us!

We discovered that they were hard to kill, let alone get rid of. After researching online, we finally found out that we needed to go to the laundromat and wash and dry everything on high heat. We spent our last day in Watertown doing laundry, and we rented a hotel room for the night.

In the morning we packed the car and headed to drop Phil off at Fort Drum. There his company would board a bus to start their long journey to Iraq. We said our goodbyes, got back in the car, and headed once more for Michigan.

The children were happy we were going back home to the farmhouse. They laughed and talked for about half of the trip. Then they decided to sleep for the rest of the way home.

When we got there, we decided not to take our stuff into the house right away. If there was any possibility that there were still any bedbugs in our stuff, we did not want them inside. We only brought in what we were sure was not infested. We left everything else outside for about two weeks, covered so that the rain would not get to it if the weather got bad.

We got settled back in and the children expressed how happy they were to be home again. Nautasha and I went out to the pasture right away to see how our horses were doing. A few weeks earlier, they had still had all of their winter fur and were just starting to lose it (we had had a bad winter, and summer came later than normal). We knew they would need to be ridden soon.

When we got to the pasture, we both looked with open mouths. You could count the horses' ribs. The pony, at least, only looked a little underweight. I hugged my horse with tears in my eyes and said, "I am so sorry, Sam. I don't know what happened. I will do my best to get you well again." Tears ran down my face.

Nautasha stood there with a stunned look on her face. Then she got angry. "How could this happen, Mom? Didn't Uncle Dean feed them? I knew I should have stayed home. This would have never happened had I just stayed here!"

All I could do was encourage her that we would fix this and find out what had happened. I touched Nautasha's shoulder and told her not to worry. Then I got on my phone to call our farrier. I explained the situation to him and asked what we needed to do. He walked me through a list of supplies that I needed to buy, then told us not to ride them until they got their weight back up.

Nautasha and I ran to Tractor Supply and got the supplements and grains needed to get our horses back to normal. When we got home, we started treating them right away. After a few months, they had gained enough back that you could no longer see their hip bones. Nautasha and I were happy that they were coming along nicely. We kept up the treatments.

Uncle Dean felt really bad. When we were living in New York, he had known that we would have extra bills and had felt that he could help us save a little bit of money. He hadn't known that cutting the horses' hay and grain intake would hurt them so badly. Because they had such a thick coat of winter fur, he could not see the weight that they had lost. But time went on, and they slowly gained their weight back. We began to ride and recondition them since they had been without for almost a year.

Nautasha seemed to be happier. She would finish her chores so that she could go riding. Nautasha loved to be on the back of a horse and to go on trail rides. If I didn't have time to go with her, she would take Tristin or Dani. When she wasn't riding, she could be found playing her guitar.

CHAPTER 60
Selfishness and Heartache

The summer and fall months went by fast while the children and I spent time with the animals. They got back into their school routine. I had decided to home-school them again instead of sending them back to the art school they had been in while we lived in Vanderbilt.

Before we knew it, the holidays were approaching again. Phil called and told me that he put in for leave around Thanksgiving, because Christmas leave was full (a lot of the soldiers wanted to be home with their families for Christmas, so those slots filled up fast; if you didn't get your papers in on time, you got what was left).

I told the children when their dad was coming home. Tristin could not wait to see him.

Phil had made plans for us to stay at his brother's house for four days and have Thanksgiving and Christmas both at once. His whole family had been invited. He was very excited when I picked him up at the airport; he couldn't wait to see everyone.

When we got back home, he hugged all the children and shook Uncle Dean's hand. Then he called his family and told them he had made it home safely and that he could not wait to see them.

A few days before we left for Phil's brother's house, I received a phone call. My husband answered and said, "Michelle, your cousin Donna is on the phone."

Donna told me that our grandma Alice was not doing well. They didn't think she was going to make it much longer. After I got off the phone, my husband's response blew me away: "I hope your grandmother doesn't die and ruin my family vacation."

I just looked at him. This was the woman who had helped raise me and who had been there for me when things weren't going well. She was the one who had made me laugh, showed me how to cook, and above all had shared her love for God with me. I loved my grandmother so dearly, and now she was dying. How could Phil say such a hurtful thing to me?

The day before we drove up to Brimley, the phone rang again. This time it was the call I had dreaded.

> The phone rang again. This time it was the call I had dreaded.

"Sis, your grandmother passed away an hour ago." My mother was sobbing. She had to pause before she could give me the rest of the news. My heart sank while Mother continued, "I will call you back to give you the dates of the wake and funeral as soon as I know."

I told her to stay strong and lean on Jesus for her strength. I knew that all my aunts and uncles would also take this hard. My grandmother was very family-oriented and full of love for everyone she met.

No sooner had I hung up the phone than Phil said, "Great! There goes my vacation time."

I yelled, "*Really?* I can't believe you are being so insensitive and only thinking of yourself. I just lost my grandmother, and all you can think about is your vacation!"

In tears, I ran into my bedroom. I slammed the door behind me, lay on the bed, and cried. After a few minutes, I got on my knees and asked God to forgive me for my outburst and to help my husband to be more like Jesus.

Phil came in a little while later (I found out later that Uncle Dean had said something to him about how he was being rude and selfish). He told me that he was sorry for the words he had said. I knew in my heart he was not sincere. I figured he was only trying to make peace before we left for his brother's house.

Once we were there, I received another call from my mother. "Your grandmother's wake is on December second, and the funeral is December third."

After I hung up, Phil started saying bad things about my grandmother. He didn't see why we needed to go. Then he said, "Just you should go, and I will stay here with the kids. She is dead anyway; there's no sense in us all going."

I already didn't want to take Tristin because of how young he was. Also, he had ADHD, Emotional Disorder, Asperger's, and Tourette's Syndrome. I felt it would be too much for him to handle emotionally. But Phil was trying to use this as an excuse to stay with his brother.

His mother spoke up and scolded him for his behavior. Then she said that she would take Tristin and watch him for the two days that we were gone. I was thankful that I had such a caring mother-in-law.

Phil gave in and went to the services with me. Dressed up in a suit and tie, he looked very handsome, but the character he displayed was arrogant. He was acting so differently that I felt embarrassed to be around him.

He also followed Nautasha around and hugged her a lot. He even had her sit on his lap. She was a young lady, and this was not the behavior a father should display toward his child. I was very uncomfortable and so was some of my family.

A few of them talked to me about this. They felt that it was inappropriate. When several members of my family and I approached him, he acted like we were all overreacting. I began to feel like I should have let him stay at his brother's house.

I saw many family members whom I had not seen in years at the wake and funeral. We all recalled the happy times we had had with Grandmother Alice.

Grandma Alice.

One of them was my brother Robin, who had flown in from Tucson, Arizona. He had been very close to our grandmother. She used to make him breakfast all the time when he lived down the road from her; his favorite was pancakes, and Grandmother Alice would make them from scratch just for him. She also did his laundry. She would spend time talking with him and listening to how his day at work went. She was a very loving woman.

I was excited to see Robin. I missed him since I hadn't been able to see him much after he moved south. He had opened up his own contracting business and was doing very well for himself. He had also learned how to fly a plane and bought a ranch. He even bought some horses. I was shocked. When we were growing up, he had always teased me by saying my horse Bridget was dog food.

Scott had decided not to come. He wanted to remember Grandmother the way she was. It was too hard on him to see her so thin and sickly-looking. Uncle Dean didn't come for the same reasons. I understood why they stayed away. I knew that they must be taking it hard, and that this was the only way they knew how to handle the death of someone who meant so much to them.

The services started, and we all sat mourning over the woman we had grown to love. As they ended, we were given the opportunity to go family by family up to the casket. When it was my mother's family's turn, all of us got up together: Phil, Robin, Mother, Ben, Nautasha, and myself.

I had kissed Grandmother goodbye earlier, but now my mother felt the need to say goodbye, too. As she did, she was lost in emotions and almost collapsed. Ben and Nautasha grabbed her and held her up. Phil started to crack jokes at the casket. All I did was look at him, and he stopped.

We went back to our seats and waited till the whole family went through the line. When everyone was done, the director of the funeral home shut the lid of the casket.

As Nautasha heard the click, she broke down, and my mother and brother comforted her. Nautasha knew that she would never be able to go to her great-grandmother's house again to see her cooking or baking. She could never again sit and talk with her about things that bothered her.

My daughter knew who God was and that we needed to trust in Him and seek His Guidance, but death was still scary to her. She did not understand why she had to lose her great-grandmother, having forgotten what I had shared with her from Thessalonians:

> But I do not want you to be ignorant, brethren, concerning those who have fallen asleep, lest you sorrow as others who have no hope. For if we believe that Jesus died and rose again, even so God will bring with Him those who sleep in Jesus.
>
> For this we say to you by the word of the Lord, that we who are alive and remain until the coming of the Lord will by no means precede those who are asleep. For the Lord Himself will descend from heaven with a shout, with the voice of an archangel, and with the trumpet of God. And the dead in Christ will rise first. Then we who are alive and remain shall be caught up together with them in the clouds to meet the Lord in the air. And thus we shall always be with the Lord. Therefore comfort one another with these words.
>
> (1 Thess. 4:13-18)

Ben was also close to his great-grandmother, and he did not take her death well at all. They had bonded from his birth, and Great-Grandmother Alice had always been a prominent part of his life. For a short time he had lived with her and cared for her. Now a young man, Ben was struggling to find his way in life, and he had just lost the one connection to God whom he could trust.

Ben had fallen away from the church and God. I tried several times to reach him, but I only made things worse, because I would try to control the situation or tell him what he needed to do instead of helping him see how much God truly loved him. While I struggled in my marriage with Phil, I had left my son behind.

As I already mentioned, I had sent Ben to stay with Uncle Robin in Tucson, where Robin put him to work for his company. After only a few months, I grew to miss Ben and told him that he could come home if he wanted to. But then, a few days later, I called him again and told him that I didn't think it was a good idea for him to come home after all, because God had communicated to me that Ben needed to stay with his uncle.

I confused my son emotionally and mentally. Ben never told my brother about that second phone conversation, and my brother became upset with me. I explained to Robin that I had told Ben to stay.

Again, as I said earlier, Ben ended up leaving and coming back to Michigan anyway. First he lived with my brother's ex-girlfriend. Then he stayed with my mother for a month, who told him that he had to get his life together; she was too old to be supporting him. That was when my grandmother took him in.

Instead of seeking in prayer for God to show me how to raise up my children through the Word, I tried to fix Ben (when I was not pushing him away). This was a mistake on my part, and because of it my son did not have the spiritual guidance he needed.

He strayed completely from the Lord and into the world. He talked to spirits and let them direct him. He got hooked on drugs, and for most of his life he would wind up jumping from one house to the next, or living in a tent when no one would take him in.

My heart breaks now, knowing that the answers to raising our children are right in front of us. It is we as parents who fail to obtain the knowledge which God has placed before us: "Train up a child in the way he should go, and when he is old he will not depart from it" (Prov. 22:6).

I wish I would have understood back then that this involved knowing the character of Christ and how He would have responded to my children, and applying it to my life. Now my goal is to help other parents seek the character of Christ while raise their children. God brings all things together for good.

Today I regret the time with Ben which I lost. He hated me at times, and as I look back, I can't blame him. He needed me, but I was so engulfed in trying to save my marriage that I just kept pushing him farther and farther away. And as I pushed, he fell farther and farther from God. In those days, Ben was seeking someone to love him where he was at, but all anyone ever did was push him away. He had lost his way with God and was hurting so deeply inside. No one but his great-grandmother Alice had broken through his walls of defense. Now she was no longer there to comfort this lost child of God.

As the funeral ended, the sons, grandsons, and great-grandsons carried the casket to the hearse. It was hard to see the casket at times because there were so many men carrying it at one time. We got into our vehicles and started the long procession from Munising to Trenary. Near Trenary I received a phone call from Aunt Bell.

"Mick," she said, "you know we are going to drive by the homestead and the old homestead before taking Grandma Alice to the cemetery, right?"

"Yes," I said, "my mother already told me. We are just going to keep following you." As I hung up the phone, I realized how deeply the loss of my grandmother was affecting all of us.

When we arrived at the cemetery, I watched the men carry grandmother's casket to the grave. Grandma Alice had so many descendants that this was another whole group of them.

Tears formed in my eyes. My daughter and I were to sing, and I knew I would have to do so with my eyes closed. If I didn't, if I watched my family's pain come flowing out through their tears, I would not make it through the song. I was grateful that my daughter was going to play the guitar. Later, I didn't know how she did it. I think she must have closed her eyes, too.

The funniest thing happened as we walked up to the grave site to sing. It started to snow: big, fluffy, white snowflakes.

My grandmother had loved snow. She used to sit for hours at her kitchen table, watching it fall and commenting on how beautiful it was.

As the snowflakes fell, so did the tears of all the people there.

We had had such a mild winter that the ground was still soft enough to bury Grandmother Alice. There was no snow on the ground at first, but she was now getting a burial with the love of God showering down. His blessings were falling upon a woman who had loved and helped many in her lifetime.

I found out later that my grandmother had stated, "I hope it snows when I am buried." Her prayer was answered. She will be greatly missed, but "heaven is cheap enough" (White, *Heaven*, p. 82).

We started back to finish our holiday celebration with Phil's family. On the way we hit a big snowstorm and had to spend the night in a motel. The next morning we got up bright and early and once more headed down the road to Brimley.

The roads were bad, but at least it was daylight out now and we could see the road. Phil mentioned that we had spent so much time away from his family that we should stay another night and head back in the morning.

This was cutting it close: Phil wanted to spend Sabbath evening at his brother's house, and they were not Sabbath-keepers. We argued over this, but finally I decided it was no use and just gave in. He wasn't going to take us home, anyway.

I studied from the Bible with the children that evening, but after we were finished Ben and Tristin went right out into the living room with their uncle and dad to play video games. Nautasha stayed in the other living area with her aunt and watched television. My heart broke. I went to the guest bedroom and cried, praying for God to help me through this time of sorrow.

When we got back home, all Phil and I did was argue. He was not living a Christ-like life, and I was upset because I knew his behavior would affect the children; they would long for worldly things instead of God.

One Sabbath afternoon Phil jumped on his computer and started to play a video game called *Diablo*. "*Diablo*" is a Spanish words that bears the meaning, "devil." The game met the standards of its name. Satan was taking control of my husband's mind; he was slipping farther and farther from God.

I looked across the kitchen counter at Phil and thought, *Lord, I don't want to be in this marriage anymore. I want out. I just want him to leave. But I will honor you, Lord: he has done nothing that biblically gives me a right to divorce him. I will do my best to become the wife that he needs me to be. I love you, Lord, and I know you will get me through this time of trouble.*

Two weeks went by and Phil packed up to leave. I took him to the airport in Pellston that afternoon. I just walked him into the lobby and said goodbye. He gave me a quick hug, then walked away to check in his bags. I exited and got into my car.

I was relieved when I pulled out of the airport parking lot, and I asked God to forgive me for being happy that he was leaving. I felt guilty for the way I felt, because he was going back to a war zone.

CHAPTER 61

Nautasha's Secret Revealed

Tristin, Nautasha, and I got back into our normal routine at home. We helped out at the church when needed and attended prayer meetings led by Pastor George on Wednesday nights. We were reading through *The Great Controversy* together as a church, and Pastor George answered all of our questions from the Scriptures.

I saw how grounded in the Lord he and his wife Barb were, and I longed to know God the way they did, so I talked to Pastor a lot. He helped me to understand the Word; his questions helped me to think about the Bible in ways I never had before. Sometimes I felt like I overwhelmed him with my own questions, but he always smiled and answer them.

Pastor George was actually retired. He was just filling in at our church in Gaylord until we received a new pastor. I know that God had placed him and his wife in my life to help me learn to follow Him with all my heart and carry His truths within me. Pastor was very blessed; I could sit and listen to the wisdom God gave him for hours. I looked forward to his sermons, and I took notes so that I could remember and take in all of God's words.

I held Pastor George and Barb dear to my heart, along with the teachings they shared so lovingly with me.

I wanted to keep the Lord's Day holy after reading in Exodus:

> Remember the Sabbath day, to keep it holy. Six days you shall labor and do all your work, but the seventh day is the Sabbath of the Lord your God. In it you shall do no work: you, nor your son, nor your daughter, nor your male servant, nor your female servant, nor your cattle, nor your stranger who is within your gates. For in six days the Lord made the heavens and the earth, the sea, and all that is in them, and rested the seventh day. Therefore the Lord blessed the Sabbath day and hallowed it. (Exod. 20:8-11)

And also in Isaiah:

> If you turn away your foot from the Sabbath, from doing your pleasure on My holy day, and call the Sabbath a delight, the holy day of the Lord honorable, and shall honor Him, not doing your own ways, nor finding your own pleasure, nor speaking your own words, then you shall delight yourself in the Lord; and I will cause you to ride on the high hills of the earth, and feed you with the heritage of Jacob your father. The mouth of the Lord has spoken. (Isa. 58:13-14)

After church the children and I would drive forty-five minutes to Camp Au Sable and walk the boardwalk around the lake. It was two miles around, and there were benches that had Scripture on them. At first we took turns reading the Scriptures, but after a while we began to play a game where the children had to remember what the next bench said before we got there. It was fun and helped them to memorize the verses. We usually went the same way around every time so that they could memorize the Scriptures in order.

"What is the first bench, kids?" I would call out as we started.

Nautasha would yell back, "John 3:16: 'For God so loved the world he gave his only Son, that whosoever believes in Him shall not perish but have everlasting life.'" This was my daughter's favorite verse for a long time; I think because it was the first one she memorized.

The children raced around the boardwalk to see who could make it to the next bench first, then they read or recited the verse before the other one got there. Since Tristin was five years younger than Nautasha, he usually lost those races. At one point, though, I noticed Nautasha lagging behind so that he could get ahead. I smiled, enjoying the beauty God had given me in the form of my children.

I loved walking the boardwalk at camp. There was a heavenly peace that I will never forget. The children loved it, as well. You could feel the presence of God even as you drove through the front gate. Coming onto the camp road brought tears to my eyes many times.

As May loomed around the corner, we decided to go to Au Sable to help out with work week. This was something they did twice a year; once in spring and once in the fall. People from all over would come to help fix, restore, or build anything that the camp needed for upcoming events.

Since I was home-schooling the children, I decided this would be one of our field trips. The kids were excited until I told them that they would have to write an essay as part of the field trip project. They were bummed at first, but then decided that it was worth it.

We packed up and headed out for a week of work and fun. After three days there, the children and I had bonded more deeply.

That third night, after Tristin took his shower, we did our prayers and devotions. As he snuggled down into his sleeping bag on the top bunk, I asked if he would be okay while Nautasha and I went to take our own showers up at the bathhouse.

He nodded sleepily, and told me, "I won't even know you're gone, Mom." Then he smiled. I had to laugh. Tristin was always the first to say it was time to go to bed.

Nautasha and I headed out to the bathhouse. After we got out of the showers, I started to blow dry my hair while she talked about the day and the fun we had had since we arrived at camp. When I finished, I pulled out my toothbrush and started cleaning my teeth.

While I was getting ready for bed, my mind was troubled by a recurring nightmare that I had been having for several nights in a row. The dream was not something I would have normally shared with anyone. Instead, I would have been on my knees in earnest prayer, asking the

Lord to take it away. I had already prayed about this dream several times; it always felt so real, and I was having a hard time sleeping because of it. Tonight I felt deeply moved to tell my daughter about it.

I didn't understand why I needed to tell her such a horrible thing, but God had put it on my heart. I knew that I needed to trust Him. I said a short, silent prayer, then I looked over at my daughter.

"I had a dream that Dad was touching you in inappropriate ways."

Nautasha looked at me in shock. Then, really softly, she said, "That really happened."

I swung around and looked at my daughter. "*WHAT?*"

Nautasha repeated herself, then slowly started to tell me of all the things her stepdad had been doing to her. My heart ached as I listened to her story. Then she got to the part where he had almost committed adultery with her.

"Mom, do you remember when Dad had surgery on his neck to remove the tumor, when we were in New York, in the small apartment?"

I nodded.

"If you hadn't called Dad when you did … " She went on to tell me the details of what had happened: had I not made that phone call to my husband when I did, he would have taken her virginity.

God had saved my daughter in that moment. I could not praise the Lord enough for using me even when I didn't realize it.

> My mind was troubled by a recurring nightmare. Tonight I felt deeply moved to tell my daughter about it.

We talked for a long time in the bathhouse that night. During our conversation, I told Nautasha that I had seen red flags and confronted Phil, but that he had always told me it was all in my head; that I had started to believe him. I said that I wished I would have listened to the warnings the Lord had given me. Maybe I could have prevented this from happening.

When we were done, I sensed relief in Nautasha. She had let go of terrible baggage she had been holding onto, which had been weighing her down emotionally. Now her healing could start, but it would be a long process.

I, on the other hand, had taken on her burden. It felt like someone had just ripped the heart out of my chest. That night, I lay in my bunk, unable to sleep, as I envisioned all the bad things my husband had done to our daughter.

The next morning, after we had eaten breakfast with the group and were assigned our work for the day, I left Tristin with his sister and went back to the cabin to grab my phone. I needed to talk to someone.

I called Carol, a sister in Christ from our church in Gaylord who was a retired nurse and very educated. She could help me through this hard time. I knew that she would pray with me and help me to do what was right.

When I told her what my daughter had revealed to me, she suggested that I talk to Pastor George. We discussed how and where to have this meeting. I asked if we could all meet at her house, because I knew I was going to need a friend as I talked to the pastor.

After I was done talking, Carol said a prayer for me. Then she said, "Hang in there, girl. God will get you through this. Trust in Him."

I had to focus on those words to keep me going, because as the day went by, Nautasha told me more of the horrible things that had happened to her. To begin with, Phil had threatened to take her life if she told anyone. But since he was in Iraq and could not touch her, she felt safe.

I was glad that Nautasha now felt more comfortable telling me what had gone on and was able to confide in me, but I became so mentally stressed that it was hard for me to function. I began to blame myself for the hurt my daughter had had to endure.

The next morning, before we left camp, I talked to the camp manager's wife. I was very grateful for her prayers and advice. I was having a hard time comprehending this terrible event. I knew it was going to pull our family apart and cause a lot of pain. The idea of my husband giving his life back to Christ and having a marriage with him that was full of the love of Jesus was now just a dream.

The children and I left Camp Au Sable and headed back to Vanderbilt. I dropped the kids off at home along with all of our luggage. I told them that I needed to run an errand and would be back soon. Uncle Dean kept an eye on them for me.

I headed to Carol's house. She had called Pastor George and set up the meeting. I was in tears all the way there. I knew that I needed to compose myself so I could be ready to hear the counsel which God had for me.

We all sat in Carol's living room, and as I told Pastor George the horrible events that Nautasha had told me about at camp, I saw heartbreak and worry upon Carol's face. When I was finished, Pastor told me that I needed to report this to Child Protective Services or else, by law, he would have to report it.

He and Carol helped me get in contact with CPS. I went down there right after I left the meeting. The man who saw me set up an appointment for me to take Nautasha to the state police station in order to write up a report. I then called Pastor George and told him what would happen. He prayed with me again on the phone.

I was thankful for the Lord's children coming to my aid with prayer, love, and His wisdom. I knew I could not endure this alone.

CHAPTER 62
Action Taken

CPS called to remind me of the date and time when I needed to be at the police station and told me the name of the Sergeant in charge of the case. After I hung up the phone, I walked to Nautasha's bedroom.

I stood in the hall for a moment to compose myself. I could hear her playing her guitar and singing. After knocking, I walked into the room.

"What's up, Mom?" Nautasha asked.

"I just got off the phone with CPS. I need to take you to talk to a state police sergeant in a few days."

She looked down. "Do I have to go?"

"Yes, honey!" I sat down and explained that this had to be done. I knew it was going to be hard on her, so I reassured her that I would be there by her side the whole way.

I prayed with Nautasha, then encouraged her to ask God for the strength to endure this battle that lay ahead of her. I gave her a hug and walked out of the room.

I could only imagine the pain my daughter was feeling in her heart. Later in the day I watched her, and she seemed to be very depressed. She spent a lot of time out with the horses and talked to them about her problems. They had become her safe place throughout all of the abuse. Now that she was going to have to relive those horrible events, she needed that safe place even more.

Each day Nautasha revealed more of the abuse that had taken place in her life during the last two years. As she did, I went into a state of deep depression. I felt like it was all my fault; that there should have been some way for me to stop what had happened.

My body was under so much stress that I could not eat or sleep. I absorbed myself in vigorous exercise to stop the pain and anger I was feeling. I dropped twenty-two pounds in a week and a half, and my friend Carol became very worried about me.

My daughter also saw the state I was in and worried that I would die from stress and starvation. She stopped telling me about things that Phil had done to her. Now *she* wanted to protect *me*; Nautasha started to blame herself for everything and felt like she was going to lose her mother because of what had happened to her.

I had not contacted Phil since I found out what he had done to our daughter. Whereas I usually went online to talk to him on messenger, now I had no desire to speak to him at all. I felt hurt and betrayed by his actions. Phil had stepped way out of bounds, and I could not talk to him until I calmed down.

He started calling my cousins and mother to find out if I was okay or what was going on. None of my family knew what was going on yet so they called me up, worried that something bad had happened to me. I reassured them that I was fine; I said I had just been really busy and unable to get on the computer to message Phil.

The day came when Nautasha had to go in and give her statement. My neighbor Ann from down the road watched Tristin while I took her to the police station. The sergeant talked to her with me in the room for a while, then asked both of us if Nautasha would feel comfortable talking to him alone. She looked at me.

"Tasha," I told her, "if you don't feel comfortable, I will stay right here. Whatever you want, I will respect."

She looked back at the police officer and then at me again. "I feel safe, Mom. I will be okay."

The sergeant pulled me aside and said, "Child victims have a tendency to tell more when the parents are not in the room. They feel ashamed when they have to tell their parents. They feel like they have done something to deserve what happened to them.

"This way," he continued, "we will get more information and be able to help your daughter. We will get through this and put the perpetrator behind bars."

I signed a statement saying that I gave my permission for the police to talk to my daughter alone, and he led me to the waiting room. I sat there for almost three hours. When they were done taking her statement, they came and got me.

This time, they asked Nautasha to stay in the waiting area while they talked to me. They gave her some food to snack on, and she talked with the officer behind the counter while I went in with the sergeant. They walked me back through the small hall into the same room where they had taken Nautasha's statement. I sat down and waited to hear what he had to say.

"Michelle," he began, "your daughter stated that your husband is in the U.S. Army and is in Iraq. Because most of the sexual abuse happened in New York, and because your husband is active in the Armed Forces, we have no jurisdiction on this case. We have to turn it over to the Criminal Investigation Department of the Army.

> "We will do our best to put the perpetrator behind bars where he belongs."

"We will do our best to work with CID to solve this case," he said, "and to put the perpetrator behind bars where he belongs."

He then took my statement regarding things I had seen and confronted Phil about. Afterward, he told us that we were free to go and that he would contact us soon.

After we got home that afternoon, my daughter headed straight for the horse pasture. I called Ann and told her Tristin could come home when she was ready. She said that he wanted to play with Legos with her son for a little longer. I just smiled. Ann's son was Nautasha's age, but Tristin looked up to him like a big brother and friend. I hung up and went for a two-mile jog. I needed to clear my head.

That evening I felt like I needed to call Phil and confront him on this matter. I got through, which was usually tricky because there were only certain places where I could get hold of him. On this tour, though, he was stationed at a desk in an office most of the time. I told him what Nautasha had told me at camp and since we returned home.

The other end of the phone was silent.

I continued, "How could you do such a thing? Was I not a good enough wife for you? Didn't I do all I could to help you and make our marriage work?"

In a soft voice, all he said was, "Michelle …. " and his voice trailed off.

"I hope you realize there is no more marriage. I am done. You have stepped out of bounds with your actions. I need to do what is best for our family now."

He remained silent as he heard my words of hurt and pain. Then he said something which I will never forget. "I never meant to hurt you."

"*YOU NEVER MEANT TO HURT ME?*" I yelled. "Then what did you expect it to do? Make me feel *better,* knowing what you did to our daughter? *A little girl* you *raised?*" Now that I had raised my voice, he was not happy. The words he said next remain stuck in my mind:

"I didn't show her anything she didn't want to see, or do anything she didn't want me to do."

I was appalled. I started yelling what he had done to our daughter and asking if he really thought a little fourteen-year-old girl wanted all those things done to her. Finally I said, "I can't talk to you anymore. You are sick."

"Michelle, please don't hang up. I am sorry."

"Sorry doesn't change what you have done." As I hung up the phone, I could hear him crying. I knew that he realized he was losing his family. He had messed up, and he realized that this was something he could not fix.

I only spoke to Phil a few more times after that. Once was at the request of the police, in an effort to get a recording of him confessing to what he had done. However, by then, he had already talked to some people and knew better than to talk about the incidents on the phone.

The next phone call was to tell him that Nautasha had filed a report against him and that I was filing for a divorce.

CHAPTER 63
Falling Apart and Angry

My nights were sleepless. When I lay down in bed, I could feel and hear my heart pounding against my chest. One night I couldn't take anymore, so I got up and called Carol.

She told me what to take to help me get some sleep, and she explained that the stress I was under was causing anxiety. That was why my heart was beating so fast and hard when I lay down. It was also why I could not eat.

Carol was still worried about my health because my weight had dropped so drastically in such a short time, thanks to not eating and excessive exercise. She told me to force myself to eat, even if I had to gag it down. She suggested some foods that would stay down. I knew she was right, so I choked down half a banana, then went to bed.

The next afternoon I went out in the woods, down into a little valley. I dropped to my knees and screamed at the top of my lungs, "*WHY, LORD? WHY?*" I started to pound the ground as tears ran down my face. I picked up sticks and branches and threw them and then fell back on my knees, sobbing uncontrollably.

"I am angry, God." I said. "How could you allow this? Why, God? Why? You could have stopped this from happening. I know you could have. Why didn't you tell me, so *I* could stop it?

"I don't understand why, Lord. My anger is great, and my sorrow is greater. I don't know if I can bear the pain anymore. I have lost my husband. I have a daughter that is hurting and confused. I have a son that doesn't understand why I am mad at his father. This is tearing our whole family apart.

"Father, please help me. Please help me." I lay on the ground with my face in my hands. Unstoppable tears continued to stream down my face.

Then, as I lay there, I heard a still, small voice: "Michelle, I will never leave you, nor forsake you. I am with you always. I am holding you in my righteous right hand. Believe in me. Trust in the wisdom I have given you. I will carry you through this. I have a plan for you greater than you know.

"Arise, and be of good courage. I will strengthen you. Stand strong on my promises, and claim them in your life."

I sat up and wiped the tears from my face. "I will try to be strong, Lord," I answered. "My pain is great, and my heart feels like it is broken in half. Please help me to stay strong in your wisdom, Lord."

I heard, "In time you will heal, and your heart will be whole once again."

I stood up and walked back through the woods to our house, feeling a sense of peace fall upon me.

A few days later, the CID came into town. They wanted to question all of us: me, my daughter, and I brought Tristin along, as well. I prayed that God would protect my children and help them through this difficult time with a peace which I knew could only come from Him. We arrived at the state police post at 8:30 a.m.

While they spoke with Nautasha, I told Tristin, "Just answer the questions they ask you. Never lie. Always tell the truth. It is what God would have you do."

"Am I in trouble, Mom?" he asked me.

"No, sweetheart. You're not in trouble. The man in the suit is a nice man. He needs your help to find out the truth."

Tristin and I sat in the waiting room while Nautasha was in back. He sat there pretty well for an eleven-year-old with ADHD. I had brought books and a little brick game for him to play with. After he got tired of the simple game, he started to read.

When it got to be afternoon, I told the officer behind the desk that we were going to get lunch and would be right back. Tristin was happy to get out of the waiting room. We went to Taco Bell and got food for all three of us.

Once back at the station, we said our prayers and started to eat. Just then, the sergeant came out and told us that Nautasha was almost done. He would need to question Tristin next, which would not take as long. I handed him food to give to my daughter, and he laughed. "We have been giving her snacks, but I am sure she will be happy to have some real food."

Half an hour later, Nautasha came out with a smile on her face. She had really liked the people she was talking with. They had made her smile after all the hard questions were over with. They called Tristin back and questioned him for about forty-five minutes. He also came out smiling, and gave the officers a high five.

I was glad that they had not interrogated my children but rather questioned them with love. This was an answer to my earlier prayers.

Tristin didn't ask me many questions about all of this or talk about what he may or may not have seen. His emotional disorder prevented him from sharing his feelings; he locked everything up inside. Only years later, at fourteen, would he finally reveal to me just a little bit of what he had witnessed, and how it had made him feel uncomfortable. Afterward he changed the subject, but I could tell it had bothered him.

The day he finally opened up, he said to me, "Mom, I am not going to worry about this. There is nothing I can do about it but pray. It is in the past."

I left it at that, and told him that I was proud of him and to keep praying for his father. "There is hope for your dad to be saved."

I would sit at the table and pray with him that day. I wanted Tristin to understand that no matter what sin we have committed, God will forgive us; that if we accept Jesus fully into our hearts and make a change in our lives to follow after Him, we can obtain salvation through His blood, and God will help us to become more like Jesus. As the Bible says:

> Then Peter came to Him and said, "Lord, how often shall my brother sin against me, and I forgive him? Up to seven times?"

Jesus said to him, "I do not say to you, up to seven times, but up to seventy times seven." (Matt. 18:21, 22)

For if you forgive men their trespasses, your heavenly Father will also forgive you. But if you do not forgive men their trespasses, neither will your Father forgive your trespasses. (Matt. 6:14, 15)

CHAPTER 64
The Move to Escanaba

Two months passed, and it was getting close to the time Phil would come home from Iraq. I became nervous. I didn't want him around me or the children.

I heard that they had questioned him while he was overseas. They had confiscated his laptop to look for evidence but hadn't found anything, because Phil had wiped it clean. He was smart when it came to computers; and what he didn't know, he asked of those who did.

I started saving up money and asking people to pray for me. I wanted out of the farmhouse and away from any chance of physical contact with Phil.

The children and I went back to Trenary for the Fourth of July. I was excited to see a lot of old friends and family. One person I ran into was Skip, one of my brothers' childhood friends. We talked for a few minutes and got one another's phone numbers.

I called him after I returned from our little vacation. Skip told me he had a three-bedroom apartment which I could rent if I needed a place to stay. We set up a day for me to drive up to Escanaba and see it. I called my mother and asked her to come with me, and I brought along money just in case I wanted the apartment.

Mother and I loved it. It had a basement where I could put my workout room and washer and dryer. The bedrooms were just big enough for the children and me, and the living room and kitchen were decently-sized. It was small compared to the farmhouse we currently lived in, but it would work for us.

I paid Skip the first month's rent and security deposit. He gave me the keys and told me he would have the rental agreement ready for me to sign when I started to move in. I was thankful that he was there to help us. He was not just a childhood friend but also like a brother to me. I knew that he cared about my children and me like family.

On the three-hour drive back home that day, I felt for the first time that things were going to be okay.

We would have to find homes for all of our animals except the birds and Annabell, so I made some phone calls. I also prayed that God would place my horse Sam where he could be a blessing to others. I loved him, but I knew he was God's horse first. While He had blessed me with Sam for a short while, now it was time for someone else to be blessed.

I offered to donate him to Camp Au Sable. The neighbor down the road bought back Meg and "Big T" Thunder. To another neighbor, who had horses and little children, we gave our pony, Little T. We found a home for our dogs, and Uncle Dean kept the cats. A man from Gaylord came and bought our male goats for his farm (our little female goat had gotten sick and died).

As for the rest of our animals, a fox killed off all of our chickens, ducks, and turkeys. Nautasha's ferret escaped after she put it in an outdoor cage with too-large holes (although, years later, Nautasha found out that a girl down the road had found her ferret and taken it in as her own pet). The rats died, and the little teddy bear hamster escaped from his cage and drowned in the sump pump hole in the basement. We could not find homes for all of the rabbits, so we decided to release them in the woods behind our house.

We had never had problems with our animals till that time. It was like God was preparing us for the move. Still, losing so many animals so close together made my daughter sad.

When the Camp Au Sable staff came to look at Sam, they said that they would like him but could not come and get him right away. My friend said he could stay in their pasture until the camp could pick him up.

I was happy for all the help I was getting, so I didn't worry about the future welfare of my horse. Sadly, a few months later, I would learn from the camp staff that my friends had mowed their pasture and Sam had not had enough to eat. The day they would go to pick him up, he was like a skeleton (looking worse than he had when I had returned from New York).

My heart would sink at the news. I felt shocked and guilty at the same time. I should have called and checked on him more, but the people I was now putting him with as I prepared to move would never once call me to say that Sam was losing weight.

This was a horse which I loved with all my heart. I would cry when I left him at my friend's pasture, knowing he would no longer be mine. Yet, ironically, many people at camp would soon be very upset with me.

Thankfully, the staff would fix him up and he would gain all of his weight back. In the end, I would be very relieved to know that he was doing better and that God wanted him to be at camp, where he could be a blessing to other children and adults.

As for belongings, I was overwhelmed with all the things I had at the farmhouse. I could not believe how much we had accumulated over the years. I left a lot behind and told Uncle Dean he could have what he needed. I showed him the things that were Phil's.

At last the children and I had packed up our things, and some friends from Trenary helped us move to Escanaba. As we pulled out of the driveway, I took one last look at the house I had grown to love. Tears rolled down my face. This chapter in my life was almost over, and I needed to move on with the Lord as my guide. I knew that the road ahead was going to be rough, but with God's strength, I would be able to conquer anything that came my way.

CHAPTER 65
Emotional Turmoil

After we got settled into our new apartment, I went and registered Tristin in the Escanaba Seventh-day Adventist School. The school only went up to eighth grade, so once again I chose to homeschool Nautasha. I also looked for work and found a job with a sister in Christ who owned an assisted living home.

I knew her well from church. Her son had attended church school with Ben when we lived in Escanaba years ago. She was very sweet; she cried and prayed with me when she heard my story. I could see that God had sent me to her for work.

I loved spending time with the ladies and gentleman whom I took care of, and I showed them God's love often. They also brightened my day; I felt like I could finally heal from the broken heart I had been carrying around for the last four months.

Nautasha, meanwhile, was going through mood swings that were like a roller coaster ride she could not get off of. She was having nightmares almost every night. My heart broke for her. I knew she needed help.

Sadly, I pushed my daughter away from God by trying to force her to forgive Phil and lay all of her nightmares and all of what had happened at the foot of the cross. I did not know what was in her heart, and I was judging her. "For the Lord does not see as man sees; for man looks at the outward appearance, but the Lord looks at the heart" (1 Sam. 16:7b). As human beings this is a hard test, but one that can be overcome by God's divine grace and love.

I was still trying to fix things by controlling them. God had to show me that this was not how our children (or our brothers and sisters) get fixed. Only the conviction of the Holy Spirit in someone's heart can make changes in them. I was shown through prayer that I was trying to take over God's work. I knew that I needed to ask for forgiveness and just be a vessel for God to use.

As parents, we generally try to fix things for our children. We try to control situations. What we really need to do is pray for them and with them, giving them guidance from the Word of God. We need to let the Holy Spirit convict their hearts so they can draw nearer to God. This is how they will see the love of the Father and the Son. Only then will they have a true and sincere relationship with God.

Our case was moved to Upper Michigan. The CPS lady who had taken over came and shared how I could get Nautasha into counseling to help her cope and heal from all that had happened to her.

The road ahead was very rough. When I filed for divorce, I had to get a state-funded attorney, and he was not very good at what he did. On top of the divorce, there was the court case the military was scheduling and the pain that my daughter, son, and I were all feeling. To cope with the stress, I still exercised, but I also started spending more time in the Word of God.

I had to trust in the Lord to get me through this hard time in my life (and to help me to trust men again). There was a sour taste in my mouth about having another relationship. Satan tried to get me to play the field while I was hurting. I praise God for never giving up on me and for helping me to recognize the crafty schemes of the devil.

Satan was not only attacking Nautasha and me; he was attacking Tristin. My son wanted to figure out why he was not allowed to have a relationship with his father. However, because he had an emotional disorder, it was hard for him to express himself like Nautasha did. I placed him in counseling as well, but the counselor could not break through or get him to talk. He just discharged Tristin after a while.

He also got in trouble at school from time to time. He could take the teasing from other kids for only so long, and then he would snap and lose his temper. One day the teacher called and told me that Tristin had bit another student on the arm. His teeth had gone right through the young man's winter jacket and drawn blood.

I learned that the other boy was hyper; he liked to wrestle a lot, and he wouldn't stop when asked. Instead of Tristin telling the teacher what was happening, he had taken the situation into his own hands, with the result that the boy tackled him again, putting an arm around Tristin's face and throat. Tristin had bitten the young man to get him to stop.

I was shocked. I went to the school and talked this matter over with Tristin, and he apologized to the young man. However, as I walked out, I heard the other boy teasing Tristin about having to apologize. I then corrected that young boy on his behavior. When we got home, I told my son to pray for this boy. "He is a child of God," I said, "and you just don't know his heart or why he does what he does."

Tristin was not thrilled about this but said that he would try to forgive the boy and pray for him. Today the two of them are friends. It's amazing how God works in the lives of children.

Satan kept placing snares in front of the three of us and causing conflict in our home. We just kept lifting it up to God in prayer. The children were not quite where I was as far as trusting in God, but I knew we could not make it through these trials and tribulations without His guidance.

One evening Nautasha asked me if she could go to Great Lakes Adventist Academy to finish high school. I asked, "Do you think you are ready to handle school away from home and your family? You do understand you will only be able to come home on leave times?"

She nodded and said, "This is what I would like to do. I have been praying about it, and I want to finish my education at GLAA. I feel this is where God is leading me."

"Well," I said, "we will have to do some research and ask around about how we can get funded. It is expensive to send you to a boarding school, and right now we have no extra money. We are barely making it here."

"I understand, Mom," Nautasha said, "but I also understand that if God wants me to be there, He will make a way for me to go."

I could not argue with her statement; I knew she was right. I asked around and learned some good information about GLAA. I discovered that Upper Michigan students got a big discount on their bill if they attended, because of the distance and the economic conditions that the people from the Upper Peninsula lived in. Jobs were scarce in our region.

> Oh, great! I thought. I hope he is not trying to ask me out.

Meanwhile, one day while checking my Facebook account, I saw that I had a message from a man who was not on my friends list. *Oh, great!* I thought. *I hope he is not trying to ask me out. I really want nothing to do with men right now.*

I opened the message and recognized the man in the picture: he was a former member of Riverside Church. The message read, *Do I know you? We seem to have all the same friends. Bob.*

I laughed with relief and responded. I learned that Bob had read a post I had made on a religious quote on a friend's page. The Lord had been prodding at his heart to send me a message for almost three weeks. We messaged each other a few times to catch up on how we knew each other, then became friends on Facebook. We didn't talk too much after that.

Later, Nautasha wanted to know if I had found out any more out about her going to GLAA. When she asked me, I remembered Bob saying that he worked at the Good News Farm at GLAA, where high school students worked to pay for their tuition. I also recalled talking to Bob about how my daughter wanted to go there. He had sent me his phone number and told me that if I had any questions, or needed help getting Nautasha into GLAA, I should give him a call, and he would help me out.

I checked my messages on Facebook, found Bob's phone number, and called him. He was glad to help us. He gave me the names of the people I needed to talk to and explained how Nautasha could work to pay most of her tuition. I was so grateful to the Lord for putting Bob in my path.

I made some more phone calls and had GLAA mail admissions paperwork to me for Nautasha. She was so happy when the packet came in. She wanted to go there to start the second semester of the school year, in January, and I had agreed that she could. We sat down together to look the packet over. Since I was home-schooling her, it was going to be a lot of work for me; I needed to make sure that I had all the information they needed me to send to them.

A few months remained before the new semester, and Nautasha's counseling was at a standstill. I talked to the staff at GLAA and let them know that she might need someone to talk to from time to time. I explained her situation, told them how she would have to testify in military court, and said that when those dates got closer, she would need someone to comfort and pray with her. They were very wonderful about the whole situation and agreed to be there for her. This made me feel more comfortable about sending her there.

CHAPTER 66

My Friend Bob, and The Proposal

---◦---

Before I knew it, Thanksgiving and Christmas had passed by, and I was taking my baby girl to GLAA. We got her settled into her dorm room and said our goodbyes with tears. I would miss my daughter, but I knew God had brought her to a place where she could draw nearer to Him. Tristin hugged her a couple of times. I knew he would miss Nautasha, too.

With Nautasha at GLAA, I needed to find someone to take Tristin to school in the morning. I had to be to work early, and I didn't want Tristin walking to school alone, because the neighborhood we lived in had a lot of drugs.

I had not known this when I first went to see the apartment; I found out a little while after we moved in. The tenant upstairs, for example, was into drugs, alcohol, and partying. This made me nervous about leaving my children at home alone. One Sabbath I petitioned the church members to pray for us about getting Tristin to school. Bob was there and heard my request.

Bob's family lived in the Upper Peninsula. He owned a small house there, in Perkins, where he stayed when he was not driving. Because he lived so close by, he was already in the habit of calling and checking in on us from time to time to see if we needed anything. He helped fix anything that was broken or needed repairing: my apartment, my car, even Tristin's toys. He was a blessing from God.

Bob had left the Good News Farm and was now a truck driver for a company in Lower Michigan. During a trip he had broken his foot getting out of his semi, and he was at home for a few months. He offered to drive Tristin to school in the mornings (Bob would end up helping with Tristin until he had his boot cast removed, at which time Bob was able to go back to work).

More than a month passed, and Natausha's February leave time was coming up. She would be home for five days, and I could not wait to see her. Tristin and I got things ready for her return, and I planned to make her favorite meal.

The two of us went to the church one Wednesday night to meet the GLAA bus. It was a happy reunion; we hugged and kissed each other, and then we talked all the way back to the apartment about what Nautasha had learned at school and all the new friends she had made. I was really happy to have her home.

One evening a stranger walked in my back door, uninvited. He was drunk and high on drugs and looking for the upstairs neighbor's apartment. I had just gotten out of the shower. Nautasha, who was scared, ran to the bathroom to get me.

> *One evening a stranger walked in my back door, uninvited. He was drunk and high on drugs.*

Thankfully Bob was in town. He happened to come by the house right then to see if we wanted to go bowling. By the time I had finished dressing and run to the living room, I saw Bob standing in the doorway between the kitchen and living room, telling the man that he was in the wrong place.

The stranger was confused and argued with Bob. I ducked underneath Bob's arms, which were spread across the doorway, and told the man that he needed to go back out and up on the left to get to his friend's house. He reluctantly left, and we heard him stumbling up the stairs.

I ran to lock my back door. My daughter had a horrified look on her face. Bob also looked very concerned. Nautasha said to Bob, "I am so glad you were here. That was scary. I don't know what I would have done, since Mom was in the shower."

Later that night she expressed to me that this event had triggered a flashback for her. She was scared and worried about how she would protect herself and Tristin.

I sat with her as she cried. I knew my baby girl still had a lot of healing to go through. At that moment I also realized that God had sent Bob into our lives to help us. He was a very good man and a wonderful friend.

Bob was so concerned about this situation that he went right to our pastor. The pastor felt that the children and I were in danger where we lived and needed to get out of that apartment. Bob asked him what his thoughts were about letting my children and me live in Bob's house while he was out on the road. The two of them discussed the details and prayed together.

Bob then came and told me what they had talked about. He asked if the children and I wanted to move into his little, one-bedroom house in Perkins. I told him that I needed to pray about it, and then I would give him an answer.

I did pray, and we ended up moving. Tristin slept in the living room on the sofa, Nautasha (when she was home from school) slept in the kitchen on a cot, and I slept in the bedroom.

During this time I also began praying that I didn't want to get married again unless God sent the man and dropped him on my front doorstep. I also told God what sort of man I needed. The second prayer was inspired by my old friend Diane, Pastor Dave's wife. She had once told me how she had prayed for her own husband before she was married: Diane had asked for the Lord to give her a man who loved Him more than she did; and I knew just how much *she* loved the Lord.

I felt very compelled to pray for the same thing. I was scared and wanted no more sin and sadness in my life. I didn't want to be alone, but I didn't want to be with another man who did not love the Lord or have a grounded relationship with Him. I had started to understand what the words in Corinthians about "evenly yoked" meant.

What I didn't know was that Bob had talked to my mother recently, asking her permission to court me. And while Bob was talking to the pastor about my using his house, he had asked *his* permission (because my father had passed away, Bob felt that the pastor was the next person he needed to go to with his intentions).

And so one day Bob came to me, got down on one knee, and asked me to marry him. He told me how he had talked to my mother and the pastor and how, through our friendship, he had found all of the things he had been praying for in a woman.

I knew in my heart that I was falling in love with him, too. I realized that this was the man whom God had sent to me in answer to my prayer. "Yes!" I said.

Bob handed me a black, leather, Remnant Study Bible. The bottom right corner read, *Michelle Gustafson*.

I looked up at him and asked, "How did you know I was going to say yes?"

Bob looked at me with a smile and a twinkle in his eye. He said, "God always gives me what I ask for!"

I playfully slapped his arm and said, "Good thing I didn't say no, or you would have had an extra Bible on your hands." We laughed and gave each other a hug, then we prayed and thanked the Lord for leading in our lives.

When I told my mother, she was so excited. "You finally found a man of God. I know this one is a good one who will take care of you and the children.

"I didn't care for your other two husbands," Mother continued, "but I knew it was not my place to meddle in your business. All I could do was pray for you that God would bless you. And now that He has ... *don't mess it up*." Then she smiled and said, "God has sent Bob to you and your children to help you all through this hard time. I can't believe the military has dragged this court case out so long. This has to be hard on Nautasha. It's been almost two years!"

I agreed that it was hard, and told her I was thankful for the blessings God was placing in my life. Then I said, "Now the problem is; when should we get married? Bob was thinking August, since he proposed to me in March. I just don't know what date to choose."

My mother said, "I have the perfect date." She held up her calendar, went right to May, and pointed to the twenty-fifth.

"Mom," I said, "that is your birthday. You want me to marry Bob on your birthday?"

"What better gift could a mother ask for than knowing her daughter will be taken care of when she is no longer here?"

I didn't know what to say. I just looked at her and asked, "Are you sure?"

"I have never been more sure."

After I left my mother's apartment, I sat in my car and cried tears of joy, because my mother wanted to share her special day from God with us.

CHAPTER 67
A Wedding and a Hearing

Bob and I understood that we would be bringing together two families. He had three grown children; one boy and two girls, along with a couple of grandchildren; and I was still raising my two youngest. Thankfully, over a short period of time, I would fall in love with all of his kids and grandkids. Additionally, Bob was almost twelve years older than me. However, the age difference was never an issue for us or for our families. We knew that God had placed us together.

The main challenge was when we were separated because of Bob's job. Neither of us liked the idea of being apart when he was on the road. For that reason, before we got married, Bob started praying that God would bless him with another job.

A friend of his called one day from Cedar Lake, Michigan, and offered Bob a position working at his company. Bob prayed about it, and the Lord led him to take the position. That meant that we would not really see each other until right before our wedding.

Our wedding day.

The day arrived; Bob and I were married on May 25th of 2011. We also celebrated my mother's birthday, bringing out a surprise cake and some gifts for her.

It was the perfect day, even though Satan had tried his hardest to break our marriage even before it started. But Bob and I had been praying, and we had known that God would work it all out. After many tears and prayers of forgiveness toward people who had tried to stop us, God had now united us, with Jesus as the center of our marriage.

We made vows to each other to serve the Lord and to keep Him at the heart of our union. We vowed to raise the children up in the Lord, to be disciples for the Lord, to go where He would lead us, to petition Him in prayer in everything we did, and to never go to bed angry.

Reflecting now, I see that God has truly blessed us both as we have kept these vows over the years. We have fallen short only a few times, and Jesus has always helped us to forgive and work together throughout our marriage. We are so grateful. God has reminded us of our love for Him and each other.

We ended up moving to Cedar Lake after we got married, where we lived for six months in our camper. Nautasha was still attended GLAA, and I decided once more to home-school Tristin.

Meanwhile, Phil was fighting the accusations my daughter had made against him. He was also changing attorneys, which caused delays in scheduling a trial. But when he could no longer delay the military court, a date was set for Nautasha, Tristin, and me to fly to Fort Drum, New York, to state our case.

We were going to tell our versions of what had happened to my daughter before a panel of JAG officers. These were Judge Advocate Generals; lawyers in the military. They kept in touch with us and prepared us for the upcoming military preliminary hearing, as they were the ones who had to prove that Phil was guilty.

My daughter dreaded that upcoming day. She didn't want to go to Fort Drum; she did not want to see Phil ever again. I felt bad for her, knowing that she was struggling with the whole situation. She had nightmares almost every night. She became exhausted, leading to mood swings and a change of character. She was not turning in her homework, and her grades were dropping at school. She became rebellious. I was very worried about her.

Bob and I sat and talked with Nautasha, and we prayed with her. She came to understand that this was something which she had to do. We told her that God would be with her the whole time.

Meanwhile, the judge advocates put a restriction on any contact with Phil until the court case was over. He was not allowed to contact the children or me, and we were not allowed to contact him. Nautasha already had a personal protection order against him, but until this military action, there had been nothing stopping Phil from contacting Tristin or me.

Now a sense of relief fell over me. I was praying for Phil, but I did not trust him with the children. But Tristin didn't understand why he could not see or talk to his dad. I explained it the best way that I could to an eleven-year-old boy.

"Your dad did something that was very wrong to your sister. It doesn't mean your dad doesn't love you or want to be with you. They are doing this to protect us and to protect all the information for the court case that is coming up." I had to answer a few more of Tristin's questions, and in the end we prayed for his father; that he would give his life back to Jesus so that we could be in Heaven together.

The day for our testimony arrived. Our friend drove us to the airport, and we left for Fort Drum. My daughter was very defiant during the trip. Anything I said or did upset her. She didn't want to sit by us, and when she did, she wanted a certain seat. No matter where I put her, she was not happy. It was a rough ride for us.

Tristin, on the other hand, was happy. I knew that he did not fully understand what his sister had gone through. He had only seen little things which he didn't understand. He could not wait to experience the airports and plane rides. Even if he could not talk to his dad (even if he saw him), Tristin was still happy to be going.

With the layovers, the flight was long, and Nautasha's attitude got worse. I just kept praying for her. Once we arrived, our friend Sheila from the Watertown Seventh-day Adventist Church picked us up from the airport and brought us to our hotel, and she loaned us her van so we could get to our appointments. Once we got our luggage up to the room, one of the JAG officers called me and set up a meeting for the next morning; this was to prep us before going before the military panel.

My daughter did not sleep well that night. She was up and down with anxiety and nightmares. All I could do was pray for her, but inside my heart was breaking for the child whom I loved so much. I could fix a cut if she fell down, make her feel better when she was sick, and talk her through a problem she was having with a friend, but this, I could not fix. It tore me up inside to watch my daughter suffer through this pain that I could only partly understand.

Again I had to realize that I couldn't fix anyone. I could only lift it up to the Father in prayer and listen for His guidance on how to help.

The next day we talked to several different officers. Then we were assigned to one who would work with us and question us at the panel. They also had a counselor onsite, Mrs. Lily, who talked with my daughter for a long time. When we were done with these discussions, Nautasha was relaxed and felt a little better. Mrs. Lily was a sweet and tender lady who was very caring and loving. Nautasha grew very close to her and looked to her for guidance.

I was very grateful for Mrs. Lily, since I would not be able to be with Nautasha or Tristin when they went in to talk to the military panel. Each of us would have to go in separately, and we would not be allowed to discuss our testimony with each other. Mrs. Lily, however, could accompany both of my children through the process, because she was neutral. She really helped them to see it was going to be okay.

The next morning when we got to the building where the meeting would take place, my daughter looked at me and asked, "Do you think he is there?"

I told her, "I don't know for sure, but I am guessing he is inside."

She looked away and became silent.

"Tasha," I said, "I will be praying for you. Trust in God, and He will carry you through this."

She didn't say a word as she opened the car door. When we entered the building, the JAGs had to find out which rooms we would be occupying and where the meeting would be held. They told us to wait at the entry.

Phil was already there and was told to wait in the same area. He stood by the wall in a parade rest position. Tristin walked over to stand six feet away from his father, then looked at the pictures on the wall. He could not talk to his father, but they hadn't said he couldn't stand by him.

As Phil remained silent and motionless, feet twelve inches apart, hands behind his back, facing straight ahead and with no emotion on his face, sadness came over me. I realized how he and Tristin must be feeling.

Then I looked at my daughter, and saw how very uncomfortable and scared she was. She stood as far away from Phil as she could.

When we were called back to where we'd wait during the hearing, Nautasha went with haste. We sat in the small room at a table, and Mrs. Lily pulled out some sketch paper and coloring books.

Both of the children loved to color and draw. As they started to draw, I saw Nautasha's body relax. When it was time for her to go in, I said a prayer for her. Then I told her, "I will be praying for you the whole time you are in there."

"Thanks, Mom," she said, then walked out the door with Mrs. Lily.

I kept true to my promise, praying for her the whole while she was before that panel. She came back over an hour later. When they took Tristin, I prayed for him, as well. He was only gone half an hour.

Then it was my turn. I entered and saw a long table. I sat at the very end, facing the general who was at the other end. On my right were the judge advocates who would be questioning me. On my left was the defense team that was representing Phil. All along the walls on both sides sat more officers.

I was questioned for about forty-five minutes. Phil looked down as I told my side of the story and what my daughter had been through. It was hard not to cry when they asked certain questions about my marriage and what had happened to Nautasha.

I saw my husband look up when I stated, "I loved my husband. I prayed for him every day. I looked forward to his retirement so we could be a family. But I could not stay with a man that hurts our children in such a way as he did."

Phil looked down again and did not look up for the rest of the time that I was in the room with him.

The hearing went on for most of the day. At the end of all of the questioning, an officer entered the waiting room and walked over to my daughter. He was holding a medal.

"Nautasha," the man said, "I want to give you a medal for bravery. I received it while serving my country in a war zone. What I did was considered brave, but what you had to undergo today required the most bravery I have seen in a long time. So I want you to have this.

"Every time you look at it," he continued, "I want you to remember how brave you really are." Then he handed her the medal and gave her a hug.

Nautasha smiled up at the officer, then looked at her medal with awe. I don't think she had ever considered herself to be brave before, but that day, she found out that a decorated soldier of the U.S. Army considered her braver than him.

We finally left the building right before supper. We ate and then went back to the hotel room. Nautasha had a sense of peacefulness about her. The weight was gone from her shoulders for the time being.

We got our bags ready and took showers. Then we knelt down to say a prayer of thanksgiving together. We did devotions, prayed our own silent prayers, and at last climbed into bed. We had to be up early to catch our ride to the airport.

The plane trip was longer than I wanted it to be. I longed to see Bob. I was mentally and physically drained, and I just wanted life to go back to normal. After landing and getting our bags, I was happy to walk outside and see my husband at the other end of the building.

The children were arguing over something. I had had enough of it and told them to start walking and do less talking. By the time we reached Bob, I was not happy and snapped at him. He knew that I was stressed out, so he was very nice to me even after my rude words. I told him I was sorry when we were on the road and heading home.

I truly have a wonderful husband. He prayed with me that night after I told him of the events in New York. We knew that this was in God's hands and that we needed to wait on His timing.

CHAPTER 68
You Want Me to Do What?

It was summertime, and our family needed some extra money. A wonderful Seventh-day Adventist family owned and ran one of the local stores in town, and they offered me a job. I thought it was where God was leading me, so I took it without praying about it first.

It was camp meeting time at Cedar Lake, and the GLAA campus bustled with staff, pastors, and their families, all setting up for hundreds of people who would attend the week-long event. One day, as I drove by the campus on my way to work, the Lord put on my heart that my days should be spent there meeting with Him. However, I had never attended a meeting at Cedar Lake before.

When I came home from work that night, I told Bob what I had felt that morning.

"I think we need to pray over this matter," he said. He took me by the hand, and we knelt at the end of our bed. We prayed to the Lord to see where He wanted me to be. We ended with, "Let it be Your will, Father, not ours, that be done."

We knelt in silence, listening for the Lord's still, small voice to direct us. After a few minutes, my husband looked over to me and said, "What did you hear?"

"That I need to be at the meetings," I said, "and that I did not pray about the job I took. Now I must tell them I need to leave and follow what God would have me do. What did you hear?"

He said, "That you should have prayed before taking the job, and that you need to attend the camp meeting."

I knew that I needed to do God's will rather than my own.

At 5:00 a.m. the next morning, my husband and I got up and started our normal routine to get him and Nautasha off to work (school was out, and Nautasha was working at the Academy to pay for her schooling). I said to Bob, "Honey, I really need you to pray with me. I need to know how to tell these wonderful people that God is leading me elsewhere. I don't want to hurt their feelings or upset them."

He grabbed me by the hand and once again walked me to the end of the bed in our camper. Once more we knelt down, and my husband held my hand tightly as he prayed a beautiful prayer over me. He asked God to give me the strength through Jesus to do what was right, and to soften the hearts of the people who had given me the job, so they would understand that the Lord had other plans for me.

I felt a sense of peace as we got off our knees. I knew that I needed to drive in that morning and talk to my employers.

I was nervous on the way there, but I said another prayer and felt peace come over me. I walked in, asked to talk to them, and explained the situation. They were very sweet about the whole thing. God had His hand on their hearts and on their business.

I left feeling relieved that God had taken care of the situation and was leading me to where He needed me. Now all I had to do was listen and follow. It sounded easy enough, but I was in for a surprise.

When I arrived at camp, I walked into one of the buildings and got a program. I didn't know what classes were available and needed the Lord to guide me.

I opened the pamphlet and scanned it, and my eyes fell upon a class called, "A Sermon in Shoes." I looked over the rest, but God kept bringing me back to "A Sermon in Shoes." I prayed, "Lord, is this one of the classes you want me to attend?"

I felt a clear impression that it was, so when the time came for the class to start, I walked into the room, sat down in front, and pulled out my Bible, notepad, and pen. I was ready to learn God's wisdom.

A well-dressed man walked in, smiled, and welcomed us. He talked with people as they continued to enter, and encouraged them to find seats.

I was getting excited. I wanted to know why God had me in this class and could not wait to find out. Just then, I saw Kyle walk in to talk to the well-dressed man, and my excitement turned to defiance. If Kyle was helping teach this class, that this was not the work that I wanted to do for the Lord.

Kyle worked for the Seventh-day Adventist Conference as the assistant publishing director. He also worked with GLOW Tracts. I knew of his love for God and of what he did to serve the Lord.

But he also did a lot of door-to-door work as a canvasser, which I did not want to do. I was ready to get up and walk out when I heard the voice of the Lord: "Michelle, this is where I need you to be. Stay seated and listen."

> *I was ready to get up and walk out when I heard the voice of the Lord: "Michelle, this is where I need you to be. Stay seated and listen."*

Again, I tried to get up. Again, the Lord spoke to me. Three times, I tried to leave. All three times, the Lord directed me to stay.

I finally prayed, "Lord, if this is where you want me to be, then I will stay and listen. I will do Your will, not my own; but I will need Your help and guidance."

I waited nervously as the class started. The well-dressed gentleman introduced himself as the literature evangelist director for the conference. He explained that this class was to help others to become disciples for the Lord.

After about fifteen minutes of preparing the class, the gentleman divided us into groups to go door-to-door. I was placed in Kyle's group. Not only that, he became my partner. God has a way of working in our hearts, even when we don't understand what the outcome will be.

Everyone went to their assigned locations and started going door-to-door. God blessed me greatly that day. I enjoyed the time I spent with Kyle going from home to home, passing out tracts, and praying with those people who allowed us to. There was joy in my heart as we sought souls for the kingdom. When it was time to go back, I was reluctant. I wanted to do just one more door; but I knew that one would turn into many.

We went out again the next day, this time to hand out books about the life of Jesus. This time I was put in a different group, The lady I was with was sweet. We took turns praying and talking with the people we met. Neither one of us wanted to stop knocking on doors. We were late coming back to the class, and we laughed when we realized that we were addicted to spreading the Word of God.

Kyle talked to the director and told him that I was a natural. He said that I needed to be a door-to-door literature evangelist.

I spent some time talking to the director, and he gave me a book to read called *Colporteur Ministry* (a colporteur is a religious bookseller). He said that when I was done with it, he would come to interview my husband and me.

I did finish the book, although not as quickly as most would have. I really studied it, highlighting a lot of information. I wanted to do my very best if this was where God was placing me. My husband and I prayed every night to make sure that this was the Lord's calling.

When the day came for the interview, it went well. A month later I became an official literature evangelist and started my training.

I needed to know certain Scriptures, and how to present books in such a way that the Holy Spirit could work in the hearts of the people who were interested in buying them. It was hard work to memorize all of the material. I was mentored by a few people who will always be dear to my heart. I cannot wait to walk in Heaven with them all.

We had now been living in Cedar Lake for six months, and Bob and I could not make it on what he was getting paid (I was just getting started with the LE work). My husband found a job back in Upper Michigan, thirteen miles from our little house in Perkins. We also learned that there was no literature evangelist in the Upper Peninsula: the Word of God needed to be spread.

At this time I decided to pull Nautasha out of GLAA and resume home-schooling her. She just was not where she needed to be spiritually;

she was acting out severely. Bob and I had prayed about this situation, and we came to feel that the Lord was telling us to home-school. I would work her and Tristin's schooling around my job. It was going to be a rough road for all of us, but with God's help, I knew I could accomplish the tasks which He put before me.

Once we got to Perkins, things fell into a routine and went a little smoother. However, Nautasha was still not happy. She had nightmares regularly, and her sleepless nights turned into angry days. I would get very upset with her and her actions, but I also felt deeply for the pain which I knew she was going through.

Tracy, a Christian counselor, offered to spend time with her on the side. This helped Nautasha out a lot. Tracy also gave me many good tips on how to deal with Nautasha's actions and on how to redirect her so she could see what she needed to change.

God sent me Tracy. She became my best friend, sister in Christ, mentor, and prayer partner. She helped me through many good and bad times, and she always helped me to remember that God had my back. When I needed to talk, she was there; and when she needed me, I was there for her.

God forms friendships and grows them to glorify His work. I know that is why He placed us together. My husband and I hold Tracy dear to our hearts, and we know that our children do, too.

CHAPTER 69

Evidence Recovered

---·∞·---

Summer approached, and the military had rescheduled Phil's court hearing several times. He did not like what his military attorneys were telling him, so the date kept being pushed back as his attorneys worked to build his case.

Every time they rescheduled, Nautasha prayed hard that she would not have to testify. Additionally, each time a new date was announced, her mood changed drastically and she became unbearable to live with. We were beginning to think it would never be over.

Then one day in the garage, I ran across an old laptop that Phil had given to the children when we lived in Watertown. I remembered this computer well.

Tristin had once asked to use it to watch some movies online. Phil had said he could, because Nautasha was on my computer. Tristin had set it on the sofa and gone to get a drink, but the computer fell to the floor, breaking some of the keys off of the keyboard. Phil yelled at Tristin, and I felt so bad for our son because I knew it was only an accident. (I confronted Phil later, and he apologized to Tristin for yelling.)

In spite of his anger, Phil thought that this gave him a good excuse to buy a new laptop. He had then given this old one to the children. However, when we moved to Vanderbilt, its power cord had somehow been misplaced. Since my own computer was different and the cords did not match, we wound up putting away Phil's old laptop and forgetting about it.

When we moved from the farmhouse to my friend Scott's apartment in Escanaba, we brought it with us. We figured that we could find another power cord for it and start using it again, but we never had the money to afford it and so we packed it back up and forgot about it once again.

Now, as I looked at the computer, I thought that maybe I should finally go and get a cord so that Tristin could have his own laptop for school and not have to use mine. But for the moment, I put it back in the drawer and went into the house.

A few weeks later, Tasha was home on a five-day leave from GLAA. We were talking about computers for school, and I remembered the one I had found in the garage. I told the children, and Tristin said that the cord for Bob's computer matched the laptop.

I plugged it in, and the children and I sat down to look through all of our old vacation and family pictures. We shared some good memories and laughs over them. Then we found pictures of our Watertown apartment.

I had been praying that God would help me find these pictures. The Jag Officers needed them for evidence, and I had figured they must be on this computer. I shut it down and sent the children to do some chores while I went outside to make a call to the lawyers.

One of the officers on our case answered. "Hello, Mrs. Gustafson," he said, "how can I help you today?"

"I just wanted to let you know we found the pictures you asked for of the apartment in Watertown, on an old computer Phil gave the children. We could not get the pictures off of it before, because we lost the power cord. We were not able to turn it on until now."

"Have you downloaded anything onto this computer or gone online with it?" he asked.

"No," I said, "we don't have internet here. I just powered it up, looked through our pictures and videos, then turned it off."

"Great! I am going to send a CID officer to pick up that laptop and put it into evidence. We would like to send it to a forensic specialist to analyze it. Would that be okay with you?"

"Yes," I said, "I would be fine with that." We said our goodbyes, and I hung up the phone.

A week later they called back to set up a meeting at the police station in Iron Mountain. This was an hour and a half from our home, and since I was the only literature evangelist for Upper Michigan at the time, I also figured it would be a good day to follow up on my leads in the Iron Mountain area.

> We prayed that God would use the computer to tell the truth of what had happened.

Bob decided to go colporteuring with me that day, so he came with me to the police station. I brought in the computer, signed it over to the CID officer, and filled out all the necessary paperwork which gave them permission to analyze the laptop. As I walked out with my husband, we prayed that God would use the computer to tell the truth of what had happened.

The CID Officer was very knowledgeable about computer technology. He found a way to identify every internet site that had been visited on a computer, by date, even when the information had been erased (in this case, it had been).

He found a lot of terrible sites that my husband had been visiting. They contained videos of children, small on up to teenagers, undergoing sexual abuse. The JAGs compared this to the police report and determined that this was some of the same material which my husband had forced my daughter to watch with him.

Along with Nautasha's testimony, the evidence all fell into place. The prosecutors sent this evidence to the general as well as to Phil's defense attorney. They then set up a meeting to give Phil a chance to take a plea bargain. The evidence was so strong against him that we knew he would have no choice but to take it.

If he did, the lawyers explained, Nautasha wouldn't have to go to the trial. They would have liked for her to go, and it would be better for the sentencing, but it would not be necessary; they explained that I could go in Nautasha's place and represent her if Phil took the plea.

Yet after the evidence was presented to Phil by his lawyer, he did not want to take the plea. Instead, he decided to hire a civilian attorney to present his case. This set the trial dates back yet again, by three months.

We remained frustrated with all of these delays. Nautasha especially was not doing well. She was on a roller coaster ride of emotions that seemed to get worse. Her walk with God was strong, but many doubts and fears flooded her mind. She had a hard time laying what had happened to her at the feet of Jesus and leaving it there. I prayed that God would bless her and help her through these hard times. I prayed He would give her comfort and peace, teaching her to trust in Him with all her heart.

As Phil fought to stay out of prison, all we could do was wait patiently for him to take the plea bargain. In the meantime, I was still doing LE work in the area where I lived.

One afternoon while I was out canvassing, I received a phone call. Phil had taken the plea, and the general had set a final court date. They wanted Bob and I to fly out to Fort Drum, New York, in about four weeks to testify in the military case against my ex-husband. The JAG office scheduled our flights and reserved a hotel room for us on post.

I was relieved that it would all be over soon. I prayed that this would bring some closure in my daughter's life.

CHAPTER 70

The Death of My Brother

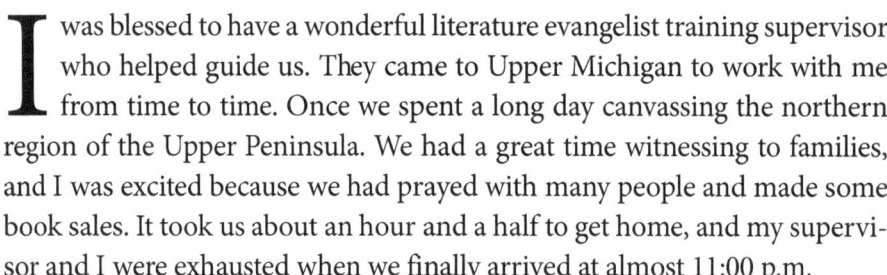

I was blessed to have a wonderful literature evangelist training supervisor who helped guide us. They came to Upper Michigan to work with me from time to time. Once we spent a long day canvassing the northern region of the Upper Peninsula. We had a great time witnessing to families, and I was excited because we had prayed with many people and made some book sales. It took us about an hour and a half to get home, and my supervisor and I were exhausted when we finally arrived at almost 11:00 p.m.

"How did your day go?" my husband asked as we walked in the door. We started to tell him all about it. Summer, another literature evangelist friend, was there to visit as well. She wanted to go out colporteuring with me because she was having a hard time and wanted to learn how to relax and let God lead. I told her I would love to go door-to-door with her. We planned to do that the next day, because she would be leaving to go back down to Lower Michigan the morning after that.

While the four of us chatted, my phone rang. I wondered who would be calling me this late at night. I saw on my phone that it was my brother Scott, and I answered in a cheery voice.

"Hello!"

"Mickey," Scott said, "are you sitting down?"

"No, why?"

"You need to sit down," he said.

As I walked over to a chair in the living room, I asked my brother, "What is going on? Is something wrong?"

His voice was serious and sad. "Robin died about an hour ago."

"No!" I said. "What? How? What happened?" I fell to my knees on the floor before reaching the chair, and lost track of everyone in the room.

"I don't know what happened yet," Scott said. "His girlfriend Tina called me from his phone at the hospital. All I know is he had a tumor on his liver. I don't think he told anyone.

My brother, Robin.

"I am flying out there tomorrow," he continued. "I need you to go tell Mom tomorrow. I can't; I have to fly out to Arizona and claim his body."

Scott's voice was filled with hurt and tears as he spoke to me. I knew the love that my brothers shared and how inseparable they were. This was going to be hard on Scott; Robin had no will and a large business. There would be a lot to take care of.

On top of this, my mother was in a nursing home recovering from lung surgery. They were going to release her to go home on Friday, which was just two days away. My heart was broken, and I felt so confused.

I hung up with Scott and only then realized that my husband was at my side. Everyone was quiet. Then Summer said, "We need to pray." She asked God to send His blessings upon my family. Afterward she said, "We don't have to work tomorrow, Michelle."

I looked at her. "Yes, we do. I need to do this in honor of my brother. I don't know if he was saved. I want to make sure others know about Jesus."

And we would go out the next day, knocking on doors and spreading the news of Jesus, in memory of Robin. It would turn out to be a great day.

But before that, I had to get up early to go to the nursing home and tell my mother the news. That night I asked my husband, with tears rolling down my face, "How am I going to tell my mother that her son died?"

I was going to have to call on the only strength I knew of that would get me through: Jesus. Bob said a prayer over me that night and held me as I cried myself to sleep. I praise God for my husband and for the love of Jesus that dwells within him.

The next morning I called the pastor and the elders from our church to have them meet me at the nursing home. My husband took the day off and came with me. The nuns who worked there came down as well. Scott's mother-in-law was there, too, with my niece Savanna, but they stayed in a waiting room until we could tell my mother the news. Even so, it was a full room.

When we all walked in, she said in a joking voice, "You all look so glum. Did someone die?" Then she smiled and laughed.

It was already the hardest day of my life; this made it harder on me. I knelt down at the foot of her chair, took her hands in mine, and said, "Yes, Mom, someone did die. Robin passed away last night."

"*No! No! You're a liar!*" She started to sob.

I hugged her close and told her, "No, Mom, I am not lying. I would never lie to you about such a thing. He really did pass away."

My mother started to have an asthma attack, and the nurses had to administer medication to her right away. After they got her breathing under control, I repeated the conversation I had had with Scott the night before.

We all hugged and cried together, and our pastor, the elders of our church, and my husband prayed with Mother.

I went and got Savanna so that she could be with her grandmother. Then I sat down and made the unwanted phone calls to all of our family. Uncle Kent took it the hardest. He and Robin had been very close; they worked together for a long time doing contracting work. Aunt Bell told me afterward that Uncle Kent cried a lot. He told her he could not believe that Robin was gone.

As I called and told each relative, the sense of shock spread to include the whole family. Many tears were shed. Many told me that it was not funny, and I had to inform them that it was true; I was not joking.

I expressed our grief and asked each of them to pray for my mother, who was deeply hurting.

Mother kept repeating, "A son should never die before his parents. He should be burying me, not the other way around."

It was a long, hard, emotional morning, but the Lord got us all through it.

CHAPTER 71
The Trial

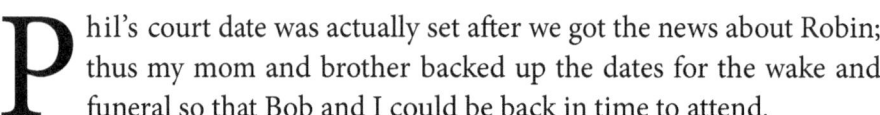

Phil's court date was actually set after we got the news about Robin; thus my mom and brother backed up the dates for the wake and funeral so that Bob and I could be back in time to attend.

When the day arrived, Bob and I headed for the airport and flew out to New York. The lawyers prepped us for the trial and offered to walk us through the evidence. I did not want to see it; I had heard enough already to know it was not of God. My husband felt that this was a good choice.

A note of explanation: military sentencing is different from the civilian court sentencing. In particular, the general who acts as judge does not know how many years of punishment are outlined in the plea bargain until after delivering the sentence which they think the soldier deserves.

If the general's sentence calls for less time than the plea bargain made between the prosecution and defense attorneys, then the defendant has to serve the minimum time described in the plea (rather than what the general determined). Likewise, if the general's sentence is higher than the plea bargain, then the soldier serves the maximum defined by the plea. However, if the general's sentence falls between the minimum and maximum of the plea, that judge's sentence is applied.

On the morning of trial, we were taken to the courtroom and placed in a secure waiting room until it was time for us to be called to the stand. The defense fought against Bob being allowed to testify, stating that he was not present during any of the events involving the accusations against their client. It was decided that he would be removed from the witness list.

When it was my turn to enter the courtroom, I was nervous. However, I knew that I would be okay; I kept claiming the Lord's promises.

The defense attorney attacked me. She tried to make me look like a bad mother and to twist events around, stating that while her client did wrong by watching things unfit for a child, I had let it happen, so I was no better than Phil.

For my part, I trusted in the judge advocate attorneys. They had told me that if a statement or question the defense asked me was going to hurt our case in any way, they would redirect or intercede by objecting on my behalf. So I did as they had instructed me to and stayed strong on the stand until my questioning was over.

Still, I left the courtroom shaking with emotions. I loved my daughter and would have never let my husband commit those ungodly acts upon her if I had known what was going on. Mrs. Lily, who was also present that day, sent me outside for some fresh air and brought me a cup of water. She reassured me that everything would be okay.

"Michelle," she said, "I have sat through many court cases. Don't worry about the defense or what they say. They are scraping the bottom of the barrel to keep their client from going to prison.

"You did a wonderful job up there," she reassured me. "It will all turn out for the greater good; you will see. Keep your faith. Do you think you will be okay to go back in now?"

"Yes," I said. "I think so. Thank you for coming and talking to me. I was shaken by the defense attorney. I just wonder how they can have a conscience and still do their job!" Then I said, "I am just going to leave this in God's hands. I want to go see my husband now. I am sure he is worried about me."

Mrs. Lily opened the door, and we walked inside. She went back into the trial, and I went to the waiting area to be with Bob and pray.

The CID officer who was testifying against Phil was waiting with us. He had the evidence that he had found on Phil's old laptop. We were not allowed to talk to each other about the case while in the witness room, or else the case would be thrown out, but we knew who he was and he knew who we were.

After hours of waiting, the officer was called to the stand. We waited a long time again before he came back. When he did, he opened the door and gave us a thumbs up. "Evidence delivered, mission accomplished," he said. Then he stepped back outside and shut the door.

> The general was a woman and a mother of two little girls.

So the general had seen the sexual abuse videos of children. It must have been heart-wrenching to watch those, and my heart was filled with grief for the judge and Phil. The general was a woman and a mother of two little girls. I knew that it would affect her emotionally and that she would have to think rationally, leaving her feelings behind, in order to judge this case.

We were released for lunch while the general decided upon a verdict. When we all walked into the courtroom after lunch, the general called the defense and prosecuting attorneys into her chambers. She looked very disturbed.

When they came back out, we learned that the general wanted another half an hour to deliberate. Bob and I went back to the waiting room to pray for the general and that the verdict placed upon Phil would be the judgment of God. We then returned and sat in the back of the room, where we waited for the general to return and resume court.

My husband and I were surprised to see Phil laughing and joking around with his friends. We also noticed that his wife was not in court with him.

Phil had gotten married in June of the same year as Bob and I. I wondered what he had told her, and if she knew the truth. I figured she had no idea or she would not have married him. I wondered if she had children of her own, and how she felt knowing that she might not see her husband again for a long time; and that when she did, it could be behind bars. I became very sad for this woman I did not know.

"Dear Lord," I said, "please bless Phil's wife. Help her through this hard time that lies ahead of her. Protect her, and help her to be comforted in Your loving arms."

My prayers were interrupted when I heard, "All rise." The general had come to a decision. She directed us to be seated again. She then addressed the defense counsel and Phil, asking them to rise. Phil's face shifted from amusement to seriousness as she recited the sentence which he would receive.

"Staff Sergeant Phil _____," she said, "this court sentences you to be reduced to the rank of E1; to forfeit all pay and allowances; to be confined for eight years; and to be discharged from the service with a bad conduct discharge. You may be seated."

The general then pulled out the plea bargain. She identified it as the "appellate exhibit three, the quantum portion of the agreement," and read the information which it contained. She asked Phil if it was correct.

He stated, "Yes, ma'am."

After all parties were in agreement with the statement and sentencing, court was adjourned, and Phil was taken into custody.

My husband and I were able to talk briefly with the CID officer. I asked him, "Where will he go to prison? When do they take him?"

He said, "He will most likely go to Fort Leavenworth prison to serve his sentence. He is already in custody now, so he will be leaving in a few days to be transported there. It is not a very nice place to be, but they do have help there for men like him."

We thanked him for all he had done and said goodbye.

The JAG attorneys came over to talk to Bob and me. With a triumphant smile, one asked me, "How are you feeling, now that the sentencing is over?"

I told them, "I am glad it is over, but I just don't know how I feel about it all."

In my heart, I was sad for Phil. This would be a rough, uncomfortable, eight-year road for him. All I had ever wanted was for him to give his heart and life to Jesus and accept Him as his personal Savior.

I also felt relief for my daughter. This would be the beginning of a different healing journey for her. Nautasha had come to forgive Phil the best she could for what he had done to her. Now she could feel safe again and start to put it all behind her.

Still, Bob and I knew that it would be a long road to recovery as long as she kept trying to deal with this pain without the help of the Savior. I told Bob all of this.

He said, "Everyone is happy for Tasha that this is over, and I am, too, but has anyone thought of how Tristin is going to react to the news? Phil is his father. I understand Tasha is hurting, but we have another child who will now be hurting, too. He will want answers and will need lots of love."

I knew that Bob was right. We prayed that night in the hotel room, asking God to give us the wisdom to talk to Tristin and answer all of his questions.

Healing would start for Nautasha, while hurt and confusion would begin for Tristin. We would have to handle this with love and care as my son grew in Christ into a young man. It would be another journey in our life that would require much prayer and guidance from our Lord.

Epilogue

Nautasha

In her senior year, Nautasha's grades went from all D's and F's to A's and B's. When she graduated, she felt like she had accomplished a great task. Her joy was immense, and she was grateful to move on in life. She wanted to go to school and start a ranch for abused horses and children, to help them both in their healing process.

However, a few years after the trial, Phil and his attorneys fought the military court system and got his case thrown out. He was released from the military prison and went back to work as if nothing had happened. It took another two years for the JAG officers to gather all the evidence back together and notify all the same people, so that they could return to court. For his part, Phil voted to have the judge advocate decide his sentence rather than a panel of officers.

In the midst of this process, Nautasha found out that Phil was not pleading guilty. That meant that there would be a full trial, and she would have to testify.

She was devastated. My daughter was scared to go to court. She did not want to have to face Phil. Her flashbacks came back, and she became very emotional and unstable. She often called me to talk, and I prayed with her.

When court started, she was the first witness. The judge called a recess when Nautasha broke down on the stand. She came out and told me what had happened, and I hugged her and prayed with her.

In the course of the trial we all took the stand. The judge found Phil guilty and sent him to prison for fourteen years. I was sad for him. He had only had a few years before his prior sentence would have been up. He fought the sentence yet again from prison, but to no avail.

Nautasha and I prayed that God would change his heart; that one day he would surrender all to Jesus and repent; that we might see him in Heaven a changed man, transformed by the blood of Christ. We knew this was all in God's hands and we gave Him complete control.

Nevertheless the trial took a toll on my daughter's life. She fell away from the church and became a lesbian. She could no longer trust men.

Nautasha remains on a rough road of recovery after all these years, and often has flashbacks to her two years of trauma. She still has dreams similar to those she had when she finished high school. She still believes in God and prays. She even picks up her Bible from time to time. However, she has never fully surrendered to Jesus.

I continue to pray for her and for the healing of her brokenness, which was caused by a man who was damaged by wars. I will always love my little girl with the beautiful green eyes and the voice of a songbird. I am proud of her and of her accomplishments. She has overcome hurdles, and I will continue to pray for her to overcome the ones that stand before her now.

Tristin

Tristin handled the news of his father going to prison well. He decided to have no contact, and stated this wish in a letter we sent to Phil in prison. But he also told me, "I will be praying for my father; that one day he may be in Heaven with me when Jesus comes to take us home."

I was proud of my son for giving all his feelings over to the Lord. It was not too hard for him because of his emotional disorder, which makes it difficult for him to process feelings, but he understood what had taken place and knew that prayer was needed for Phil, the sinner. Today he still misses his father, hurting in his own way over what happened, even if he doesn't know how to show it emotionally.

A very smart young man who wants to do all he can to better himself, Tristin decided to take some courses with a friend of ours and learned how to repair computers. At first he wanted to be a computer technician or a chef. Then he decided to take an aptitude test to see what he would be good at. He ultimately realized that God was calling him to be a missionary.

Tristin attended and graduated from Laurelbrook Academy (LBA) in Tennessee, where he got A's and B's. This Seventh-day Adventist Missionary School trains youth to be servants of God through all types of missions. While in school he went through their canvassing program and also helped out at the church as a junior deacon and in the sound booth.

He went on his first missions trip to Mexico with LBA, where he helped to build five churches and assisted at a health expo for the Mexican people. While there he also helped with a Vacation Bible School.

Tristin went to college for a little while, where his grades were lower, sometimes even failing. Then he decided that he would rather work and see where God was going to lead him. With his disabilities, finding a job was not easy; his brain does not process like ours, even though he is very smart.

Many people pushed him to work at places where he didn't feel comfortable, but he overcame. While Tristin finished his Bible studies in Escanaba, Michigan, he worked the audio system at the Escanaba SDA church and waited upon the Lord to send him into the mission field.

Around the time Tristin was to be baptized, he was struggling with giving some things up. Then one day while driving home from work, he was in a terrible car accident. He turned in front of a truck that was towing a camper, and the back end of his vehicle was ripped off.

The only part of Tristin's car that was not totaled was the driver's seat. It was like God had placed a bubble of protection around my son. Most of his belongings, meanwhile, had been in the back of the car. When my husband arrived at the scene of the accident, they were scattered down the road for about a quarter of a mile.

All of Tristin's video games, movies, and whatever else he was struggling with was destroyed by the crash. However, something strange happened.

Of a box of glass dishes that was in the back of the car, only one bowl broke in half, down the middle. The rest of the dishes were intact.

Tristin knew that God had spared his life, and that He was showing him that the things which he was addicted to had to go if he was going to serve the Lord in missions. This knowledge was in his heart when he was baptized.

Bob and I are so proud of Tristin; of how he has overcome his trials of heartache and loss by giving everything to Jesus; and of how he wants to move forward in his life to honor Jesus in the mission field.

Ben-Oni

Ben lost all hope and faith in God and walked away from most of the family. He began doing drugs and bouncing from house to house, living with whoever would take him in. Many times he has been homeless, living in tents outside of the city. He struggles to hold down a job and has been in and out of jail many times. Ben blocked me from his life and does not call me Mom; I am Michelle to him.

Ben has a lot of past hurt. My heart breaks for my son, and many prayers have gone up for him. I trust in the Almighty God to lead, guide, and direct Ben's steps. Anyone can overcome if they surrender all to Christ and give their will to the Father.

I encourage all of you parents out there to claim the promises of the Lord for your children. Seek to raise them according to the Word of God and in His character; not by pushing religion on them but by showing them the Savior's love for them, in order that one day they might have a relationship with the Father in Heaven.

Bob and Michelle

God has used us to spread His Word in many places around the United States over the past several years. Bob was an elder of our old church in Escanaba, Michigan, where both of us served as personal ministries leaders. While there we began to pray for God to place us in the mission field.

He sent us as staff to the same missionary school that Tristin attended, LBA. There Bob was asked to be vice president. He did many other jobs for the school as well, including being work coordinator for the men, the Automotive Service Excellence teacher, and direct manager of the farm.

I was also asked to serve in several positions at Laurelbrook. I was the woods and grounds manager, work coordinator for the students, manager of the farm, and secretary for the vice president. I did advertising for LBA, set up booths at GC, ASI, GYC, agriculture, and more, and even managed the academy's kitchen. I taught vocational classes, agriculture, and horsemanship, was the director of music for our music department for one year, and the assistant music director the next.

While at LBA we stayed active in the church. Bob was the head elder, I was the Sabbath School superintendent, and we worked as a team to teach Sabbath School for LBA's youth department.

God sure has surrounded us with a lot of gifts; and He has blessed us with the chance to help so many young people find Jesus.

We left LBA in June of 2017 after Tristin graduated. We were burning out and needed to spiritually rejuvenate, so we moved back to Michigan and lived there for eight months.

During that time the symptoms of Bob's mercury poisoning came back. He experienced muscle weakness and tremors, bad headaches, stomach pain, memory loss, and several other medical issues.

Bob had first contracted this condition in the Army National Guard while following orders to remove leaking mercury gauges out of heavy equipment. In 2002, he had almost lost his life due to this poisoning. All his organs were shutting down, and he got no help or answers at the hospitals.

Finally in 2004, the same year that he retired from the National Guard after twenty years of service, he had gone to Battle Creek Sanitarium. There they found out that his mercury levels were off the charts. They showed him how to change his lifestyle through diet and exercise. They also administered intense hydrotherapy and sauna therapy.

The hydrotherapy involved the doctors wearing welding gloves and placing fomentation towels under him and on top of him. They used the largest organ in Bob's body to pull out the mercury: his skin. When they took those towels off, they were loaded with an inch of yellow, green, and gray slime. They gave him an ice bath right after that. For the other therapy, they placed Bob in a sauna with ice on his head to protect his brain from overheating. After they brought him out, they gave him an ice rub. Then at bedtime they wrapped him from head to toe in charcoal poultices.

All these wonderful, natural remedies from God saved my husband's life. Had he not been treated in 2004, long before we met, he would have passed away, and I would not have had the wonderful opportunity to call him my husband.

Now we were together in Michigan, and as I said, Bob's symptoms had returned. At the beginning of April, we packed up our fifth wheel and hit the road for Florida, where it was warmer and where, we were told, there was a good VA hospital close to the military bases. We drove with Bob's daughter LeeAnn and our grandson Mason. Since LeeAnn is a registered nurse, she helped me care for her dad while we traveled.

In Florida they found out that my husband had prostate cancer. When we looked up the side effects of long-term mercury poisoning, we learned that cancer was one of them. His organs also started to shut down again.

LeeAnn and I did all that we could to help him, but the biggest thing we did together was pray. We knew God was the true healer. Another reason that we knew we needed to rely fully on God was that the VA would not help us, either directly or by assisting us with getting Bob treated at a lifestyle center. The VA did not recognize organic mercury poisoning, since it could not be detected in urine or blood as with inorganic poisoning.

We contacted Wildwood Lifestyle Center, and they said they wanted to help Bob. While we got the details worked out for him to go through their program, we moved back to Tennessee and lived at LBA. We had no money and did not know how we were going to pay for this.

But God knew.

I posted about my husband's needs on a prayer warriors website. Our friends and family started asking where they could donate money to help, so I started a project for Bob on the prayer site. We gave people an address to send money to, and we also told them they could call Wildwood Lifestyle Center and donate that way.

The Wildwood Business office told us that they would barely hang up the phone after talking to one person when they'd receive a call from another who was asking to donate. We all saw firsthand how God was providing. The donations came in amounts anywhere from $50 to $2,000.

We needed around $10,000 to get Bob his treatment. God provide that and a little extra for further treatments after the initial program. It was a blessing that we will never forget. God showed us that He is able to care for all our needs, and that I should never doubt what He can do.

After hydrotherapy treatments, doctor visits, and diet changes, my husband's mercury symptoms were gone. His skin color was back and his strength was back.

The Wildwood staff wanted us to come and work for them. After much time in prayer (and them asking us three times), Bob and I knew that God was leading us to go there. We accepted their offer, and within a week we pulled our camper onto the grounds of Wildwood Lifestyle Institute. We stayed for seven months.

Then God moved us onward again. We started our own ministry, called Never Alone Ministries. We did an evangelistic series on the character of Christ and also on helping hands.

We were in Florida when COVID hit the world and all the lockdowns started. We stayed there for two years, doing the best we could. The standstill didn't stop us from being able to reach others. Bob and I kept helping as many people as we could, sharing Jesus everywhere we went, even though we could not do our seminar.

When COVID began to let up, my husband's health was not doing well; the mercury had built back up in his organs. We prayed for God to heal Bob while we stepped forward in His work in the mission field.

We ended up going to Eden Valley for treatment. We did not have the funds to go there, but God provided them through our brothers and sisters in Christ at the Live Oak Seventh-day Adventist church in Florida. We will forever be grateful for their love and for their support of Bob's health and our ministry.

God blessed Bob at Eden Valley with the extraction of enough mercury from his system for him to function. The cancer in his prostate also shrank, and we now believe it is gone (we are waiting for Bob to get tested again to confirm). He feels like a new man.

God has shown us so much about health and healing through the eight laws of health and how they reverse many diseases. We have seen amazing things happening in our lives by applying these rules. We have also learned to wait upon the Lord for help. We trust in the Father and know that the plans He has for us are to prosper us. He has shown us this over and over again. We truly serve an awesome God.

Bob and I are praying for the Lord to reveal where we can purchase a house and some property. We plan to have an RV outpost for missionaries to come and recuperate, relax, and spiritually refuel. We also want to teach people how to garden and use home remedies for healing. And we plan to continue our helping hands ministry in the community and eventually start back up our seminars on "The Character of Christ."

The Gospel must go out before our Lord's return. God has call us to preach the Word to a dying world: "Then He said to His disciples, 'The harvest truly is plentiful, but the laborers are few. Therefore pray the Lord of the harvest to send out laborers into His harvest'" (Matt. 9:37-38).

It is our longing to work for the Lord. We want to stay in the mission field no matter where God sends us. Therefore we pray for Him to send us out to the lost, hurting, widowed, sick, and wandering sheep.

Then we heard the voice of the Lord, saying, "Whom shall I send, and who will go for Us?" Then we said, "Here we are! Send us."

Bibliography

Robert Lowry, "Shall We Gather at the River?", 1864, Public Domain.

White, Ellen G. *Counsels for the Church*. Nampa, ID: Pacific Press Publishing Association, 1991.

White, Ellen G. *Heaven*. Nampa, ID: Pacific Press Publishing Association, 2003.

White, Ellen G. *The Ministry of Healing*. Mountain View, CA: Pacific Press Publishing Association, 1905.

About Never Alone Ministry

Never Alone Ministry & Helping Hands Ministry: Bob and Michelle established these ministries with the goal of sharing seminars and meeting practical needs for church members and others whom the Lord places in their path.

Their seminars focus on the character of Christ and the need for our characters to reflect His in all we do. They believe that when we learn to be like Jesus we are nurtured by the Holy Spirit and prepared to carry out the gospel commission.

Learn how to implement your gifts to work for the Lord as this couple come alongside you in ministry. They will help you exercise practical Christianity as you serve those within your church or meet needs in your community. In addition, they are available to help in practical ways, whether making needed repairs or completing unfinished projects.

The Gustafsons have worked in the mission field for the last nine years and served in a variety of church roles. Both served the Michigan Conference of Seventh-day Adventists, Michelle as a literature evangelist and Bob in camp ministry. Michelle's love for sharing the word through evangelistic, motivational speaking came when she presented a health seminar in Watertown, New York, at the request of her pastor.

For three years, Bob and Michelle worked at Laurelbrook Academy in Dayton, Tennessee, where they enjoyed teaching the youth God's word. Their favorite part was watching the youth surrender their hearts to Jesus. Often tears of joy would stream down their faces as they watched the youth respond to altar calls and commit to baptism.

With Jesus as their guide, Bob and Michelle plan to follow His light and continue to share the Savior's love in training and service, teaching all who will listen for the calling of the Lord. There are many lost sheep and time is short. Let us labor together for the Master.

TEACH Services, Inc.
P U B L I S H I N G

We invite you to view the complete
selection of titles we publish at:
www.TEACHServices.com

We encourage you to write us
with your thoughts about this,
or any other book we publish at:
info@TEACHServices.com

TEACH Services' titles may be purchased in
bulk quantities for educational, fund-raising,
business, or promotional use.
bulksales@TEACHServices.com

Finally, if you are interested in seeing
your own book in print, please contact us at:
publishing@TEACHServices.com
We are happy to review your manuscript at no charge.

www.ingramcontent.com/pod-product-compliance
Lightning Source LLC
Chambersburg PA
CBHW052049230426
43671CB00011B/1845